BODY IN THE BUSHES

The boy was naked, lying on his back with legs spread outward, knees in the air, and a cast on his right arm. Nearby, soccer clothing was stacked together, and next to his left hand lay a huge two-by-four with a protruding nail. The intense heat of the past few days had dried and darkened the skin.

Twelve year old Sean Dannehl, missing for six days, had been found.

The three and a half hour autopsy revealed multiple puncture wounds. The small circular hole in the right frontal section of the skull was the kind the nail in the two by four would make. The shape and depth of the punctures in the left chest and between the fourth and fifth ribs were consistent with an icepick.

The body was too decomposed to determine if the boy had been sexually molested by his killer. The blow to the head was enough to knock him unconscious, but death had come from the deep wounds to his heart.

Police compared the facts of Sean Dannehl's murder with the brutal death of another local boy. If the two cases had the same assailant, he was becoming more proficient at killing his victims. They would have to find him before he could strike again.

Before he could kill another innocent child.

THE BOY NEXT DOOR

Gretchen Brinck, MSW

Pinnacle Books
Kensington Publishing Corp.
http://www.pinnaclebooks.com

Some names have been changed to protect the privacy of individuals connected to this story.

PINNACLE BOOKS are published by

Kensington Publishing Corp.
850 Third Avenue
New York, NY 10022

ISBN 0-7394-0513-6

Printed in the United States of America

This book is dedicated to the boys who died:

John Davies
Lance Turner
Sean Dannehl

and to those who survived:

Steve Murphy
Monti Hansen

Part One

Lance Turner
October–November 1984

Chapter One

Dead and alone, he lay in a scarlet tunnel of poison oak.

His cheek rested against his left shoulder. His arms were extended along his sides and his right ankle rested on his left.

The alligator on the pocket of his green pullover shirt indicated that he, or his mother, knew the most popular styles. His shiny black shorts defined him as a member of the Belmont Oaks Soccer League.

Nicks and slashes gouged his black shin guards. Blood smeared his defenseless bare thighs and gleamed through the brush scattered on his chest.

On the field three hundred feet up the hill, five Belmont Oaks teams noisily practiced soccer. His friends hadn't yet noticed that he was gone.

An hour earlier, at four o'clock on Tuesday, October 2, 1984, four Belmont Oaks boys—Lance Turner, Thomas Russell, Ian O'Brien, and Mark Quintero—had arrived at the Ralston Intermediate School playing field, chauffeured by Ian's father, fireman Tim O'Brien. Normally they would have come at five o'clock, but car pool problems today meant they'd have to fill an hour before practice while Mr. O'Brien coached a younger team.

The boys had grown up together in Belmont, a town about twenty-seven miles down the Peninsula from San Francisco. Blond, blue-eyed Lance and dark, brown-eyed Thomas were especially close. Happy and confident, studious and athletic, they were beginning to attract girls' attention, though they themselves had barely begun to shift their interests from sports and Dungeons and Dragons to romance. Still, at last week's seventh-grade dance, Lance had spent the evening with a redheaded girl. From across the room, his mother, Margo, a chaperone, watched and thought, *They really like each other.* Lance's older sister, Tracy, told friends, "He's only twelve, but he's such a stud. Girls call him up all the time."

While Mr. O'Brien coached his young team, the four boys kicked a soccer ball around, wearing their practice uniforms of black shorts and short-sleeved shirts. Soon they were "hucking" dirt clods.

"This is boring," said Lance. "Let's play on the rope swing."

The Ralston School campus backed up to the Water Dog Lake Recreation area, a chunk of California chaparral ringed by schools, a tiny industrial complex, and blocks of apartments and condominiums. Water Dog Lake had been created in the 1870s to provide water for millionaire William Ralston's mansion. In the 1920s, the Sisters of Notre Dame du Namur took over his property and eventually leased the lake and its surrounding woods and chaparral to the town that had grown around them. Joggers, dog walkers, hikers, picnickers, mothers with strollers, and whole families frequented its paths.

What began as a rich people's vacation town was now a cushioned bedroom community that attracted hardworking, affluent middle- and upper-middle-class families. More

Republican than Democrat, more Catholic than Protestant, more white than anything else, its citizens worked to maintain a good life. Narrow, tree-shaded roads meandered past yards landscaped with juniper, jade plants, oak trees, ivy, and lush flower beds. Doves cooed in Belmont trees, raccoons raided garbage cans and drank from backyard pools, and at night, deer clattered along the roads to munch on rose bushes.

When Belmont's junior high students were released each day, many crossed the Ralston School's basketball courts to the gate that opened onto one of Water Dog Lake's trails. They'd hunted pollywogs there as children; they returned as adolescents to experiment with cigarettes, beer, marijuana, and love. Some, like the four Belmont Oaks soccer boys, often played on the old rope swing, straddling the knotted rope and spinning wildly between sky and water.

Today, though, a chilly wind was rising. "It'll be cold by the water," Mark said.

"I can go alone, then," Lance said cheerfully.

"If that's what you want," Ian said, shrugging.

Lance jumped the fence, flashed a grin at his buddies, and ran down the trail. His friends watched until he vanished around the giant oak known as "the smoking tree." Lance had strong legs; he was the team's fastest runner.

When Lance Turner passed the smoking tree, four eighth-grade girls from the popular crowd noticed him, thinking how cute he was for a seventh grader. Then they turned back to the stranger with whom they'd shared a little beer and pot. "We've gotta go," said Heidi and the others chimed in, "Me, too." No way did any of them want to be left alone with this guy—"John" or "Don" or whatever his name was. They waved good-bye and strolled away giggling and leaning against each other.

Beyond the oak, the path entered dense trees and brush.

Lance ran in dappled sunlight along the switchback that led to the swing. Later his father, Quincy, speculated that Lance had treasured this final moment of quiet and solitude.

At 4:50, Ray Williamson, head coach and creator of the Belmont Oaks Soccer League, paced Ralston field and gathered the boys aged ten to sixteen. A down-to-earth Irishman, he felt nearly as attached to his players as to his own sons, fifteen-year-old Sean and twelve-year-old Padraic. "Come on now," he shouted, his accent making it sound like "nigh."

Lance's buddies grabbed their Belmont Oaks bags, which were black with each player's number printed in gold. "Who's number ten?" thought Mark Quintero, and grabbed that one, too.

Clusters of boys covered the field. Mentally disabled young men from a board-and-care home watched them practice, as did a thin, middle-aged, brain-injured man called Charlie, who strode shouting around the perimeter. His Ichabod Cranelike figure was familiar to everyone.

By six p.m., thirty or forty parents had pulled up in the parking lot. Boys poured off the field, torsos sweating, legs chilled. Thomas, Ian, and Mark ran to Thomas's father's car and started to pile in.

"Hey," said Ian, "where's Lance?"

Thomas Russell's father, Bill, formerly a district attorney and now a lawyer with a private practice, listened with growing alarm. Like many parents, he didn't know the trails and had never heard of any rope swing. "You'd better run down and find him," he said.

As the boys dashed across the basketball court and disappeared down the hill, Bill Russell thought how odd it was for Lance Turner to ditch practice. He was the most carefully raised child in this group of watched-over kids. His days were tightly scheduled—school, soccer and basketball practice, homework, weekend games, church. In his free time he played with friends, painted Dungeons & Dragons figures, and sometimes visited a disabled neighbor child. When he did well in soccer or basketball, he caught the eye of his mother on the sidelines as she clapped and cheered. The love between them was obvious.

The boys returned. "We went all the way to the swing. We didn't see him."

Bill Russell walked over to Ray Williamson, who stood in the parking lot making sure his players all had rides. "Hmm," said Williamson when Russell told him the problem. "Some lads don't show up and their mothers don't call, but never Lance. He's not flaky like some. Tim and I will go down, have a look."

But they soon returned. "It's nearly dark," said Williamson, "and I don't know my way about. That lake—Lance is surely a strong swimmer?"

"I think so," answered Russell. "I'll get these boys home and phone his mother."

Williamson nodded. "Perhaps he just walked on home for some reason."

Thomas Russell called his friend Lance's parents, then reported, "Dad, his mom's really upset. He's not home and she says, 'Some little boy is going to get spanked.' "

During dinner, Bill Russell watched the Turner home, which was clearly visible through his large picture window. When he saw a patrol officer walk to the Turners' front door, he threw down his napkin. "I have to get down there."

Belmont Patrol Officer Banks documented, "At 19:13 I proceeded to the above address re: a missing child. Mrs. Turner stated that her son Lance disappeared from soccer practice. . . . The husband was at Ralston School searching. Mrs. Turner very upset, nearly in tears. She stated that

Lance was not the type to come home late. Tim O'Brien, coach, was present."

Banks feared that the boy had fallen from the rope swing. He might be lying injured on the hillside or, God forbid, he could have drowned. Several years back, Water Dog had claimed a teenage boy.

Officer Banks and Tim O'Brien drove the short distance to Ralston School and began searching the hillside.

While Margo Turner was reporting to Officer Banks, Coach Ray Williamson was gathering fathers and older team members into a search crew. By seven-fifteen, he had divided the hillside into a grid and instructed his men to cover their assigned areas thoroughly. He stationed a man in the center of the field and another at the gate to relay information. He himself waited in the parking lot in his Bronco, prepared, if necessary, to haul Lance up by rope in a makeshift stretcher. He'd heard Margo Turner call the police and thought they hadn't taken her seriously.

When Bill Russell arrived at the Turner home, he found Margo there with Ray Williamson's wife, Carole.

Margo Turner was a tall woman with blond hair falling to her shoulders in a wave. Born in England, she spoke with an English accent and had a friendly yet reserved manner. Anxiety was making inroads on her usual poise. "I can't help but think of that poor boy Kevin Collins," she said. Eleven-year-old Kevin had disappeared after basketball practice in San Francisco eight months before.

"It's too soon to think of things like that," said Carole, trying to hide her own fears.

Lance's father, Quincy Turner, burst into the house. "Where's the big flashlight? There's a whole mess of trails. I don't know where to go."

"Thomas knows the trails," said Russell, reaching for the phone.

By eight, Russell, Turner, and twelve-year-old Thomas Russell, all carrying flashlights, reached the school. Flashlight beams dotted the hillside and everywhere voices called, "Lance! Lance!"

Thomas led his father and Mr. Turner across the basketball court. "Here's the trail Lance took." He leaped the fence. The two fathers followed through the gate.

Bill Russell swept his light across the trail and up and down the dense brush. Close behind him came Turner's footsteps.

Beneath a shrub about twenty-five feet back from the path along the switchback, his light caught what looked like a tennis shoe. He stepped closer. Yes. Legs and feet. He kneeled and aimed the light through a tunnel in the bushes.

Lance lay there on his back, fully clothed, shirt neat and smooth over his chest. Russell saw a little blood on Lance's neck. The boy must have fallen and gotten hurt. "Lance," he said softly, placing his hand on the boy's leg.

It felt cool and hard. Russell knew death when he touched it. Never able to cope with blood, despite growing up on a farm, his mind immediately filtered out the sight. He focused on the ants covering Lance's body. Nature was cruel. She allowed no dignity.

With the protective filter came another defense. Russell began to shift from his role as Thomas's father and Turner's friend to that of a former DA at a crime scene. He flicked his light over the area. Near Lance's body he noted a faint print in the dirt, the toe of a shoe as if someone had "leaned Lance down." Looking up, Russell found himself looking into a window of Wadsworth Publishing Company. *What a strange place to commit a murder,* he thought.

"What are you doing?" Turner asked from the trail.

Russell's professionalism dropped away. He turned and

put his hand on his friend's shoulder. "Quincy, your son is dead," He stepped back to allow the man a few minutes alone with Lance.

From the trail, Thomas Russell saw Lance's legs up to the knees. He heard his father tell Mr. Turner that Lance was dead and then Mr. Turner dropped down beside the body, crying, "Oh, Lance, who did this to you?"

Thomas bolted. He ran as fast as he could to the school, a familiar place now made strange by lights and shouts and horror. Men and boys' voices rose from the trails and his father called out with firm authority, "Stand back, stay back, we have to preserve evidence!" As always, his dad knew what to do.

Thomas paced near the gym. Inside, rowdy rock and roll accompanied women in bright leotards performing dancercize. He was still there when the fire engines, ambulances, and police cars arrived.

Chapter Two

Sergeant James Goulart, head of Belmont's Detective Bureau, stood on the path and peered at the body. A few years earlier Belmont had been listed as one of California's ten safest cities. Twelve-year-old boys weren't supposed to get killed here. This murder violated not only the victim but his family, his friends, and the whole community. Belmont officers would take this case very personally, taking greater pains and working harder than many of their more experienced and hardened big-city counterparts.

Already, though, the investigation suffered from small-town limitations. "We're waiting for lights," Detective Joe Farmer told Goulart. "The county fire department is rigging up a light tower." He pointed toward the Wadsworth Publishing Company parking lot on the other side of the trees. "They're putting a generator over there."

Farmer, the first detective on the scene, had been an officer for barely four years and a detective less than one, but he was doing a good job of coordinating the immediate investigation.

"Fire department lights," grunted Goulart. As usual,

Belmont police didn't have the right equipment. Officers' flashlights sent out dusty illumination totally inadequate for investigating a crime scene at night. The small police department served a town whose citizens felt cushioned from crime. The city council refused luxuries like unmarked cars, updated equipment, and a photo lab, and councilmen regularly demanded that the chief justify the existence of the three-man detective bureau. One officer, Cinquini, developed evidence photos in his own garage.

"I don't know if we exactly have a preserved crime scene," Farmer went on. "There was mass confusion here. Men and boys ran up and down the trail for hours trying to find the kid. The man who found him went all the way in. So did the father—"

"The *father?* God."

"And a paramedic. Everybody tromped down here to take a look."

"Damn." Goulart had often told his men, "You get just one shot at a crime scene. Mess that up and you've messed up the entire investigation."

He glanced at Officer Pat Halleran and Sergeant Don Mattei, who waited impatiently with their evidence kits and cameras. Fixated on detail, meticulous to a fault, they made an excellent evidence team.

Light suddenly flooded the trail as the generator kicked on. Tree branches made silhouettes against the dark sky and shadows puddled the ground. Halleran hefted his camera, preparing to flash-photo every detail of the scene.

Goulart left them to it and headed up the trail to confer with county officials.

"There's blood on the edge of the trail here," Officer Banks said. "Here's a bloody rock, too."

Halleran photographed them both and bagged the rock while Farmer jotted notes. Then Halleran opened his metal tape measure, dropped to his knees, and tackled the first inch of the brushy tunnel. At 9:37, he noted a trail of leaves spotted with blood, which he photographed and collected—they might show up later on a suspect's clothes. The leaves proved to be from a typical group of California chaparral plants: oak, soap grass, honeysuckle, juncus, mugwort, coyote bush, monkey flower, yerba buena—and, of course, poison oak, whose effects would soon torment the very allergic young officer.

By 9:41, Halleran and Farmer had progressed twenty feet into the tunnel and were five feet from the body. Farmer wrote, "There are deep lacerations on Left forearm, Right arm, Left leg." He figured these to be defense wounds received while the boy fought his attacker. "The body is flat with the arms straight down by the sides with the face resting on the Left ear. There are many ants."

Meanwhile, Halleran noted that branches lay over the bloody torso roughly in the shape of a cross. Farmer wrote, "Beneath the body, twigs are bunched as if the body was slid along on the back."

They inched closer to the body, mentally functioning like robots. They kept emotion on the back burner with the lid down tight. Halleran aimed the camera at the body from every angle, while Farmer documented, "The majority of wounds were produced by an instrument consistent with a knife with a blade somewhere in the vicinity of an inch wide."

Halleran moved behind the body and continued inch by inch through the dense brush, photographing beer cans, cigarette butts, junk food containers, and soil samples. Two hundred and seventy-six inches in, he came across a battered, rotting mattress.

Detective Mattei crept into the tunnel behind Farmer and Halleran. When he had arrived at the scene, all he knew was that a "stabbing" had occurred. He had thought the victim to be a teenager till he stood on the switchback and saw the feet, legs, and shin guards. "Oh, man!" he burst out. "It's a kid! He's just a kid!"

A generation of Belmont children knew Mattei as "Rock," their counselor at summer day camp. Before joining the police force, Mattei had been a recreation specialist for Belmont Parks and Recreation. A man of medium height, Mattei had the athletic intensity and thick-shouldered build of a football player. Every afternoon he ran the fourteen mile cross-country trail from Carlmont High School up Water Dog Lake trail and back, a rugged up-and-down trek over rough paths. Today, though, he'd skipped this 3:15 to 5:00 P.M. routine to repair his father-in-law's car. For years this would torment him. He felt that if he'd run that day as usual, he'd have seen the killer.

Inching his way through the bushes, Mattei photographed everything, just as Halleran did. When he reached the body, he noted the indignity of twigs and brush and ants all over it. He surveyed the wounds and bruises, the blood on the chest and neck. Then he raised his eyes to the narrow, lightly freckled face, and the blond hair. He saw bright blue eyes staring fixedly upward.

"It's Lance!" he cried. "Oh, my God! Lance Turner!" He'd known and coached Lance for years and considered him a bright, athletic, wonderful kid.

From that moment forward, Don Mattei dedicated himself tirelessly to catching Lance's killer. It would prove to be a much harder and longer mission than anyone imagined.

After the coroner left with the body, Goulart had to tell his men that county evidence and lab experts would be assisting them. "If there's an expert to use," he said, "we use the expert. We have to make sure. They've got the experience of dozens of murder scenes. We don't." He couldn't allow some defense attorney down the road to claim that inexperienced Belmont cops had botched the evidence.

Still, once the crime lab specialists reviewed the scene, Goulart knew his men had missed nothing. The coroner department's criminalist Mona Ng later told them, "You did all that could be done here."

Belmont and county officers spent the whole night conducting a grid search of Water Dog Lake's paths, hills, and flora. They feared that if they left this until morning, the night fog and morning dew might damage evidence. They found countless bits of trash, beer and soda cans, and one set of keys, but did not recover a possible murder weapon or bloody clothes. Around five a.m., they agreed to stop temporarily. Goulart posted men to guard the trail and all entrances. Some men then dragged themselves home for a few hours of disturbed sleep.

At 10 a.m., Detective Farmer attended Lance Turner's autopsy, representing the Belmont police and taking evidence photographs.

Dr. Peter Benson, assisted by criminalist Mona Ng, first examined Lance's clothing. It wasn't until Benson removed the shirt that Farmer fully grasped how vicious the attack had been. The killer's knife had plunged so deeply into the left side of the chest that the lung protruded. The throat wound penetrated the esophagus and a three-inch gash penetrated the heart.

Dr. Benson agreed that the deep cuts on the arms, wrists, and hands looked like defense wounds. Stabs and gashes on the buttocks and backs of the legs suggested that the boy fell down, held his legs up against his chest, and kicked at his attacker. Lance had fought long and hard. The abrasions at the waist and hips indicated that once still, he had been dragged headfirst into the bushes.

There's a lot of anger in those wounds, thought Farmer.

Chapter Three

Hours before Detective Farmer attended the autopsy, evidence techs Sergeant Mattei and Officer Halleran resumed their labors. "Oh, hell," Mattei said as he and Halleran headed across the basketball court. Reporters and cameramen crowded the gate to the trail.

Mattei, like some fellow officers, despised interviews and publicity, believing that reporters wasted officers' precious time, distorted events, and quoted the police out of context.

Grumpily, Mattei and Halleran headed down the path, followed by some reporters. Teenage Explorer Scouts, youths specially trained to serve on search-and-rescue missions, waited near the crime site with some officers from the county sheriff's department. Mattei had divided the Water Dog Lake area into exact grids, which searchers began to examine inch by inch. The scouts, smaller and more agile than adult officers, prowled the thick brush on their hands and knees. Everyone bagged knives, butts, trash, keys. Halleran found a green pump handle. While Mattei spent the day filling in details on his careful grid diagram, helicopters whirred overhead taking aerial photographs.

At the base of the dam that created the lake, the men discovered two culverts designed to carry off the lake's overflow.

"Great place to stash a murder weapon," said Halleran.

"And how can we search them? Look how narrow they are," Mattei said.

Halleran glanced over at the scouts.

"Jeez," said Mattei, "it's dangerous. They'd have to rappel down these slimy walls here."

Two Explorers eagerly volunteered. Wearing safety lines that officers held secure, the boys clambered down the dam's algae-covered sides like experienced rock climbers and disappeared into the dank culverts. After a while, they emerged, slimy and stinking, to be hauled back up. They had found nothing, but had managed to eliminate the culverts from the search.

Thomas Russell arrived at Ralston School at eight-thirty that morning, about an hour after Halleran and Mattei returned to the trail. He saw that the flag hung at half mast and yellow crime-scene ribbon barricaded the trail entrance by the basketball courts. Some students huddled in whispering groups, but others were laughing and joking as usual. Kids who weren't connected with the Belmont Oaks Soccer Club didn't seem to have heard the news yet.

Teammates surrounded Thomas. "You found Lance's body? What did he look like? What happened to him?"

A part of Thomas felt thrilled to be living this adventure. But when he visualized Lance's legs beneath the bushes, words locked in his throat. "I didn't see anything," he muttered.

When classes started, the principal, Joseph Fruwirth, entered Thomas's homeroom and perched on the teacher's desk, sleeves rolled, his pleasant features sad and earnest. "I have to give you some very bad news," he said, and told the students about Lance Turner while a TV news crew filmed him from the doorway. The video's sound track caught cries and sobs.

Through a haze, Thomas heard Mr. Fruwirth say that counselors were available in the building. "If any of you can't handle this, you may call your parents and go home." He also spoke of safety: "I don't want you to panic, but we urge you not to go anywhere alone. Walk home in groups."

Reality broke through the numbness Thomas had been feeling. He covered his face and sobbed.

The scene in Thomas Russell's homeroom replayed itself all over the school as Mr. Fruwirth and other administrators addressed the students. Early that morning Fruwirth and county school district officials had prepared the teachers, and San Mateo County Mental Health therapists had come in to help the school handle the large volume of distraught children.

The counselors found the kids confused. Girls fell back on sincere, but melodramatic sobs and embraces. Boys shielded themselves with macho bravado: "I'm riding my bike wherever I want. He'll be sorry if he comes after *me.*"

An eighth-grade girl resented the other girls' histrionics. "They weren't even Lance's friends," she complained. "They're just being fake." She acted out her disapproval by ripping off a piece of crime scene tape and tying it in her hair.

A boy wrote to Lance's mother that he felt very sad for her and wanted to come be her son.

Dozens of Belmont children, even those from the seventh and eighth grades, didn't sleep in their own rooms for many weeks; they camped in their parents' bedrooms. Many of Lance's peers never outgrew the fear. As young adults, they remain vigilant about locking doors and watching over younger siblings.

* * *

When the school administrators announced Lance's murder to the students, they urged that all those who had been around the fields, basketball courts, or the Water Dog Lake area the afternoon before to go the principal's office and meet with police.

Sergeant Goulart assigned Sergeant Jerrold Whaley and Officer Lisa Thomas to interview the Ralston students. As Belmont's juvenile officer since 1981, Sergeant Whaley had diligently built up relationships with kids and school officials. Unknown to the BPD and himself, another case with which Whaley had struggled and suffered for the past three years would turn out to be linked to Lance's murder.

Of Belmont's two policewomen, patrol Officer Lisa Thomas was the less threatening to kids. Slender, with shoulder-length hair, she hid a vulnerable sensitivity beneath her uniform and swagger.

Sergeant Whaley and Officer Thomas faced some problems with the interviews. Apart from Joseph Fruwirth, who reported speaking to an unknown man on the basketball court the previous afternoon, the witnesses were frightened, excited children, aged eleven to fourteen.

Some were so nervous they couldn't attend to the questions.

Other students resisted answering questions about their own activities, as if they considered their secret vices more important than murder. Clearly, they feared that stories of their drinking or smoking would get back to their parents, who remained sublimely ignorant of the sex, drugs and rock 'n' roll realities of their children's daily lives.

"What were you doing on the trail?" Whaley asked Mike Brent, the leader of a group that had played around on the switchback trail right next to the brush tunnel an hour before Lance had been killed.

"Oh, nothing. Hanging out with my friends."

"A lot of beer bottles and cigarette butts are down there."

"I don't know anyone who smokes."

When pushed, twelve-year-old Mike angrily asserted, "I quit smoking last year!" Whaley and Lisa Thomas couldn't make the kids understand that the detectives had to account for every scrap, butt, bottle, can, ZigZag paper with traces of marijuana, and other trash anywhere around the crime scene.

When not hiding their own vices, kids poured out exaggerated rumors and local lore. The officers painfully documented the tales of illicit marijuana gardens, war games that might include real weapons, knife-carrying troublemakers who sassed teachers, and older guys who sold drugs next to the school grounds.

The most common rumor was related to the battered mattress found near the body. "There's drug addicts living in the canyons and around Water Dog," kids told the officers. "There's a *mattress* in the woods!"

Others reported that the brain-injured man called Charlie had been in a bad mood the day of the murder and that "scary" handicapped youths had watched soccer practice.

Using these first interviews, plus details gleaned from repeated follow-up interrogations by Mattei, Goulart, and other officers, the police eventually put together the scenario of activities on Water Dog Lake trail the afternoon of Lance Turner's murder.

Several groups of kids had gone down the trail when school let out.

Mike Brent and his crowd ran down to the giant oak called the "smoking tree" because kids sat and smoked on its lowest branch, which paralleled the ground like a cozy bench. Brent then led his buddies to a more secret spot down the switchback trail. They stopped at the leafy tunnel and he reached into a juniper bush to retrieve the battered Marlboro pack he'd hidden there. They shared a smoke, snacked on Melon candies, and shared a soda. Brent touched a match to the empty Marlboro pack.

Randy Boynton charged up the path with his crowd. The boys bristled like tomcats, shouting insults and pelting each other with rocks. Boynton's gang raced on up the hill while Brent's headed down to the lake, passing the rope swing. Brent saw a teenage boy he knew sitting on the pier with a girl and drinking champagne. Mike Brent skidded down the hill on prickly oak leaves and joined them. While he and his friends shared champagne and a beer, they saw a man jog past on the trail, wearing a blue running suit with white stripes; a bit later, they saw a guy go by in jeans and a gray sweatshirt.

While Brent and his friends were skirmishing with Boynton's crowd, about three-thirty, two twelve-year-old boys approached the smoking tree. One took advantage of the momentary privacy to unzip his pants and aim a stream into a bush.

"Get the fuck away from here!" shouted an angry voice.

Startled, the boy fumbled with his pants. He and his friend looked up and saw a guy sitting on a branch above them. Light, greasy hair hung to his shoulders and he held a tall beer can in his hand. Single-band retainers were on his stained teeth. He had bad skin and an unwashed look.

The boys took off.

A few minutes later, perhaps 3:45, while Mike Brent and friends were settling down on the pier, four eighth-grade girls, members of the popular crowd, chased each other to the smoking tree. Heidi dug her painted fingernails into a hollow above a root and pulled out her stash—a cigarette pack and a personalized blue matchbook with silver lettering from a wedding.

"Hi," said a male voice.

"Oh!" The girls giggled as they discovered the guy who sat above them on a branch, swinging his feet. His gray LSU sweatshirt and blue jeans were rumpled and he had pimply skin and a dirty look. Still, they calculated that he was between sixteen and nineteen, and he qualified as "An Older Boy" on whom to practice flirtation techniques. When he offered his beer can, Heidi and Taylor took sips.

"Eeeyooo," said Taylor. The beer was warm and flat.

"So what's your name?" asked Heidi, handing the guy the blue matchbook. Later she and the girls weren't sure if he answered "John" or "Don."

The wind kept blowing matches out. "Hey," the guy said to Taylor, "let me use your jacket as a windbreak." She handed it over—it was a Patagonia, the in-crowd brand at the time—and he draped it over his head and invited her underneath it to light the cigarette.

"No," she said, giggling.

"You, then," he said, pointing to Heidi. None of the girls agreed to get that close to the scuzzy guy. They had begun to notice his red eyes and beery smell.

When he'd lit the cigarette, he passed it around.

"Do you go to Carlmont?" asked Taylor, naming the nearby high school.

"I graduated last year," he said. "I used to go to Ralston. Do you know Mr. Smith?"

They shook their heads and exchanged glances. They took puffs while Taylor climbed around the base of the tree and Heidi sprayed everyone, including the guy, with her Jean Nate perfume.

Lance Turner ran past them around four-fifteen. By then the girls wanted to get away from their creepy companion. Two of them headed back to school for cheerleader practice. The other two left for home.

While Sergeant Whaley and Officer Thomas interviewed junior high students and Detective Farmer witnessed the autopsy, other Belmont officers questioned homeowners and renters whose homes overlooked Water Dog Lake trail or its surrounding streets. They also spoke with anyone they saw on the trails themselves. Only one lead with any promise emerged from the first day's contacts: At about four-thirty p.m. the day before, the approximate time of the murder, a husky youth had parked his beat-up Karmann Ghia at the lower gate of the Water Dog Lake trail.

"He had brown hair to his shoulders, and bushy eyebrows, and maybe he had sideburns," said the informant, who added that the car was gone by five.

It bothered the investigators that no one reported hearing Lance cry for help. How could that be?

At about four-thirty on this second day, Mattei and Halleran conducted an experiment. They stationed men and scouts at various points along the trail and in the athletic field above. Then they positioned a scout next to the leafy tunnel and asked him to shout and scream.

Not one person could hear the scout's cries. That section of the switchback trail was a sound pocket.

Chapter Four

Wednesday afternoon, twenty-four hours after the murder, Goulart reviewed the information gathered thus far. Though several of the boys who had been by Water Dog Lake had behavior problems and a few carried pocket knives, investigators had cleared them of suspicion in the murder. Sergeant Goulart listed people sighted in the Water Dog Lake area on October 2 who remained unidentified.

- The male jogger wearing a blue track suit with a white stripe;
- A "wild" old man reported to chase boys in the woods (though he wasn't seen the day of the murder);
- The mentally disabled youths, especially one reported to have followed a Belmont Oaks boy;
- The angry youth with shoulder-length light hair who chased two boys away from the smoking tree. He seemed to be the same person as:
- The possibly drunk youth at the tree who chatted with four girls and/or:

- The husky youth with shoulder-length brown hair who parked his Karmann Ghia at the Lake Street trail entrance from four-thirty to five.

Goulart sighed. Eyewitnesses were notoriously unreliable, and in this case most of them were junior high school kids. Were the smoking tree youth and the one with the Karmann Ghia the same person? He decided that he and former Juvenile Officer Floyd Cinquini needed to reinterview the kids from the smoking tree immediately. He ordered them brought to headquarters.

The two boys were concerned Lance's killer would come after them if they told the police anything.

Eventually, the boys gave out bits of information, describing the guy's irrational anger at them, though leaving out the worst of his language. They repeated their description of his braces, bad skin, fleshy look, and scuzziness.

The girls had spent enough time with the young man to have noticed a lot about him. They reported that he smoked Marlboros, hard pack, and had a large, warm can of Budweiser beer.

They added details to the story they had already told.

Goulart and Cinquini glanced at each other, silently agreeing that these girls had flirted big time. Vivacious and attractive, they struck poses and bounced around provocatively while seemingly naive about how their sexiness might affect a guy. This young man chose to hang around where he would meet kids several years younger than he. By exciting him, had the girls inadvertently set him off?

Goulart brought in Frances Caine, mother of an officer and a volunteer police artist. Following the girls' descriptions, she produced a portrait of a spotty-faced teenage male with stringy hair to the shoulders. The girls didn't like it, but couldn't explain how to change it.

* * *

The media were screaming for information, so Goulart decided they could help. He prepared a press release using selected information about the significant unidentified Water Dog Lake people, plus the composite drawing, making it clear that none of the people he sought was a suspect, "merely persons as yet unaccounted for."

One newspaper fulfilled Sergeant Mattei's expectations about reporters: It said officers wanted to speak with a long-haired youth who wore a blue jogging suit with white stripes and drove a Karmann Ghia.

The composite drawing reached a huge audience. The Bay Area includes three major cities—San Francisco, San Jose, and Oakland—which experience many crimes against children, yet even their jaded populations responded so strongly to the murder that years later many people still remembered Lance Turner's name.

His murder violated deeply held myths. *It wasn't supposed to happen to him.* He had been a good-looking, well-behaved child who lived in an apparently idyllic town, an innocent place compared to the big cities that surrounded it. In FBI parlance, he was a "low-risk victim"; to the public, he symbolized innocence. He was Good destroyed by Evil.

Reporters slanted their coverage to satisfy this unspoken subtext, pouring out human interest stories for weeks, even months, after the murder.

BELMONT STUNNED BY TRAGEDY, said the front-page headline in the Thursday, October 4 *San Mateo Times,* describing the "Back To School Night" at Ralston School that had proceeded as planned the day after the murder, a day that teachers and administrators had spent consoling students. Principal Joseph Fruwirth addressed an auditorium overflowing with upset parents, presenting the facts as he knew them, and describing the counseling and security steps being taken.

In one classroom a teacher assured the parents, "You

can be proud of your kids. Things were rough today and your kids handled themselves well."

A few days after the murder, a *San Mateo Times* reporter interviewed Quincy Turner. Portraying Lance's father as a down-to-earth foreman in construction, the reporter said that Mr. Turner expressed the philosophy that when the Lord comes for you, you must go: Lance's time must have come and the family must accept it. He said he hoped whoever harmed Lance would not harm anyone else. The person could do no more harm to the Turners. The father repeated that the Lord must have just decided He wanted Lance now. That was the only answer Mr. Turner could think of to explain how this could happen.

His words revealed a father still in shock, a man who had yet to suffer the full impact of the terrible thing that had happened to him. Except for a brief statement a few days later, at the funeral, Quincy Turner never again appeared in print or at public events related to the murder.

Bill Russell continued his leadership role after finding Lance's body. The first night had been agony. He would never forget the anguished screams inside the Turners' home nor his helplessness to temper the family's grief. By the next day, though, he was ready for action. He went to police headquarters and met with Sergeant Goulart.

"God!" Russell said. "I can't bear to think of his last moments." He would, in fact, find himself obsessed for years with such images, which drove him to work ceaselessly alongside the investigation till it ended. "How can I help the police?"

Citizens' offers to help were clogging police phone lines, but Goulart didn't consider Bill Russell a mere citizen; he saw him as an attorney and former DA, someone capable of harnessing all this local good will into useful areas for the department. Goulart and his fellow officers soon trusted Russell as a go-between with members of the community.

Goulart told him about the composite drawing of the male at the smoking tree. "We're not calling him a suspect," he warned, knowing the former DA would understand.

"I have a friend with a high-speed copier," said Russell. "Volunteers can hang the signs. Someone must have seen something. We need to encourage them to come forward. I'm setting up a reward fund."

By Saturday, four days after the murder, volunteers had posted the composite drawing in hundreds of windows and Bill Russell had met with Belmont Oaks fathers, the mayor, the city council, and a local bank to organize the Lance Turner Reward Fund, which was to be awarded to anyone whose information led to the apprehension and conviction of Lance's killer. Volunteers collected donations at shopping centers, while newspapers inspired the rest of the Bay Area to contribute. Within two weeks the fund had risen to $45,000.

Russell would continue to meet frequently with Goulart and other officers. Two years later, a hero behind the scenes, he would play a more direct role in bringing the killer to justice.

On October 6, Lance Turner lay in an open coffin in Duggan's Mortuary, a short distance from Ralston Intermediate and Carlmont High Schools. He wore black, gold-trimmed Belmont Oaks running pants and jacket. Beneath the zipper jacket, the rolled collar of a black turtleneck covered his throat wound.

Carole Williamson, the coach's wife, spent the day in the viewing room, overseeing the guest book. It meant a great deal to her and her husband that the Turners dressed Lance in Belmont Oaks clothing. The Turners, as well as most other families, had made it clear that they in no way thought Ray Williamson hadn't supervised Lance properly. No one blamed Ray at all for the murder, thank God, thought Carole, who knew that the crime had utterly devastated him.

Watching the guests, she noticed that all day, junior and senior high school kids were coming in and laying flowers in the coffin—not formal, store-bought bouquets, but flowers picked from private yards or possibly lifted from the nearby Carlmont Nursery. "Well, I don't care where they got them," she decided. If the kids needed to remember Lance with flowers, let them steal flowers. Anything that helped the kids feel better was all right with her.

By the end of the day, the coffin overflowed with blossoms.

Ray and Carole Williamson met Lance's team members outside the Good Shepherd Episcopal Church the day of the funeral. All the boys wore the Belmont Oaks running suits. Ray's son Padraic had suggested black armbands, so Carole had made them and now pinned one around each boy's arm. "You're welcome to sit with us," she told them, "or if you'd rather stay with your parents, that's fine, too."

The boys clustered together. Soon the American Youth Soccer Organization (AYSO) team they were to play the next day joined them, wearing their team's bright red-and-blue running suits. When the church doors opened, the Williamsons found themselves leading a parade of boys inside, where they sat as two color matched units in the front.

About five hundred Belmont citizens followed, crowding into the church and spilling out the doors. Belmont officers observed the crowd, scanning it with video cameras, hoping to spot the face from the composite.

Ray Williamson gave a eulogy. "Lance was the best," he said, his Irish accent thickened by emotion. He made no effort to hide his tears. "Lance was a jewel." He announced that Lance's player number, ten, would be permanently retired.

Reverend Royston Auelua said, "We ask the question, 'Why? Why did God do this or allow this to happen?' I can only answer you, God had nothing to do with it at all. He has given us free will and it is in our hands where our destiny lies. Lance was not killed by God, but by a fellow human being exercising his free will which God gave to him. I do not know why this happened. I only know there is pain. . . .

"This service today is not for Lance. Lance is fine. It is for all of us who are left behind in pain."

When the service ended, the pallbearers, Belmont Oaks coaches and fathers, lifted the blue coffin and began the slow walk down the aisle to the door. Ray's tears fell heavily onto the lid. The Turners followed, then Carole Williamson. Behind her came the Belmont Oaks boys, then the AYSO team, making a spontaneous and striking processional.

Outside, Lance's mother turned and saw the boys. Some of them were crying and clearly they all felt awkward and didn't know what to do next. Margo Turner smiled and opened her arms. In ones and twos, she embraced them all.

Chapter Five

While Belmont mourned Lance Turner and struggled with fear, police officers worked around the clock, putting in massive overtime and sacrificing routine business. "We were so focused on Lance," Officer Farmer said later, "if a burglary came in, or a fraud, it got put into a box. We never heard the yelling and screaming about these cases. Chief Sanderson told us, 'Don't worry about it.'"

When Sanderson began ordering officers to take a day off after two weeks of this intense pace, they resisted. "There was so much emotion in this department about Lance Turner," Sergeant Goulart recalls, "that if you went home, you couldn't rest anyway." When officers did make it home, they couldn't stop hugging their kids.

One by one, the "persons unaccounted for" turned up.

The jogger in the blue track suit arrived at police headquarters as soon as he heard his description on the news. He was a middle-aged man who jogged daily. He reported that he had seen nothing unusual on October 2. Officers photographed him for the mug book they were assembling, but did not consider him a likely suspect.

Belmont officers knew the "old man who chases boys"; he sometimes slept in Twin Pines Park near police headquarters. When they brought him in for questioning, they reassured him that they didn't object to "different life styles." He denied chasing boys on trails. On the day of the murder, he had just received his benefit check, enabling him to seduce a sex partner with food, booze, and new shoes. They spent a happy day and night in a motel. The police easily verified this.

The city manager phoned in with information about the disabled young men who watched soccer practice. Sergeant Mattei visited their group home and cleared them; for one thing, none had the physical strength or coordination to do what had been done to Lance.

Three days after the murder, gritty-eyed with exhaustion, Officer Halleran took a break at Belmont's Chuck's Donuts. In the tiny parking lot on the town's main street, Ralston Avenue, he saw a battered Karmann Ghia. He called in the license number and ran a registration check. The seventeen-year-old owner, Peter Williams, lived in Belmont.

That evening Mattei and Banks drove to the address, finding the Ghia in the driveway. A black martial-arts uniform lay in the backseat.

A dark-haired, husky teenager answered the door. "Oh, oh," he said. "I've been expecting you for a half hour, ever since I heard you were looking for my car."

"It's been on the news three damn days."

"It has?" Williams glanced over his shoulder. "We can't talk in front of my parents."

"Want to follow us to the station, then?"

At headquarters, Williams admitted that on October 2 he parked by the trail entrance from four-thirty to five. "I was listening to the radio and studying," he said, not meeting anyone's eyes. He said the only person he saw was a man with two dogs.

"Do any smoking or drinking while you were there?" asked Mattei.

Williams studied the ceiling. "Maybe I had a clove cigarette." He said he stepped out and jogged a hundred yards. "Usually I jog the whole trail, but I felt sick that day. I just went back to the car."

What was he hiding? Mattei said, "We'd like to arrange a polygraph."

"Oh, God."

Mattei made an educated guess. "We don't want criminal charges about drugs or something. What we want is information on this murder here."

The teenager pondered. "Okay, look, I never got out of the car. I went there to smoke a couple joints. Then I left."

"Okay. Who'd you buy the pot from?"

"I can't say."

Mattei was worn out. He could barely contain his frustration. Testily, he repeated the spiel about no charges for drugs.

"Okay, Okay," groaned Williams. "It was Willie Soriano."

Before sending Peter Williams home, Mattei snapped a Polaroid photo of him for the thickening mug book. Later Williams passed the polygraph, and the smoking tree girls agreed that he was not "John" or "Don" from the smoking tree.

Checking Willie Soriano's record, the officers learned he was on juvenile probation. They paid him a visit, finding him alone at home, watching a children's program. He was a short boy with blondish, shoulder-length hair, and braces on his teeth. He had pinpoint pupils and smelled of alcohol.

"How old are you, Willie?" asked Mattei.

"Fifteen." He admitted he'd been suspended from

school, which he hated anyway because he couldn't "read so good and the kids are all stuck up."

He told them that on October 2 he'd slept till ten-thirty a.m., when his supplier phoned to say he had scored some marijuana. Later Peter Williams called and Soriano said he'd have some pot to sell him that afternoon. He brought out the clothes he'd worn that day. Mattei documented: "jeans and a gray cutoff shirt with a red, green, brown, and blue picture of Iron Maiden with the Beast surfing on the head of a shark."

That afternoon Soriano skateboarded down Belmont's twisting roads to a church parking lot, where he met his moped-driving drug supplier and bought marijuana.

Back home, Soriano sold some pot to Williams and took a couple of hits from the first joint he rolled. "I got sick," Soriano said. Mattei and Banks glanced at each other. The marijuana had made Williams sick, too. These boys needed a better supplier.

Soriano said Williams left about three-thirty. He watched TV till his mother came home at five. When she left for exercise class at five-thirty, he skateboarded to a pizza place, where he ate supper, and then poured his drug profits into video game machines. While in the liquor store buying cigarettes at eight-thirty that night, he watched police cars and fire engines speeding up to Ralston School. The next morning, while eating breakfast at Heidi's Pies, he read about the murder.

Though Willie Soriano superficially met the description of the smoking tree youth, the timing didn't fit. The officers added his photo to their book. They doubted he was the killer. However, because they could see that he was sliding fast into addiction and crime, they notified his probation officer "of his condition." Like Williams, Soriano later passed polygraph questioning about the murder.

The BPD had now identified and tentatively cleared every person known to have been at Water Dog the day of the murder, with one exception: the strange youth at the smoking tree. Not wanting to scare him away, they continued to tell the media they simply wanted to account for him. In house, though, they called him "The Suspect."

Their problem wasn't lack of leads, but an excess of them. Since public emotion ran so high over this murder, the composite drawing generated hundreds of leads, ranging from highly probable to highly lunatic. Unable to keep up with the volume of calls, the department installed an answering machine.

The dispatcher documented each lead on a form, which Goulart then reviewed and assigned a priority level. Every lead had to be investigated and its outcome written on the form. Uncleared leads could jeopardize the case later if The Suspect went to trial.

Though most of the young men cooperated, some resisted. Weary officers struggled to be diplomatic. Farmer tried "to make them feel sorry for *me,* I'd say, 'I don't think you'd kill anyone, I have no proof. I wouldn't bother you except for this problem we've got. Can you prove where you were? No? Okay. May I take your picture?' "

Officers expended hundreds of hours following leads that rose purely from citizen panic. Terror had stripped layers of enlightenment from Belmont residents, who suddenly suspected the mentally ill, the retarded, and the unconventional, much as their superstitious ancestors had accused misfits of witchcraft.

The police checked dozens of boys with behavior problems or who had records for molesting younger children, many of whom now lived in group treatment homes hundreds of miles away.

Besides investigating the hundreds of leads, which felt like trying to stop a tidal wave with bare hands, officers found more imaginative methods to identify the suspect.

Since the guy wore retainers on his teeth, Farmer mailed the composite and description to orthodontists all over California, tediously tracking the responses for months.

Mattei presented the composite drawing to high school

students in Belmont and neighboring towns and visited the schools' offices numerous times over the next few months to study yearbook photos of every recent graduate named John or Don.

Sergeant Goulart contacted the Department of Motor Vehicles and requested drivers' license photos of sixty-four youths reported as possible suspects. By the end of October, Polaroid pictures and driver's license portraits filled several mug books.

Meanwhile, Mattei and Halleran continued to work as evidence techs. The afternoon after the murder, when they learned about the suspect at the smoking tree, they knew they had a second crime scene to process. They strung yellow tape around the tree and conducted an inch by inch search of the area, bagging candy wrappers, Marlboro butts, ZigZag papers, pop bottles, a Bud Tall can, and the personalized wedding matchbook.

The cramped police headquarters lacked space for so much physical evidence, so the evidence techs barged into the Belmont Arts building next door and commandeered a conference room. Soon they had covered several large tables with bagged items. To protect the chain of evidence, Halleran and Mattei carried the only keys to this room. Whenever they had time, they studied the items, documenting an overwhelming number they couldn't account for.

Goulart assigned Mattei and Cinquini to reinterview Ralston kids and soccer team members in order to refine the information. "We have to know exactly who was where when, who held which beer can, and dropped which bag of Cheetos."

Mattei honed his approach with the kids: "I don't care if you were smoking. I don't care if you were drinking. I don't care if you were smoking dope. If you were and are honest with me, I'm not going to tell anybody. What you say stays here."

Mike Brent didn't trust this. He still claimed he had quit smoking the year before.

Mattei sighed. "See, what we care about is stuff found on the cutback trail where you hung out with your friends that day. Now, a lot of kids told us you smoked there and had a beer."

"We ate Melons candies. There was one soda." Finally Brent admitted he tried to burn a Marlboro cigarette package. He agreed he'd gone down to the pier where his friends had champagne and beer. "I didn't have any," he continued to maintain.

Mattei heated up. "This is a very serious thing. Got that? It's not somebody stealing a pack of cigarettes from the damn store. It's a young boy that's killed. I want to know what you did and who you did it with and I'm not going to beat around the bush. I want to know now. What you say here is not going to go any place."

"I just had a taste."

"You're holding back on us."

Brent stayed tough. "Don't believe me, then."

Eventually he admitted that he drank two beers, though he claimed he took the empty cans out with him.

Struggling through numerous such sessions, the detectives narrowed the information down to a few bits of possibly significant evidence: the wedding matchbook the girls shared with the suspect; a Bud Tall can found beneath the smoking tree that had a partial latent print on it; and a Marlboro butt whose saliva, ideally, could reveal if the smoker was a secretor or non-secretor.

In the end, the matchbook gave up no fingerprints, the partial print from the Bud can proved too fragmented to be useful, and the butt didn't yield enough saliva for testing.

* * *

On October 14, a San Francisco police officer notified Goulart that a seawall at Land's End in San Francisco was spray painted with the words, *I'm very sorry about that boy in Belmont but he called me a faggot.* The officer added, "We have a suspect in custody who lives right by there. He and another guy just confessed to killing two young white males."

"This is it!" Belmont detectives shouted. But when Officer Cinquini questioned the murderers in the San Francisco jail, they denied writing the graffiti, had no idea where Belmont was, and proved to have no connection with Lance Turner.

By the second week, Bill Russell saw that even with reinforcements from the San Carlos police and county sheriffs, the overwhelmed Belmont police couldn't get to the basic task of canvassing the Water Dog Lake neighbors. He and other Belmont Oaks fathers worked out a plan with police that would allow volunteers to do this for them.

On many weeknights and three cold, rainy Saturdays, volunteers, including Carole Williamson, knocked on doors and interrupted people's dinners and TV hours to ask prepared questions. Most residents responded eagerly with tales of wild drinking and drug parties in the woods, drug sales, peculiar neighbors, and the mattress in the shrubs. No one, however, reported seeing a male, with or without blood on him, leaving the trail between four-thirty and five the day of the murder.

The volunteers compiled several thick notebooks of data. Their findings prompted the city council to step up security in the Water Dog Lake area but, like the massive police effort, the canvass did not bring investigators any closer to the unknown killer.

On Halloween, the Belmont police doubled the number

of patrol units on the streets. Dozens of children normally paraded the streets at night in elaborate costumes their mothers had created. Groups of parents would follow their offspring, socializing and carrying pitchers of cocktails. If Lance's killer felt like snagging a child, tonight was his night.

But when darkness fell that Halloween, Belmont turned into a ghost town. Goulart stopped at an intersection and saw black-and-white units on all four corners.

No one was out except cops.

Chapter Six

Besides sifting through and accounting for the physical evidence and clearing hundreds of possible suspects, Sergeant Goulart knew that investigators needed better data about Lance Turner's killer. What did he really look like? How did he act? What went on in the guy's head?

The one-dimensional composite drawing portrayed a pimple-faced kid who vaguely resembled hundreds of males between the ages of thirteen and forty-five. On October 9, Goulart brought in the four girls to study a modified version. They didn't like it much better than the first, but it went to the newspapers. The third refinement, made a few days later, didn't satisfy anyone either.

Goulart discussed the problem with the DA in early November, then with his detectives. "The composite is shit. We're going to have to hypnotize one of the girls, but the problem is, whoever we hypnotize, we sacrifice." California law considered hypnotized witnesses "tainted," unduly influenced, and they could not testify. The three detectives decided to use Heidi.

Goulart contacted Tom Macris, the police artist for the

San Jose Police Department. Macris agreed to help. Macris had an excellent reputation. He had worked several times with Bay Area psychic Kathryn Rhea and in the late seventies, their joint efforts had helped solve some murders.

Heidi sat at a table with Belmont Lieutenant Scales, who was trained in hypnotism, and Tom Macris. Once Heidi went under, Macris systematically offered her sets of shapes for eyes, lips, facial structure, and other details. Gently he eased information from her, and as she hesitantly answered, a face took shape beneath his hand. The portrait differed from the others—the hair was darker, the complexion less spotty, the eyes rounder.

"Does this look right?" Macris showed her a three-dimensional face nearly as complete as a photograph.

"It's him!"

Goulart tested the picture with the other smoking tree girls and boys. They all agreed, "That's the guy."

The first time Goulart saw Lance Turner's body, he knew that the crime met the guidelines for FBI assistance. Not long before the murder, he had attended a workshop in murder investigation methods that included the FBI Behavioral Science Unit's (BSU) preliminary findings from its study of psychological profiles of serial killers and rapists.

The public of the 1990s is familiar with FBI psychological profiling, but in October 1984, when Sergeant Goulart requested a psychological profile of Lance Turner's killer, he was using a service that had been available less than a year.

In the late seventies, the media, plus grass roots movements by and for crime victims and parents of missing children, pushed for improved methods of tracking and stopping criminals. In 1980, President Reagan set up a task force on Victims of Violent Crime, while his attorney general, William French Smith, called for each agency of the Department of Justice to submit reports on how to curb crime. The task forces universally urged a centralized system for tracing serial criminals, a recommendation that paralleled demands by parents of missing children. The recommendations led to the creation of the Violent Criminal Apprehension Program (VICAP).

Connected with that, the task forces demanded generous funding for the FBI's Behavioral Science Unit so it could develop a formalized Crime Analysis and Criminal Personality Profiling System. Detailed, lengthy interviews with known serial killers and rapists were teaching the BSU agents a great deal about modi operandi, rituals, motivations, and predictable behavior. They learned to determine if a criminal was "organized" or "disorganized," whether one or more perpetrators were involved, and whether or not the killer knew the victim. Such insights would enable investigators to understand and manipulate perpetrators so they could be caught.

The BSU's preliminary insights had just begun to be shared with law enforcement in 1983. With FBI profiling in mind, Goulart had made sure that the original crime-scene data included such details as weather conditions, wind direction, and aerial photographs of the area and its surroundings. He assigned the overworked but thorough Sergeant Mattei to compile the rest of the materials the FBI special agents wanted: photos of the crime scene, body, and autopsy; the medical reports including all lab results; a map of the victim's movements before the murder; detailed background about him; and socioeconomic data about the community.

On November 6, Goulart sent a memo to his men describing the FBI's preliminary impressions. The murder was "a youthful type of crime" committed by someone with an "exploding type of personality." The severity of the wounds indicated great anger. The perpetrator wasn't an aggressive, abusive person, but one who tried to impress kids. He might have lied to the girls about his name and high school. He had an alcohol and substance abuse problem. This was not the first time he had approached someone, but it was the first time he had killed.

Tell me something I don't know, thought some Belmont officers.

They reacted differently to the completed report that arrived December 10, though.

Special Agent Patricia Lee Kirby had completed the profile in consultation with one of the BSU study's experts, John E. Douglas, later to become well known through his own books about profiling. The report was broken down into sections.:

Victimology: *"The Victim" was from an "upper-middle-class suburban California city." He was well adjusted, had no evidence of substance abuse problems, was a good student, popular, and had speed and coordination. "It is felt that he would flee from danger rather than confronting it."*

He was "an exceptionally good-looking boy with blond hair, blue eyes and long dark eyelashes. He was comely to the point of pretty." He had a normal interest in girls. He should have been a "low risk victim. Given the location of the crime scene and the number of other children in the area, he was definitely a victim of opportunity." He was probably not known to the offender, though they could have been familiar to each other.

Medical Examination Report: *The cause of death was exsanguination (bleeding to death). After describing the number and size of the wounds, the report notes that the abrasions on the right forehead "were the result of the killer striking the victim with a rock in order to control and silence him. Also consistent with the attempt to silence is the deep penetration of the thoracic cavity and esophagus." The killer had tried to cut Lance's throat so he couldn't scream. The rock and the effort to silence the victim would both become modus operandi identifiers later.*

The report verified that Lance fought hard: "The multi-

tude of slashes on the buttocks and right thigh suggest the Victim was on his back with legs raised to kick. There were also defense wounds on the ankles, hands, wrists, and fingers."

Crime Scene Analysis: *Describing the scene so familiar to Belmont officers, the profiler said that the crime "was not painstakingly concealed" and speculated that the first blood was that on the trail and the further blood spots came "from the Victim fighting off the assailant. The location of the bloodied rock is probably the point at which the offender made his initial approach to the Victim."*

The probable sequence was: "The offender approached the Victim, the Victim was less than receptive, the offender became angry, picked up a rock and swung at the Victim, hitting him on the forehead." He fell to the ground or tried to flee. He was killed at the spot where the body was found.

"The Victim was approached because of his age and appearance. The offender was roused: he may have believed him a girl at first sight.

"The Victim was alone and vulnerable." It was a "high-risk crime" because it was done in daylight with many people nearby. It was "not preplanned but occurred because the perpetrator panicked and tried to seize control. The assailant was fully prepared to take advantage of a young child, but he was not prepared to murder the Victim."

Offender Profile: *The murder was sexually motivated despite no evidence of sexual assault. The "offender was in a known juvenile area when school was out and athletic activities were occurring; this timing ensures exposure to young boys and girls. Because of maximum exposure to teenagers that day, there was very high risk to the assailant. To lower his risk and get highest results he must be quite familiar with the area."*

The profiler concluded, therefore, that the perpetrator probably lived in the immediate area.

"Such crimes are intra-racial," she went on, "so the perpetrator is white, statistically seventeen to twenty-two, single,

lives with a family member on whom he is dependent financially and emotionally. . . . He is an underachiever with average to low IQ. He is not a shrewd or cunning individual."

The killer would have problems with interpersonal relationships. He "has no truly positive sexual relations in his own peer group. He is not confident with males or females his own age; he was considered an oddball in high school and now by those who know him casually."

He would have poor self-image and would not be physically attractive. He would be a loner. "If he dates, it is with younger girls. He can't control or impress a girl his own age. He is possibly a latent homosexual since he is attracted to early teens, a time when the sexual differences between males and females are minimal.

"He probably finished high school or has his GED.

"He abuses drugs and alcohol and may have a prior criminal record for this.

"He did not bring the knife for the purpose of killing, but because it is part of his daily attire. It was used in panic or anger; he failed to establish a relationship to the Victim and was angered by the Victim's attempt to flee." Excessive alcohol or drug use contributed to his actions.

Post Offense Behavior: *He went directly home or to a close relative's home. "His clothing was bloody so he had to go immediately to a safe place. He thoroughly cleaned the knife but didn't throw it away. He might have destroyed his clothing. He probably still carries the knife."*

He would have behavioral changes after the murder. He wouldn't return to the crime scene or attend the funeral. He would become more isolated and might miss work. Sleeping poorly, feeling nervous, he would drink and do drugs more. "He will probably alter his appearance. He will be highly stressed by the crime and publicity. He will try to leave the area for a legitimate reason. The knife is for 'macho-ism' so he may try to enlist in the military."

The profile became a valuable tool in the ongoing and intense investigation. By the time it arrived in its final, typed form, the Belmont police had found a person who matched it in virtually every detail.

On November 14, Mattei had returned to Carlmont High School to conduct yet another mind-numbing search for "Johns" and "Dons" in the school's old records. When he entered the school office, he tossed the Tom Macris composite drawing onto the desk of one of the school secretaries.

He sat down and dug into the latest stack of folders. A few moments passed before he noticed the secretary's intense silence. He looked over at her. She was staring down at the picture with her hand pressed hard against her mouth.

Chapter Seven

"You know him?" asked Mattei. The secretary looked shocked, and tears had appeared in her eyes.

"This looks a lot like— He was a student clerk. I supervised him for years." She shook her head. "He had a lot of problems, but I just can't believe—"

In bits and pieces, she told Mattei about a former student who had severe learning disabilities that interfered with reading and math, yet the educational psychologist had found that in areas not requiring reading, he had tested in the 130-IQ range. Part of the student's special education program required him to earn job experience through working as a student clerk. She and another secretary had supervised him for years.

"He was usually very sweet," she said. "We were friends. I trusted him so much I let him house-sit for me twice when I went on vacations. He did it for several of my friends, too."

She said the young man had been socially immature. Most students had disliked him. Not only had his learning problems set him apart, but he had zero social skills. He tried to impress schoolmates with wild stories. He'd claimed he was a drug informer for the Belmont police and that he had connections with the Mafia and the CIA. He'd acted like a little kid who claimed to know Superman. Often he would become frustrated in class, burst into rageful tears, and run to her or other staff members for comfort. Several middle-aged female staff, and the psychologist Robert Kauk, had been as close to him as she had, had tried to help and comfort him, and still went out to lunch with him when he came to town.

"Who is he?" Mattei asked again. "We'll check him out. If he's clean, we'll clear him."

She sighed. "This picture looks a lot like Jon Dunkle."

Mattei took the picture around to the other staff members the secretary had mentioned. They reacted with shock and near tears and named Jon Dunkle.

On November 16, Goulart stood at the flip chart again, continuing the tedious work of logging cleared leads and adding the new ones that poured in daily. The Macris composite had stimulated a new rush of calls. The investigators took turns reporting their latest activities.

Mattei said, "Some Carlmont High staff say it looks like a guy named Jon Dunkle."

"That's odd," said Juvenile Officer Whaley. "I've been trying to reach him the last couple of weeks in this reinvestigation of the John Davies case. He keeps shining me on."

Fifteen-year-old John Davies had disappeared three years before, creating a nightmare case complete with bad press, recent FBI involvement, and angry, activist parents who badmouthed the department on TV whenever possible.

On the surface, the Davies disappearance had nothing in common with Lance Turner's murder. The Davies boy had been a brainy but unpopular boy, reputed to experiment with drugs. The first investigator determined quickly that the kid ran away and passed the case on to Whaley, who bore the brunt of the family's anger for almost three years. Right now a VIA flow chart of the Davies investigation covered three walls of the staff conference room. Jon Dunkle's name appeared often on that chart, next to Mrs. Davies' stock phrase: "When my son vanished from our lives, so did our friend Jon Dunkle."

If Jon Dunkle proved to be the link between the Davies disappearance and Lance Turner's murder, the police had handled the Davies case wrong from day one.

Part Two

John Davies
November 1981–
November 1984

Chapter Eight

On November 7, 1981—his last normal day—John Davies rose mid-morning. It was Saturday and he needed to catch a ride with his mother to the library. In the kitchen, he greeted the family's Portuguese exchange student, Carlos, in the backward talk the Davies boys used: "Hi, Solrac."

Seventeen-year-old Carlos Marquez smiled, then returned to his sheet of figures. His Junior Achievement Club was setting up a mock corporation.

"John, I'm leaving by eleven," called Joan Davies. A program director for a high school district across the bay, Joan would monitor a swim meet all afternoon.

John hurried through his usual two bowls of Cheerios, then brushed his teeth, flashing a no-metal smile at himself in the mirror. Two days earlier his braces had come off. Better, but still no prize. His freckled face had no hint of a beard and his body carried remnants of baby fat. Two years earlier, the eighth grade class at Ralston Middle School had named him Boy with Best Hair. The joke, which John hadn't caught for a while, was that he had the oiliest, geekiest hair in school.

This fall when Joan transferred John and his seventeen-year-old brother Mark into Serra, the prestigious Catholic boys' high school, John's social life got even worse. His big words and physical immaturity earned him catcalls like "Fag!"

Desperate to fit in, John shadowed Mark. Four years earlier when the Davies family had transplanted itself from the Midwest to Belmont, California, Mark had learned that high school cliques consisted of jocks, brains, or stoners. He'd chosen stoner. At Serra, John followed Mark to the "smoking pit" and eagerly befriended boys who smoked pot and played Dungeons & Dragons. At home Mark let John tag along to wild neighborhood parties and to drinking bouts in the nearby hills.

Social experimentation brought John friends, but wrecked his usually high grades. His mother scolded him, and John himself wanted to do well. He intended to become a doctor. Today, he'd research two history papers before visiting his new and best friend, Larry Roche.

He pulled on dark blue corduroy pants and a T-shirt with the Kansas rock band logo. Then he jammed his feet into his Nikes, the only shoes left besides his church shoes since he and his mother had thrown out his old ones. She planned to take him on a "shoe run" soon.

John gathered his binder, Dungeons and Dragons notebook, and the "pet calculator" he carried everywhere and ran out to the car.

Joan Davies watched John's uncoordinated dash down the driveway. Her beloved youngest son didn't have an athletic bone in his body.

Joan held high expectations for herself and her family. Her father had created the Hallmark slogan, "When you care enough to send the very best," and she strove always to match that standard. When John's grades recently nose-dived, Joan's heart dove with them. He'd read full sentences by age three, rattled off human physiology at ten, yet now he was dipping his toes into his brother's troubled waters of drinking, drugs, and wildness.

"John," she said impulsively as she drove, "do you wish we'd stayed in Chicago?" She'd nearly divorced her husband, Jim, when he accepted a high-level job with Varian Associates in San Francisco in 1977.

"Serra High is flu city," said John. "But I like working with Dad on the Victorians."

"Let's pray they make a profit," said Joan. A year after uprooting his family from Chicago to California, Jim had quit corporate America. He had foundered and Joan, climbing toward a vice principal position, currently supported the family. Jim was now launching a one-hour photo business and renovating Victorian houses in The City. After rocky high school years, their oldest son, Jimmy, was rising in the navy. Mark and John seemed to be settling down in Serra High School. Joan believed her family was mending.

Joan pulled up outside the San Mateo Public Library. "Don't forget to clean up that three feet of debris tonight," she reminded John.

"No problem," John answered. If nothing else would goad him to clean his room, his beloved Grandma Bell's upcoming visit would.

He walked away with a hint of teenage male lope. Joan realized that soon her baby would have peach fuzz and a cracking voice.

He stepped into the library and she never saw him again.

At five-thirty, Jim Davies played back a message on their new answering machine. "Hi," said John. "I'm running late."

Jim had been banging around hardware stores. Since he was financing the photo business by borrowing against the heavily mortgaged Belmont home on Winding Way—

their dream house—he needed to profit soon from the Victorian houses he was renovating in San Francisco.

Like many Belmont homes, the Davies house hung over a slope, its deck perched on stilts above a slice of California countryside so steep that the home could only be entered from the front door.

In the main level, vaulted ceilings and oversize windows supported a forest of house plants. The three bedrooms included a luxurious master suite at the end of a long hall. Equipped with pool table and video games, the family room encouraged the boys and their friends to stick around rather than go drinking and driving.

Downstairs, Mark and Jimmy had built their own bedrooms. Jimmy's was now Jim's office.

Jim changed for the dinner party where he was to meet Joan. He and she always drove separately, their busy lives keeping them at opposite ends of the earth.

In the kitchen, he found John at the table, while Carlos clowned and Mark whipped something up at the stove. Jim checked John's history notes. "Looking good," he said.

"Dad, remember church tomorrow," said Mark. They attended Belmont Baptist and last summer Jim, Mark, and their friend Jon Dunkle were saved together by Billy Graham.

At the dinner party, Jim and Joan watched the movie *Ordinary People.* The portrayal of marital dysfunction and a mother rejecting her surviving son in favor of the dead one depressed them both.

After supper Mark took two friends to his room, which felt like a tree fort. At night he could watch San Francisco glitter, and in the mornings the sun rose over the crown of the buckeye tree.

Ordinarily, Mark would go through a few six-packs with buddies, but he hadn't recovered from the party he'd taken

John to the night before. As soon as Mark flopped on his bed and started schmoozing, John butted in. Mark usually enjoyed being the kid's guide to teen life, but tonight he wasn't in the mood. He snapped, "Hey, scram."

"I can stay if I want."

"Go clean your room."

"Later."

"Jesus, you're a fucking shadow. Get a life, why don't you?" Mark hauled himself up and grabbed him. God! That high-pitched screech! When would the kid's voice change?

John flailed his arms. "You still fight like a girl," Mark said, wrestling him through the door. "Beat it."

John stomped up the stairs crying. Soon Mark heard furniture banging around. Around ten, he went upstairs and checked John's room. "Hey, great job!"

John refused to answer.

At eleven, Mark fell asleep. John walked Mark's friends home. Then he and Carlos watched a TV movie. At twelve-thirty, they said good night. Carlos saw John shut his bedroom door, then heard John's tape deck start up with a new album by the rock group Yes.

At one-thirty, Jim and Joan entered the dark house and closed the door behind them.

In the morning, Joan found the door ajar when she went outside for the paper. *Mark,* she thought. He was always sneaking in late and leaving the door silently on the latch.

At nine a.m., Joan peeked into John's room to wake him for church. He was not there.

Joan Davies thought, *Something is terribly wrong.* Subliminally, she noted the details that she and Jim would tell police for the next five years: "He left his money, his new jacket, his pet calculator, his only shoes. With his touchy feet, he wouldn't go past the driveway in socks. He laid out his church clothes."

But that first morning she distrusted her premonition and woke the family to demand a sensible explanation. "Mark, did John sleep down there with you?"

Mark stumbled up, confused. "He's probably just trying to ditch church."

Could John have fallen from the high deck? Jim descended the rough stairs carved into the incline outside. No John.

Joan rounded on Mark. "Did you and he sneak out last night?" It was an open secret that Mark, sometimes joined by John, slipped out with certain friends in the middle of the night to go drinking in the hills.

Mark's face registered a *Shit! No secrets!* look. "I went to bed early."

Though Joan prided herself on being tough, tears trembled in her eyes. "Something's happened."

"Come on," said Jim. "We'll find him here nursing a hangover when we get back from church."

After the service, Jim hurried home, while Joan stayed for the fellowship potluck, greeting friends, serving food, praying for Jim and a shamefaced John to appear.

But at home, Jim was calling the police.

Officer Joe Farmer, who in 1984 was the first detective at the Lance Turner scene, was in 1981 a tall, handsome Belmont boy on the police force about a year. He'd been taught that missing kids either came home or contacted someone within twenty-four hours.

Farmer found Jim Davies concerned, but "not totally mystified. Mr. Davies was a very jovial guy, real nice guy. *Real* nice . . . . I sat there for a long time with him, as you usually do with these questions. . . . They had an open door policy in that house; they didn't lock doors. It seemed like a lot of times they just wouldn't know who was in the house."

Farmer classified John as a 601, "a youth who has broken a law that pertains only to his status as a minor," i.e., a runaway. He wrote, "For the past few weeks, according to John's father, John has been acting a little belligerent toward parental control. The father did not think too much of this, as he has experienced the same behavior with the other boys on occasion. This is the first time John has run away." Farmer listed John's friends and noted that John had left without ID, shoes, or wallet.

For "Disposition" Farmer wrote, "Refer to Whole Earth," an experimental teen counseling project. After the question, "Investigation Completed?" Farmer checked "Yes."

Later, Jim Davies insisted that he said, "John would *never* run away," and that he didn't call John "belligerent." He returned to church believing he'd set off an investigation. It was the first of many bitter misunderstandings between the Davies and the Belmont Police Department.

The Davies brainstormed. John must have sneaked out with friends, probably Jon Dunkle or Larry Roche, to drink beer and been sick or hurt, like when Carlos broke his arm.

"Ah, yes!" joked Carlos. "My first lesson in the U.S.: never get drunk at the top of a cliff!"

"Some of the party places in the woods are pretty rugged," said Mark.

Joan said, "I can't believe his friends would just leave him." Yet she did believe it—she worked in a high school.

Jim and Mark checked with neighbors, while Joan phoned everyone listed in John's Dungeons & Dragons notebook. No luck.

To get more Serra students' phone numbers, Jim phoned the president of the Serra Dads' Club, but couldn't make him understand that John might be injured and a Serra kid might know where. "Your son running away doesn't have anything to do our school," the man insisted.

* * *

Mark slipped into John's room, shut the door, and examined the decorative Gallo Wine bottle in the corner. The film container in which he and John kept LSD tabs was still lodged in its long neck. Mark worked the container out and opened it.

The LSD was gone.

Oh, damn, oh, damn. Angry with Mark, John must have swallowed it and wandered off high. Last week, when John tried LSD for the first time, he'd peered at Mark and asked, "Who are you?" He couldn't handle hallucinogens at all.

Mark snagged a bottle of wine from the liquor cabinet and headed for his room. What would he tell his parents? And where would John go if he'd been tripping? Mark had searched the wooded areas and called everyone he could think of.

He drank all the wine, but couldn't get drunk and kill his fears.

"I'm going to make flyers," said Jim, who had never seen a missing child poster. Joan nodded, grateful. "He's changed since this was taken," Jim went on. The school photo exaggerated John's freckles , and he no longer had those ugly braces.

As Jim printed MISSING TEEN on a sheet of paper, Joan's premonition swelled to painful certainty: *John is either dead or it will be a long, long time before I see him again.*

Chapter Nine

That night, fog spilled over the hills into Belmont's canyons and blanketed yards in a wet, cold cloud. When Detective Sergeant Tompkins walked into headquarters Monday morning, dew drenched his shoes.

The dispatcher signaled and Tompkins grabbed the nearest phone. "What's happening in the search for my son?" a man asked.

"Name?"

"John Davies."

"Age?"

"I told you people all this yesterday! He's fifteen."

"Oh. A runaway."

"John would *never* run away! He's out somewhere hurt and—"

Tompkins cut off the tirade: "I'll be right there." He checked yesterday's reports. Nothing on a "missing" kid. He headed out.

* * *

Mr. Davies opened the door—a tall, stout, bearded man. There was a large, solid woman standing behind him. Their swollen eyes revealed sleeplessness and tears.

Tompkins followed them down a long hall while Davies insisted, "John isn't the type of boy who would run away; that's the last thing he would ever do."

"Mm." Tompkins glanced around the boy's neat bedroom, taking in the Gallo bottle.

Davies pointed to a pair of Nikes. "Those are his only shoes. Do you really think he would run away in his stocking feet?"

The wife whispered, "Shh."

"You can't know how many shoes he has," said Tompkins. "Kids are tricky."

The father said, "He slipped out with someone and they abandoned him or something."

The mother added, "They might have gone out to try marijuana."

Tompkins glanced at the ZONED sign on the wall. Drug culture. He jotted names, asked about places "frequented by the juvenile," and flipped his notebook shut.

Mrs. Davies touched his arm. "John is dead," she said, "or else it'll be a long, long time before I see him again."

"Oh, he'll come home when he gets cold and hungry," Tompkins reassured her. "I'll be in touch."

A short teenage boy hovered in the driveway. "I'm Mark," he whispered. "Listen, there's LSD missing. Maybe something happened to him while he was on a bad trip."

Chasing runaways wasn't a detective's job, but the Juvenile Officer position had been vacant one and a half years and it appeared "to be rather unusual circumstances on the missing juvenile," Tompkins noted. Teletypes with John Davies's description went to the closest cities, San

Mateo and Foster City. They mentioned "possible LSD" and John's "belligerence."

On Wednesday, Tompkins received a blast from Jim Davies. "You haven't notified other counties? You call that a wide net?"

Tompkins documented:

> The report was taken from the file secondary to the father's call due to circumstances suggesting to Lt. Scales to update the missing person teletype ASAP and to have dispatchers send out verbal broadcasts for next 3 days each shift to ensure officer awareness.

Tompkins contacted the Serra High School principal, who wouldn't allow him to question students. Since Serra was in the next town over, San Mateo, Tompkins had no authority there. Instead he questioned a few of John's friends at their homes. All said John was "too chicken" to run away. Larry Roche reported that John phoned him the night he disappeared, "all weird, like he wanted to tell me something, but I hung up. A friend was waiting outside."

On the second day, Jim Davies urged Tompkins to explore teen party places at Edgewood Park and Vista points, all of which lay along Highway 280, a scenic four-lane that ran past the grassy hills behind a row of linked towns: Belmont, San Carlos, Redwood City, Woodside, and Palo Alto. Tompkins, Farmer, and a dog conducted "an area search by foot" of wooded areas within Belmont city limits, but not along 280 because it lay outside Belmont's jurisdiction. Tompkins documented that the Belmont locations were "thick with vegetation, very steep and very hard to maneuver around." The dog found nothing.

On the fourth day, Belmont Officer Gorran explored the local Sea Scout base, pool hall, and abandoned radio station.

* * *

Tompkins kept hearing from Joan Davies. "We really think John possibly went out to meet with Jon Dunkle to perhaps smoke some dope. We can't reach him. Please could you speak to him soon?"

"Right," grunted Tompkins. He tried several times, but the young man's parents always claimed he wasn't home.

On the fifth day, Tompkins took another irate call from Jim Davies. "John would have gone out with Dunkle, no questions asked. Why the hell haven't you questioned him yet?"

At six p.m., Tompkins knocked on the door of the Dunkle family's ranch-style house in Belmont. Several years earlier, he had arrested their older son, Jeff, for dealing drugs. The youth had become Tompkins's informant. In the process, however, Jeff allegedly "burned out" through bad drugs and his bitter father blamed the police. Jon would have been about ten at the time.

The drapes were closed and the house was dark, but eventually a short, dark-haired man cracked open the door.

"I need to speak to Jon," said Tompkins.

"My boy is at work."

"Where?"

"You'll just harass him and make him lose his job." Mr. Dunkle slammed the door.

Tompkins phoned Jim Davies back. Davies exclaimed. "They won't tell you where he works? *I'll* tell you where he works! For the third time!"

Tompkins went to Toys "Я" Us in Redwood City. Dunkle was a short, brown-haired, slightly clumsy youth with chipmunk cheeks, immature for his twenty-one years. Shyly cooperative, Dunkle acted embarrassed and took Tompkins into the storeroom.

"The last night I was at the Davies' house was the fourth or fifth. I went about midnight to take Mark out." He'd never heard of Mark or John using LSD. He couldn't imagine what happened to John and would do whatever he could to help.

Dunkle's supervisor said Dunkle had started the job on Monday, November 9, and there were "no juveniles" hanging around him.

Tompkins checked Dunkle's name off.

Near the end of the week, Officer Gorran noticed, "Evidently, posters have been transmitted about the area. . . ." The publicity was producing sightings. People saw John in the next county, barefoot in the rain, or fifty miles away in Santa Cruz, on a pier or street, or in a van, or over the San Mateo hills in Half Moon Bay.

LSD and pot. Slipping grades. Age fifteen rebellion. Sightings in hippie runaway havens. No evidence of foul play, accident or injury.

Tompkins and Gorran agreed that all signs pointed to RUNAWAY.

Jim and Joan Davies were raised to accept authority without question and to believe that "the system," like a wise parent, would guide and assist them in time of need.

This belief began a long, slow crumble when John disappeared. "Why doesn't he respect us?" Joan wondered, deeply offended by Tompkins's remark, "He'll come home when he's tired and hungry." She couldn't believe officers would disregard a parent's knowledge that her son was not the type to run away.

Jim's reaction was, "We have to take care of this ourselves." During the first weeks, paralleling police efforts, the Davies ran their own investigation.

On Monday morning, the copy shop clerk refused Jim Davies's credit card. "For God's sake," cried Jim, "my son is missing!" After much negotiation, the man allowed them to run the posters. MISSING! MISSING! MISSING! Joan visualized John soaked and bone cold somewhere. She fled to the car to weep in private.

In the kitchen "command center," Joan took calls. Most came from crackpots or private detectives offering expensive services. When she phoned reporters, they said missing kids were "too common to be newsworthy," but suggested she place ads for seventy-five dollars.

Sacrificing teen secretiveness for John's sake after Tompkins's visit, Mark told his parents about party places in the woods. Then he confided, "John's too naive to run away, he's got no street smarts. But a couple weeks ago he tried to sell a sheet of two hundred LSD tabs and a guy stole them. The dealer's probably after John for the money."

Jim Davies agreed that about the only thing that would scare John more than running away itself would be an angry drug dealer. But was this tale real, or teen hysteria?

He phoned Roger Asti, a friend from Marriage Encounter, who had spent his teen years on the streets. Asti brought over a friend, Chui, a six-foot-six, bearded, tattooed Mexican-American, who clumped into the Davies middle-class home in battered motorcycle boots. Before back injuries forced him off his Harley, Chui wielded power with bikers. "I ain't workin' for free," Chui announced.

"Okay," said Jim, agreeing with some misgivings to an hourly fee well above minimum wage.

"Right. I gotta make some calls."

While Asti searched John's room for clues, Chui banged numbers into the phone. "You hear anything about someone's out to get a kid in Belmont?" he growled. "You know, Belmont. By fuckin' San Mateo! Don't give me that shit. You better know something by tomorrow."

Jim listened with disbelief. "This guy is threatening the

Mexican Mafia!" he whispered to Joan. "We're in *The Twilight Zone!*"

Jim Davies's mother, the petite, religious, hardworking Grandma Judith Bell arrived from Colorado. She quickly formed her own opinions: "The biker was just taking Jim for a ride, and that other man kept saying there were indications that John had deep problems and used drugs." Her John was a gifted, loving boy who'd helped her teach Bible classes back home in Colorado Springs last summer. The deep and special love between John and Grandma Bell was legendary within the family.

Each day, after a couple of hours' rest, Jim Davies and Roger Asti, with help from Mark and Mark's friends, distributed posters in widening circles that finally included several counties. Asti took Davies to San Francisco streets and parks, where they met ageless runaways. They snooped around boats, sheds, large drainpipes, and oil drums along the mid-peninsula mud flats. Fast food containers and moldy sleeping bags indicated that people lived in these places, but Davies couldn't imagine John there.

When Tompkins wouldn't search wooded party spots outside the Belmont city limits, Davies did it himself. Several nights between midnight and four, he, Asti, and Chui hit Vista Points along Highway 280. Then they tried the teens' favorite place, Edgewood Park, a preserve of rolling hills and chaparral a few miles farther south on the same route.

One morning at three a.m., the men stumbled up a dirt track in the park. Their flashlights lit on empty beer cans, whisky bottles, snack wrappers, and condoms. Ahead, pink rectangular buildings stood side by side: the old Hassler Home, "the Morgue" to teens. Inside were rusted hospital beds, and one room contained stainless steel tables that must have been used for autopsies. Mark had reported that Jon Dunkle loved going there. The boys would wander through the dark halls, drinking, opening doors, joking about death.

Now, crunching across broken glass, Davies, Chui, and Asti explored a hall. Their flashlight beams converged on a short, wide-eyed security guard. "What're you doing here?" the guard stammered.

Chui flexed his tattoos. "We want to know something and we want to know it now." He thrust John's poster at the guard. "You seen this kid in here or up there on the hill?"

"I don't know what goes on out there."

"There's beer cans, bottles, trash all over the damn place!" said Davies. "You never go up there and chase kids off?' "

"No. I'm scared of them. I feel safer right here in the building."

Jim Davies and his helpers searched for several more nights. They found no trace of John.

The Davies ran into the same resistance at Serra High School that Tompkins had: The principal would not allow them to speak to John's classmates or Dungeons and Dragons friends. The principal questioned kids himself and notified Joan that they knew nothing.

Mike DeLeon was scared. His parents weren't home and he'd opened the door to a red-eyed, bearded man who looked like some raging patriarch from the Old Testament, plus a tattooed criminal type wearing murderous boots. These crazy dudes demanded that he tell about drug dealers at Serra High School and midnight drinking bouts in the woods.

"I don't know anything about drugs," he said.

When DeLeon realized the bearded guy was Mr. Davies, and they were searching for his Dungeons & Dragons friend John, he said he'd heard that John had planned to turn in an LSD dealer from biology class and to escape his wrath, John was holed up in the Richards's house.

Jim Davies remembers his bullying now with much embarrassment. "We did some crazy, crazy things. Scaring hell out of those boys wasn't exactly nice. But what kid will give information to the dean of a Catholic school?" If John lay injured somewhere, time was running out.

Chapter Ten

When Sergeant Tompkins informed the Davies he'd cleared Jon Dunkle, they had trouble accepting it. "Our son would have gone out with Jon Dunkle, no questions asked," they told everyone. As time passed, they added, "When our son disappeared from our lives, so did Jon Dunkle." Their other friends couldn't do enough to help, but the young man who had been almost a family member for four years didn't even return their phone calls.

Four years earlier, in 1977, during Fellowship at Belmont Baptist Church, the Davies' oldest son, Jimmy, introduced a shy youth to them. "This is Jon Dunkle," Jimmy said. "We're in the same P.E. class."

Dunkle ducked his head and smiled up at them, seeming younger than seventeen. Joan instantly picked up on his need for care and love. "Come have Sunday dinner with us," she offered, and his surprised, joyful smile rewarded her.

Dunkle's Sunday visits spread to weeknights. Sometimes

he told vague stories of abuse and trouble in the family. "My problem [with learning disabilities] started when my brother pushed me out the window when I was two," he would say. "He was a police informer and I am, too." When he stumbled in drunk with Jimmy Davies, he said, "My father will beat me if he sees me like this," and Joan let him sleep it off in the family room.

Like all the Davies' friends, Dunkle entered the unlocked house at will. Soon he called Jim and Joan "Dad" and "Mom." On Christmas Day, 1980, when his own father gave him a white Honda Civic, Dunkle burst into the master bedroom where Joan was napping. "Mom, Mom! Come see my car!"

He brought gifts like foreign coins or gold jewelry. Once he sold Jim an unusual gold and jeweled scarab pin for Joan.

Trained in Special Education, Joan tutored him when he prepared for an air force exam. His dyslexia was severe and he often exploded in rage and tears.

Dunkle and Jim sometimes shared beer and man talk at the kitchen table. "What other dad can you sit around and BS with like that?" Mark asked his buddies.

Jimmy Davies had befriended Dunkle out of pity. The guy didn't know how to act. His father seemed a strict, mean, suspicious man who kept his son away from other kids, so Jimmy had decided to "get him out of that house and teach him to be a teenager." This meant including him in beach parties and in drinking bouts at the Hassler Home, Vista Points, and Edgewood Park. "That's why his father hated me," Jimmy said later.

The Davies boys and their friends tormented Dunkle. "Your folks are the Munsters," they would tease. "Your sister's the Bride of Frankenstein." Sexually active themselves, they figured Dunkle "must be queer" since he never had a girlfriend. "Who'd have sex with *him?*"

He was a lightweight with alcohol. He would get giggly,

then fall asleep in his parked car, his greasy hair leaving a smear against the window.

When Jimmy Davies and his friend Don Wolfe graduated and left home in 1980, twenty-year-old Dunkle turned for friendship to their fifteen-year-old brothers, Mark Davies and John Wolfe. They used him to buy alcohol and take them to party spots in the woods and learned things about him their parents didn't know.

"I stole thousands of dollars worth of gold jewelry from Belmont Lapidary," Dunkle announced one night. "I hate that mean lady owner. She fired me." Mark then realized where Dunkle's jewelry gifts came from. Dunkle also bragged about stealing tiny gold parts from a computer firm that employed him in security.

Once Mark went to his room and caught Dunkle staring at Mark's naked girlfriend, who was too terrified to pull up the covers. Dunkle acted as if he were in a trance till Mark manhandled him out of the room.

During Thanksgiving week, 1980, Mark got in trouble for fighting with John and took off in his truck. When he returned, Dunkle was parked in the driveway, wearing his security guard uniform. "You'd better not go inside yet," he said. "Hey, got money for beer?"

"Sure! Let's go!" Mark jumped into Dunkle's car. They loaded up on beer and Jack Daniel's and headed for a Vista Point. Mark kidded around with some other guys, while Dunkle pouted, got drunk, and fell asleep in his car.

Later, Mark shook him awake. "Hey, move over, I'd better drive."

Dunkle's right arm lashed out. "No one drives this car but me!"

"Okay, fine, man."

Wild and uncoordinated, Dunkle careened up 280 and hit Belmont's narrow streets at eighty mph. Sirens sounded.

"Shit, the cops," cried Mark.

Dunkle laughed. "I'll ditch them."

"No! Stop the damn car!"

"Hell, no."

Mark clutched his head, preparing to crash. Up ahead, he saw flashing lights as the cops cut off the intersection. The car fishtailed.

"Step out of the car, both hands up!" An officer slammed Dunkle against the car. "It was the old combat boot in the back, they roughed him up pretty good," Mark said later.

Mark told them, "I kept asking him to stop. I want to live to a ripe old age."

Joan ruled that Mark and John mustn't ride anywhere with Dunkle anymore. A month later, when Dunkle's father gave him the Honda Civic, Joan only allowed her sons to sit in it in the driveway to listen to its excellent sound system.

In spring of 1981, Dunkle got an airport security job. One night he told Jim Davies he was ordered to watch for a serial killer believed to be flying in. "God knocked me down to the ground. He told me, 'Get out of here!' So I walked off the job, right then, and you know what? On the bus going home, I met a born again Christian! See what he gave me?" Dunkle held up a pamphlet about Youth for Christ, a fundamentalist missionary organization.

In May 1981, Dunkle entered a Youth for Christ training camp in Oregon. The Davies received a couple of semiliterate notes from him over the summer.

One evening in September, Dunkle walked into their house. "Surprise!"

Joan hugged him. "When did you get back?"

"Yesterday." He helped himself to a beer. "I quit. They make you work too hard in that place." Joan figured he'd blown the Bible and pamphlet reading.

"Hey, come look at the computer!" John and Mark showed Dunkle the Apple that Joan sometimes brought home from work. "Type your name and then punch this key here."

Dunkle did. The screen responded with "Dunkle is a shithead."

John and Mark laughed. "Look what it says about Wolfe," Mark said. The computer flashed jokes about all their friends.

A few nights later, Dunkle threw pebbles against Mark's window around two in the morning. Mark and John slipped out the front door, leaving it slightly ajar so they could sneak back in silently. They partied at Hassler, but Mark was tiring of Dunkle, who had never matured. Dunkle began taking John out alone and listening to music with him in the driveway. John acted thrilled.

A couple of weeks later he vanished.

Five days into the disappearance, Dunkle showed up at the Davies'. Grandma Bell reproached him. "Jim and Joanie have been so good to you. Why haven't you helped them?"

"I'm busy. Could you give me some posters?"

Jim Davies came to the door. "I've been leaving messages with your parents since Sunday."

"I started that job at Toys 'Я' Us," said Dunkle.

"Did you take John out Saturday night?"

"No."

"What's happened to him?"

"God, I wish I knew." Dunkle glanced at his watch. "I gotta go."

Davies watched Dunkle drive off. Dunkle had practically lived with the Davies for the past four years. It was very strange that he'd suddenly stopped coming around. A little later Sergeant Tompkins phoned to describe Dunkle's father's refusal to say where Dunkle worked and Davies gave Tompkins the information.

That night, after Tompkins questioned Dunkle at Toys

"Я" Us, Mr. Dunkle phoned Davies. "Quit siccing the cops onto my son! You're a bad influence. Taught him to drink. Get him drunk. Your fault."

Davies hung up on the weird guy. Tompkins had cleared Dunkle. Jim and Joan tried to accept it—for a while.

Chapter Eleven

On Saturday night, one week after the disappearance, the Davies boys' friends John Wolfe and Brian Loftis went with Dunkle to Edgewood Park. Dunkle said, ''This dumb cop questioned me about John Davies.''

Wolfe, at fifteen, was already six feet tall and participated in sex, drugs, and rock 'n' roll. He considered Davies brainy but childlike—miles ahead of him academically, miles behind him in experience.

''They going to arrest you?'' Wolfe joked.

''Go to hell,'' said Dunkle.

Wolfe exchanged glances with sixteen-year-old Brian Loftis. They didn't think Dunkle had anything to do with the disappearance, but they did know he was capable of violence. A year earlier, drinking and smoking pot in Wolfes' kitchen, Wolfe and Loftis ''fucked with'' Dunkle, laughing at his hair, his odor, his general dorkiness. Suddenly their scapegoat screamed, ''Shut up! Shut up,'' pulled a butcher knife from the rack, and charged Wolfe, eyes peculiar and glassy.

Wolfe thrust his arm beneath Dunkle's wrist to force the knife upward. The blade sank into the web of his thumb.

"Oh, my God, you cut me! You cut me!" Wolfe sank to the floor and clamped his gushing thumb between his knees. Dunkle dropped the knife and burst into hysterical sobs.

Wolfe had gone to an emergency room the next day. It was too late for stitches and he would carry the scar for life.

Tonight, Dunkle parked by a wooden gate chained across the dirt road. Beyond it, in the darkness, lay the shrubby hills of Edgewood Park. The boys grabbed six-packs of Bud Talls and followed Dunkle over the gate and up a hill. Eastward lay the lights of the entire Bay Area. To the west, beyond a power plant, cars flashed by on Highway 280. The boys and Dunkle joked around and drank on the dark hillside for hours.

Afterwards, Dunkle dropped the boys off. Later that night, in the neighboring town of San Carlos, police chased Dunkle to a screeching halt on a narrow residential street near the eastern border of Edgewood Park. John Davies's MISSING posters hit the floor in back.

Dunkle stumbled from the car. There was blood all over his hands. "I tried to change a tire drunk," he explained. He lost balance when asked to stand on one foot

The cops arrested him for drunk driving. No questions were asked about the blood.

The following morning, after a week of pursuing newspaper and TV reporters, the Davies taped a television interview in their home with Linda Schack, a Channel 7 newscaster.

Joan came across grief-stricken but tough, Jim as a hollow-eyed wreck. Judith Bell, the diminutive grandmother, seemed worried but dignified. Dark and skinny Carlos, gazing sadly at the camera, could hardly look less like a member of this hefty, blue-eyed family.

The camera scanned John's cozy room while Joan's voice-over said, "You've got to understand this kid. His friends say he's 'too chicken' to run away. He's not your normal teenager. He's the last kid on earth who would run away."

The next day, Belmont police documented, "spots on TV have been utilized by the father." Tompkins pressed the Serra High School principal and this time was permitted to question John's classmates. He learned nothing new.

The new publicity brought both help and pain to the Davies. Newspaper articles mentioned the Davies' theory that John was hurt while out with friends, but emphasized the police position that he ran away. A police spokesperson was quoted as saying that John had been upset about his grades and hadn't been seen since November 8.

"They twisted my words!" Jim told Joan. "All I said was John's grades dipped."

Joan regretted her honesty with Tompkins about John trying marijuana and with reporters whom she'd told John probably went out with friends "to perhaps do things they shouldn't." Her straightforwardness led to John's being presented in the wrong way. Cops and reporters made him sound rebellious, when in reality he was naive and immature. Yet now Belmont gossips called John "a bad kid who used drugs," as if his bit of experimentation rendered him unworthy of neighborhood or police concern.

The next time Tompkins mentioned pot, Joan answered, "John never touched dope!" It was the beginning of a Davies policy that would madden police.

In the second week, Joan asked Tompkins if she should hire a private investigator. Instead, Tompkins suggested Kathlyn Rhea, a psychic who provided consultation to police departments.

Cautiously hopeful, Joan, Jim, and Mark went by appointment to Mrs. Rhea's home, bringing with them John's yearbook, some pictures, a piece of his clothing, and cash. Mrs. Rhea asked about their backgrounds, listened to the story of John's disappearance, and presented sharp insights about family issues.

Then she concentrated on John. "I see a grassy area and a wooden gate with a chain. I see John in a white car with one or two other young men. John is still alive," she said slowly, "but he is in bad company."

The Davies knew two people who drove white cars: a friend of Larry Roche, and Jon Dunkle.

On December 2, the Davies heard that John was seen in Half Moon Bay and Santa Cruz with a scruffy, bearded man in a battered white van with lettering on the side.

Davies phoned Detective Tompkins, who said, "Check with the reporting parties about time and place." He asked for posters and dental records.

After Davies did so, he couldn't reach Tompkins. Grandma Bell couldn't sit still. "Please, Jim, let's go look for white vans."

They drove to Half Moon Bay and crisscrossed muddy back roads down the coast to Santa Cruz. Once Jim got stuck. The day didn't improve.

Eight days later, when Jim took posters and dental records to headquarters, he learned the case had been transferred.

Chapter Twelve

When Sergeant Jerrold Whaley entered the San Mateo Police Department in 1957, he stood one disappointing inch shy of the five-foot-nine height requirement and qualified only as a dispatcher. Twelve years passed before height requirements relaxed and he became a patrol officer for the Belmont Department. In December 1981, he reached his lifelong goal: He won the Belmont Juvenile Officer position.

An old-fashioned Baptist, he didn't party with fellow officers or share their crude humor. His knack for imitating cartoon voices endeared him to small children, but his stiffness alienated teenagers.

Jerry Whaley leaped into the John Davies case with zeal, but he would continually bump into what he called "the proverbial brick wall." The most frustrating case of his career, it brought him stress-related illnesses, humiliation, and divorce.

Whaley met with Jim Davies for an hour on December 10. Loyal to his good friend Tompkins, Whaley remained neutral when Davies grumbled, "After a whole damn month, police are going to send posters to other departments?''

Whaley called a Santa Cruz juvenile officer about the white van lead and mailed posters out. The Davies' blitz had made John's face familiar, but Whaley's contacts gave the case a whiff of official recognition.

When he recontacted Santa Cruz a week later, he learned that the white van belonged to a professional gardener who had no beard and denied any contact with John Davies. Whaley reported back to Davies, who said, ''Can't they dust the van for fingerprints?''

Whaley sighed. Detective work differed from its portrayal on TV. He had no probable cause to search the van, and its grimy surface wouldn't yield a usable print. Even if it did, how could he use it? ''Did John ever have his fingerprints taken?'' Whaley asked Davies. ''I would need those for comparison.''

There was a stunned silence from Davies. Whaley sympathized. He could imagine no pain greater than losing one of his beloved daughters. Still, he needed to present Davies with an unpleasant reality. ''If John is a runaway, I can't bring him in or force him to tell you his whereabouts.'' John would be considered a ''status offender,'' not a lawbreaker, and as such he could not be detained.

A few days later, Davies called him back. ''You could get John's fingerprints from his license plate collection. He has hundreds. He reorganized them just before he disappeared.''

Whaley didn't need John's fingerprints. There was no body to identify.

Davies also notified Whaley of a hang-up call to the house. ''What if it was John? Maybe someone forced him to hang up.''

Tompkins had installed a phone trap to document the origin of all incoming calls. Whaley met with the phone company's special agent and traced the hang-up call to an address in the Santa Cruz Mountains town of La Honda.

Checking with the homeowners, he learned they had been out of town the day the call was made and had no children. Whaley believed the culprit was a teen "crank" caller.

He pulled in Mark Davies.

Mark lurched into Whaley's small office, flopped into a chair and presented a shit-eating grin. He looked drunk and answered questions impatiently. "Of *course* I didn't make the hang-up call. I couldn't do something so cruel to my parents. No, I didn't take John out that night. No, I didn't hear anything after I went to bed."

He stood up, made a *Pssh* noise and swiped the air as if brushing something away. "You're fuckin' wasting your time. Go do your damn job and find my brother."

Whaley looked hard at him. "What aren't you telling me?"

"I already told you cops all I Goddamn know!" Mark slammed out. Whaley would dog him to find out what he was hiding.

Whaley gradually ruled out the rumors that John lived in a canyon tree house, had joined hippies in Santa Cruz, was snatched, was murdered by a drug dealer over $200.

On December 18, the Carlmont High School security officer, Bill Lufrano, told Whaley, "A kid says, 'John Davies is wasted, dead and buried.' "

"Thanks." Whaley interviewed the boy, who was on the periphery of the Davies boys' crowd. "It was just idle talk," the kid muttered. He didn't say where he'd heard it.

The same week, Robert Kauk saw Dunkle smiling shyly in his office doorway. "Come in!" As the special education counselor at Carlmont High School, Kauk had known Dunkle for years and had determined that Dunkle's IQ was 130, despite the serious learning disabilities and emotional problems. Kauk had felt the pull of Dunkle's deep, yearning needs, seen him through rages and sobbing spells and heard years of his wild stories about undercover drug spying, the FBI, homosexual orgies.

Now Dunkle sat in his usual chair. "You know what, Bob? John Davies is wasted. He's dead and buried in the hills where no one will ever find him."

"Uh-huh." Kauk considered this one of Dunkle's typical flights of fancy and didn't bother the police with it.

Whaley kept hearing, "John Davies is heavy into D&D." The role-playing game from TSR, Inc., received national attention in 1979 when sixteen-year-old genius and D&D player Dallas Egbert disappeared and investigators discovered he'd played the game in real life in tunnels beneath the Michigan State campus. Other youths had died of wounds from homemade lances or maces in mock D & D combat.

In mid-January 1982, Whaley met with Serra teacher Robert Stark, who headed Serra's Dungeons & Dragons club. "It attracts loners: intellectuals, nonathletes, book worms, fat boys," Stark said, flipping through John's D& D notebook. He said he refused the boys' requests to set the game up three-dimensionally.

Whaley found the D & D players "anything but cooperative." With attitudes conveying "leave me the hell alone," they denied drugs and midnight D & D games in the woods. He kept after them.

All Joan wanted was to be the buffer between police and her family. Jim and Mark were falling apart and their home had become a minefield of volatile emotions. She had returned to work, which structured her days and provided comforting friends, but Jim had fallen into angry depression when his tireless search efforts proved useless. Neglecting his fledgling photo business, he continued obsessively trying to find John.

Religion's clichés didn't touch Joan's anguish and she quit church. She couldn't let off steam in the Marriage Encounter support group, nor could Jim call the Belmont police "Keystone Kops" there—Whaley and his wife also attended.

A family therapist prodded for "the root of your depression." When Joan responded, "The root is that *our son is missing!*" the counselor said his training hadn't covered working with parents of the missing.

Meantime, Mark was drinking to deaden his fears and guilt over John. When Serra suspended him for being drunk at swimming practice, his parents had to persuade the school to let him complete his senior year and graduate.

The final straw came when Serra banned Dungeons & Dragons because of Whaley's investigation. D & D kids blamed Mark. To make matters worse, Jim and Joan brought in San Mateo narcs to investigate LSD dealing at the school because of the rumors that John ran away to escape a dealer. "Everyone hates us now!" Mark shouted at his parents. "You're sacrificing me for John! Don't you give a damn what you're doing to me?"

Between Mark's outrage and Jim's constant criticism of the police, Joan Davies decided she should be the family spokesperson.

On February 4, she called Whaley and said, "The investigation is disrupting my family. Please communicate only with me, at my work number."

Whaley felt he was working himself into the ground on the case. How could Joan put up walls like this? Whaley sat down with Sergeant Tompkins. "What should I do with this crazy damn Davies family?"

"I can't do my job if I limit my contacts to one family member," said Juvenile Officer Whaley, confronting the

Davies in their living room. "I need *everyone's* cooperation." He eyed Mark.

"Why haven't you guys searched the Hassler Home and Edgewood Park?" Mark demanded. "Pshhh." But then he related a new rumor: "Larry Roche split to his mother's place in Alaska. He didn't even take December finals. Kids say John's with him."

Nine days later, Whaley sent a letter and photo of Larry Roche to the Juneau police and followed up the next month. On March 17, Juneau officers questioned John's friend. Roche claimed to know nothing about John Davies or Dungeons & Dragons, insisting he'd never played the game. He denied involvement with drugs, though he claimed that John was "heavy into" pot and LSD, and said Mark Davies probably knew where John went.

Whaley read the statement and fumed. It was *Larry* who was "heavy into pot and acid," and Larry and John had played D & D all the time.

But no way could the department send him to Alaska to confront a lying boy about a runaway.

While Whaley pursued Larry Roche, Joan Davies was learning that what religion, Marriage Encounter, and psychotherapy couldn't do for her, activism could.

It started with a phone call in March from Eileen Luboff of Santa Cruz. "I have a missing son, too," Eileen said. "Do you know about the Vanished Children's Alliance?"

Joan drove to Eileen's home that Saturday and learned that since around 1975, grassroots organizations like the Vanished Children's Alliance in California and Child Find in New York had been springing up all over the country. They helped parents publicize a missing child, gave leads to police, taught prevention and child safety, and testified at congressional hearings. They wanted faster police response when children disappeared, and coordination (instead of rivalry) among jurisdictions.

"Two hundred child and teen murder victims are unidentified every year because police agencies don't communicate," said Eileen. "Most are presumed runaways."

"Oh, God!" cried Joan. The women's eyes met, and for the first time since John vanished, Joan experienced the full and deep understanding of another human being. Within a couple of weeks, she and Eileen had formed a missing teen and youth subcommittee in the Vanished Children's Alliance.

Following Eileen Luboff's advice, Joan asked Whaley to list John's name with the National Crime Information Center (NCIC).

"Of course," he said crisply, though he'd thought NCIC only tracked stolen cars and violent criminals.

A few days later, she notified him that Child Find would publicize the disappearance and forward information to him about sightings. "We appreciate your continued investigation!" she wrote, drawing him a happy face.

On May 9, 1982, Joan Davies was featured with several other mothers in a *San Jose Mercury News* article titled, FOR MOTHERS OF MISSING KIDS, THE PAIN PERSISTS."

Shortly after the article came out, Whaley met with Larry Roche's father in Foster City.

"Why did Larry move to Alaska so suddenly, before finals?" asked Whaley.

Mr. Lewis dropped his eyes. "It was just a family problem." In July he admitted, "Larry took off to get away from a drug supplier, an older man, who was hassling him for money he owed."

The old rumor about John running away to escape a drug dealer was roosting on Larry's perch.

Three days later, the San Mateo county coroner requested John's blood type, medical records, and skeletal X rays. A headless male body, estimated age twelve to fourteen, had washed up on shore in Santa Cruz.

* * *

"John's medical records don't have his blood type!" a very frustrated Joan Davies told Whaley the following week. The missing children's movement trained parents to keep identifying information on their children, but Joan was learning this too late. In August, Whaley notified her that the body was identified: not John's.

In September, Whaley followed Jim Davies's suggestion from the previous December: He dusted John's license plate collection for latent fingerprints. "No usable prints obtained," he documented.

In October, missing children's organizations wedged a toe in the federal door: The first National Missing Children's Act passed, allowing the FBI to create its own files on missing children so that state and local law enforcement could compare their cases with the national data bank. Joan hoped this would give Whaley another tool for locating her son.

Chapter Thirteen

Jon Dunkle had his own problems during 1982. He pled guilty to the Driving Under the Influence (DUI) charge he got the week after John Davies disappeared, when blood smeared his hands. The court ordered a probation study. The report showed his prior DUI with Mark Davies in the car, and a recklessness citation, but not that one month after this first DUI, Dunkle's father bought him the white Honda Civic.

Mr. Dunkle's responses on the probation questionnaire blamed others and denied Jon's problems. In odd, dyslexic-sounding phrases, he wrote that his son's problems in school were "normal" except for "some different" in learning. He claimed Dunkle stayed out of trouble more than the average kid and that his son's biggest problem was peer pressure, which he was sure would be outgrown.

The court placed Dunkle on eighteen months probation and required him to attend the Responsible Drivers Program.

By now he had lost his Toys "Я" Us job because, he

told friends, "I was fucked up all the time on LSD." In April, he started working for The Bubble Machine, a car wash franchise. Unable to work fast enough, he would storm out or burst into tears.

The probation officer and the Responsible Driver Program teacher believed Dunkle had stopped drinking, but on August 15 he got back in trouble.

As he described the incident in 1985, "I was cruising along, had one of the bottles of Jack Daniel's, one of the great big ones, twelve-dollar ones. Friend of mine, we drank it together. We were at the beach. I took him home. I thought 'shit, I want to cruise,' heh. I had my Sony stereo, seven speakers, blasting away. I was cruising along this park and I ran a stop sign and I went up this hill and pretty soon all I see is a blur—my eyes were all, you know, fucked up. And it was a moped, I pushed this moped twenty-two feet of scrapes up this hill and that means like thirty-five feet I pushed him."

The Vespa's driver, a young man in a white suit, struggled to his feet, screaming, "What the hell are you doing?" He stepped toward Dunkle, who cut his lights, backed down the hill, and sped to a friend's home to beg for an alibi.

But the victim gave Dunkle's license plate number to police, who tracked Dunkle from his parents' home to his friend's. "I don't know what you're talking about," Dunkle said. "I was here the whole time." His drunkenness was not documented.

The next day, since his friend wouldn't back him, Dunkle confessed and was arrested for hit and run. After the arraignment, his probation officer, a woman, documented: "1) aside from the hit and run offense, he has been a model probationer, and 2) his Responsible Drivers counselor reports that the defendant has been an extremely good example to the other members of his group, as he has taken his need for sobriety seriously."

Dunkle remained on probation.

* * *

In November 1982, three months after Dunkle pled guilty to hit and run, a crime occurred that remained unsolved for four years.

The Alameda de las Pulgas, the Avenue of the Fleas, runs through miles of Peninsula towns, each merging seamlessly into the next. A teenage boy named Steve Murphy lived near the intersection of Alameda and 42nd Avenue in San Mateo, a few blocks from the invisible Belmont border. Forty-second Avenue is split level, its upper and lower tiers separated by a grassy slope.

On Friday night, November 5, Murphy and his close friend and neighbor, Kelly Moroney, set out walking to a party on 24th, using residential backstreets. They bought beer at a friendly store. Drinking was chancy for Murphy. Since age eight, he had been an insulin-dependent diabetic, but he rebelled periodically against his diet precautions, determined to live like a normal teenager. If he had to juggle his insulin tomorrow, so be it.

At the party, he joined a group playing "quarters," a drinking game. Later his older brother arrived with his girlfriend, and Murphy hung around with them for a while. From that point on his memory was lost forever. Moroney later provided police with details about the next two hours.

Police broke up the party around eleven-thirty. Murphy and Moroney walked to the Round Table Pizza restaurant. Friends observed that Murphy was a little tipsy. Then the boys walked back to 42nd Avenue.

Now the beers were catching up with Murphy. He threw up in some bushes, then said he felt dizzy. He lay on his back on Moroney's porch. A white van drove past, doubled back via the lower tier, and came by again. The driver called, "Everything okay?"

"Yeah," said Moroney. The van left. "Come on in. Why don't you sleep here?" Moroney asked Steve.

Murphy sat up. "No, I'm supposed to work for my stepfather in the morning, and besides, my insulin is at home."

He had less than a block to walk to the corner of Greenwood. Moroney watched him start up the hill, then went inside.

Deanna Baldwin, Steve's mother, was surprised when Steve didn't show up at breakfast the next morning. He was reliable when he had a job with her husband, Wallace. She went to his room. "Steve? It's getting late." His bed hadn't been slept in.

She called Moroney. "Would you tell Steve to come home?"

"He's not there?" Moroney panicked. "God, what could happen to him in half a block?"

Mrs. Baldwin called the San Mateo police. An hour later, an officer arrived. "He probably slept over at a friend's and forgot to call you," he said.

"He'd be home by now. He needs his insulin."

"There isn't much I can do," said the officer.

Steve's parents, brother, and Moroney began calling friends and searching the neighborhood.

Around noon, Mrs. Baldwin heard a siren scream down Alameda from Belmont toward Chope, the nearby county hospital. She clutched her husband's arm. "Follow that ambulance! Steve's in there, I know it."

He doubted her—the ambulance could be for anyone—but he followed it to the emergency room.

Half an hour earlier, a man living two miles away in Belmont saw a young man crawl out of a ravine onto the Marburger turnaround, which intersected with Upper Lock, near where the Davies had lived before buying their Winding Way home. Only nearby residents and local teenagers seeking party spots knew the area.

Blood covered the youth's head and face. He pulled himself onto the turnaround and collapsed backward beneath a NO DUMPING sign. The homeowner called 911, then rushed to the shivering, moaning boy.

Officer Gorran, who had assisted Sergeant Tompkins during the first week of John Davies's disappearance, responded to the "Man Down" call. Fire trucks and an ambulance filled the turnaround. Gorran found the location "comparatively desolate . . . uncut bushes, weeds, trees, brush, etc., with the dirt road making a tight turn (nearly a U) to continue down to San Juan Blvd."

Paramedics unbuttoned the boy's shirt. Across his bruised torso ran a black mark resembling a tire tread.

"He's nearly unconscious," the paramedic told Gorran, "but he says his name is Steve Murphy." The boy whispered and the paramedic shouted, "He's diabetic! We need orange juice!" The man who had called 911 ran home and returned quickly with a mug and a juice pitcher.

"What happened?" the paramedic asked as Murphy sipped.

"I don't know."

The paramedic showed Gorran a deep, long gash across the top of Murphy's head, exposing the bone.

One of his shoes was missing, and his socks were caked with mud and weeds. "Looks like he walked or crawled awhile in the underbrush," Gorran said. The BPD cordoned off the area and searched the turnaround and ravine. They could not find Steve's missing shoe or wallet.

Wallace Baldwin ran into the emergency room right behind Steve.

Steve mumbled, "He forced me into his car. Beat me up. I'm freezing." He lost consciousness again and later did not remember what he had said.

The emergency room doctor documented that the injuries were "consistent with MVA (motor vehicle accident)."

Murphy's pelvis was fractured in four places; his duodenum was bruised, his bladder ruptured; he had a broken rib; and his skull was fractured. His lacerated spleen and kidney could not be saved. He was rushed to surgery.

Because it looked as if a car hit Murphy on 42nd in San Mateo, Officer Violett of the San Mateo PD took over the case. He and Belmont detectives Farmer and Goulart agreed that after the person ran Murphy over, he put him in the car, sped the two miles to the secluded turnaround, and dumped him into its deep ravine. The act was vicious. If Murphy hadn't crawled out, he would have died.

Yet investigators found no physical evidence along 42nd—no blood or glass, no tire marks from slammed-on brakes. "This SOB didn't slow down," Goulart said. "He ran Steve down on purpose."

Moroney told police about the white van, and the Upper Lock homeowner reported seeing a black, beat-up Chevelle drive in and out of Marburger Road earlier that morning. An APB was put out for the black Chevelle, and the next day the police circulated posters. They cleared an acquaintance of Murphy's who drove a similar car, but Murphy's crowd roughed him up anyway.

The BPD learned that another hit-and-run victim, Paul Andropoulos, sixteen, had been found the same night Steve was hit. Andropoulos was lying on Coronet in Belmont, just off Alameda in a direct line from 42nd. Like Murphy, Andropoulos was hit while walking home at night. His injuries were minor, but included a concussion. He knew he had been sideswiped, but couldn't remember details. The two boys knew each other, but attended different schools and were not in the same crowds.

San Mateo and Belmont detectives investigated the apparently related cases for weeks, reconstructing Murphy's and Andropoulos's activities, digging into information about their friends, school contacts, possible drug or gang connections, old grudges—anything that could explain these attacks by car.

Murphy spent about two weeks in the hospital and left a week before doctors thought he should. He couldn't return to school for several more weeks, though he refused to stay home. Walking bent over because of his rib fracture and abdominal surgery, he went out with friends. He and his mother believed that what happens happens and life must go on.

When he did return to classes, he found himself far behind, and his head injury interfered with his ability to catch up. One day, his abdominal incision opened and he had to have stitches again.

He told friends to touch the ridged scar on his head and laughed when they said, "Yuck!" Inside, he wasn't laughing, though. He fantasized about revenge. He'd beat the bastard to a pulp, stomp him into the ground, and see him in hell.

The cops drove Murphy crazy. "You're lying," accused an officer when Murphy repeated that he remembered nothing.

"Why the hell would I lie? I want you to get this asshole." Mrs. Baldwin jumped up. "I'm sick of you blaming Steve for this. If you don't believe him, give him a lie detector test. Now!"

The officer conferred with others behind a closed door. They agreed to give the lie detector test. Murphy passed.

A few weeks later, Belmont's Sergeant Scales hypnotized Murphy and documented, "Steve's memory appears to get worse instead of better."

The only part that came back was a cloudy picture of rough ground in a dirt circle. "Was I found in a place like that?" he asked his mother. "Or am I making it up?"

She drove him to the turnaround. "Yeah, I recognize this!" he said. Its isolation upset him. The hit-and-run driver must have wanted him to die there.

Murphy's diabetes was harder to control now, later causing him to lose jobs. He couldn't overcome his rage. The hit-and-run was unfinished business.

Chapter Fourteen

During the first year, Joan Davies strove to remain civil with the Belmont police. When weeks passed without contact from Juvenile Officer Whaley, she phoned him politely and sent happy face notes, "to keep the investigation alive." But in early December, when she felt the police didn't take a mysterious phone call seriously, she silently declared war.

On December 2, when John had been missing thirteen months, Joan heard a muffled, whispering male voice on the answering machine. "Lllle-e-e-e-h, ni-i-i-i, s-i-i-i, n-a-a-a-jjjj, d-eh-eh-eh-d, s-i-i-i, n-a-a-a-j," and more unintelligible garble. Joan caught one word: *Naj*. In the kids' backward talk Naj meant John.

Joan phoned the Belmont Police. Whaley was out. She pushed: "I need to speak to someone immediately about the John Davies case."

"What kind of case is it?" asked the dispatcher.

John's poster had hung on every local store window and telephone pole for over a year. "Give me a superior officer," Joan said coldly.

Tompkins came on. ''Someone will pick up the recording.''

The next day at noon, Joan reached Whaley and asked, ''When will you be by for the tape?''

''What tape?''

Angry tears sprang into her eyes. To her, the phone message was the first concrete clue since John had disappeared.

When Whaley did listen to the tape, he seemed to agree. ''This is important,'' he said. Joan's relief lasted only seconds. As he dropped the tape into his shirt pocket, Whaley warned, ''Don't tell Mark.''

''No way did Mark make that call!'' she said bitterly.

Whaley was determined to prove Mark was the mystery caller. He interviewed Mark on tape for a voice sample to compare to the mystery call and requested funds for the phone tape analysis and voiceprinting. He also arranged for a voice stress expert to analyze Mark's taped interview.

Meanwhile, Joan and Eileen Luboff prepared for a Vanished Children's Alliance press conference scheduled for December 20.

Afterward, when Joan tried to reach Whaley for an update, she learned he'd gone on a two-week Christmas vacation and the tape analysis hadn't yet begun. She took a five-by-seven-inch notebook and started a detailed log. She was declaring war.

Sixteen-year-old Monti Hansen spent New Year's Eve, 1982, baby-sitting for his ten-year-old brother Nathan, in their San Mateo home. Late that evening, Jon Dunkle called. ''Hey, Monti, okay if I come over?'' Hansen and Dunkle had met through a mutual friend of John Wolfe and Brian Loftis. For a while they went drinking together a couple of times a month, but lately Hansen was pulling away. He thought Dunkle was pretty peculiar. Tonight, though, Hansen was bored.

"Yeah, what the hell, come on over if you're in the neighborhood," he said.

Around midnight, Dunkle arrived, obviously drunk. "I was partying at my house with Wolfe and Loftis," he said. "They barbecued some steak and it was good, but I got really bored. They have girls with them."

Hansen nodded. Dunkle never had a girl himself—who would want him? "Man, I'm fucked up," Dunkle said, plopping down in the family room. Hansen returned to his parents' bedroom where he had been watching a karate movie on TV. Eventually, Dunkle walked down the hall to join him, glancing into the room where young Nathan lay sleeping.

"I'm so bombed I'm dizzy," said Dunkle.

"Go drink some water. Flush the alcohol out of your system."

When the movie ended, Hansen went into the backyard to smoke a cigarette. He strolled among the piles of lumber and bricks his father kept there for his construction business. After a moment, Hansen sensed that Dunkle was standing behind him. He turned.

"I drank some water," Dunkle said. Then he swung a two-by-four high in the air like a club.

"What are you doing?" cried Hansen, but Dunkle just stared at him, eyes glassy, mouth set in a strange grin. He slammed the two-by-four into Hansen's brow.

"Jesus!" cried Hansen. Blood poured down his face. He covered his head with his arms as Dunkle kept bashing him with the two-by-four. Not daring to turn away, Hansen backed up toward the fence, where a gate stood open. Once there, he warded off the next blow, then turned and ran through the gate and around to the front of the house. He found the front door locked. Then he heard the back door slam and realized Dunkle was inside.

Hansen crept up to the kitchen window and peeked in from the side. Through the glass, inches away, Dunkle was putting a large-bladed kitchen knife into the knife rack.

Hansen realized that Dunkle had intended to knock him out with the two-by-four and then kill him with the knife.

And now Dunkle had locked himself inside the house with Nathan!

Hansen went wild. "Get the fuck out of there!" he screamed. He ran to the kitchen door and beat on it. "You hurt my brother and I'll kill you!" He kept up the noise until he heard Dunkle burst out the front door. Hansen snatched up an armload of bricks and intercepted Dunkle. He threw a brick as hard as he could into Dunkle's chest. Dunkle slid his hand toward his pocket and Hansen remembered the Buck knife Dunkle usually carried.

He hurled another brick. "Get your hand away from there!" Dunkle snatched his hand up. He looked scared. Hansen saw that the way to save himself was to keep up the attack, so he screamed nonstop curses at Dunkle. "Beat it! Get away from here, you son of a bitch!" Dunkle turned and ran. Hansen chased him down the street, hurling bricks, till Dunkle dove into his car and peeled out.

Hansen wiped the back of his hand across his eyes to clear away the blood. His head, arms, and body throbbing, he ran to the house to check on Nathan. The child was covered up and sound asleep, absolutely unharmed. He had slept through everything.

Now Hansen's adrenaline rush faded. He called the friends whose New Year's Eve party his parents were attending. "Tell my dad to come home!" he cried. "This guy tried to kill me!"

Next he phoned John Wolfe. "Don't let him in over there!" Now he was trembling and cold and losing strength. His voice shook. "He's fucking crazy! He had this board and this knife, he tried to kill me. There's blood all over my kitchen!"

Hansen's father took him to the emergency room, where a doctor put twenty-five stitches into the lacerations on his head. Then his father called the San Mateo police. Five days later, two officers came by to take a report. Hansen told them about "the demonic look" he'd seen on Dunkle's face. "It was a murder attempt," he insisted. "Dunkle had a butcher knife on him when he was beating me up with that two by four."

The officers considered the incident a New Year's Eve brawl. Dunkle's probation officer never heard about the incident and continued to believe that Dunkle was clean and sober, "a highly motivated probationer."

She still believed this three weeks later, when Dunkle called her from a hospital.

"I had surgery for a lump in my side," he said. He called her again a week later. "I'm still in the hospital. They're giving me radioactive injections and X rays."

She documented that he was behaving in a reliable manner, notifying her that he would miss his appointments. She did not learn that, while loaded on alcohol and LSD, Dunkle had obsessed on his small penis and injected it with bacon fat. To the doctors, he blamed his weird act on bad LSD.

Out of the hospital in February, Dunkle resumed his Responsible Driver course and started working at a gas station.

Chapter Fifteen

On January 6, 1983, Joan Davies launched her battle with the police. Presenting herself as an intimidating bureaucrat armed with a typed agenda, she met with Juvenile Officer Whaley and Chief Sanderson.

"John's picture will be in the *People Magazine* article about missing children, and I'm appearing on *20/20* and *Merv Griffin*. What will you do about the new leads this will generate?"

"An officer can assist Sergeant Whaley," said the chief.

Check mark. "I requested a phone trap a month ago in case we get another mystery call," Joan continued.

"We'll get right on in it," said Sanderson, "but it's a public service the telephone company provides. It's difficult to convince them it's necessary in some cases."

Next she brought up the need for an age-enhancement to portray John as he might look now. Computer techniques weren't available yet, but the Vanished Children's Alliance had an age-enhancement artist.

"We'll use ours," said Sanderson.

Joan brought up Mark. "Can't you give him a lie detector test and clear up the doubts about him?"

Whaley mentioned he was setting up the voice stress test but asked her not to discuss it yet with Mark.

"Okay," said Joan, doubtfully. She and Mark both wanted the lie detector test.

Then Sanderson and Whaley described a new investigative tool. The Department of Justice would diagram dates, leads, individuals interviewed, sightings, and so on onto a specially designed flow chart called the VIA, to highlight clues buried among meaningless details.

Wow! thought Joan, *they're finally taking this case seriously!*

When Joan left, the chief said, "Install that phone trap tomorrow. And make weekly contacts with her."

"Yes, sir," said Whaley, thinking, *Now how the hell can I call her every week with forty child-abuse cases on my desk?*

Reporters kept calling about sightings he hadn't had time to clear, making him appear behind on the job, but public criticism wasn't as harsh as his own. John Davies invaded his sleep, interrupted his thoughts in the shower. Whaley talked about John into a pocket tape recorder when driving.

Obsession and failure were building a wall between him and his wife. By the end of the year, they were living apart.

"The Santa Cruz Coroner's Office has an unidentified skull of a young teenage boy," Eileen Luboff told Joan.

"Oh, God."

Posters of John had saturated Santa Cruz and he was listed with NCIC and Child Find, yet officials hadn't made the connection. Joan could see how the U.S. ended up with two hundred unidentified child victims a year.

Joan went with a woman friend to the Santa Cruz Coroner's Office and handed a poster to a Sergeant Bird. "My son has been missing thirteen months. You need to contact Sergeant Whaley in Belmont."

Bird studied the picture. "I certainly will, Mrs. Davies. This looks like a possible ID."

Outside, Joan's friend burst into tears. "How can you bear this?" she sobbed.

Sergeant Bird's call to the Belmont PD about the skull added another prong to Whaley's investigation. To help search for a living John, he took Davies family photos to the police artist for the age progression. To identify a dead John, he sent dental X rays to the Department of Justice and Santa Cruz. And he still had Mark's lies to expose.

When Whaley showed Joan two age-enhanced portraits from the same volunteer police artist who in 1984 would make the first composites of the smoking tree youth, Joan said, "John would still have freckles now. I don't think his hair would be so dark." She sighed. "Jim will make up the posters."

Before he left, Whaley warned, "The voice on the phone tape will be someone we recognize."

When Whaley met with Sergeant Beam, the voice stress analyst from the Burlingame PD, Beam said, "The boy gets 'stressful' whenever he talks about his missing brother." Then he squelched Whaley's soaring hopes. "The analysis is inconclusive as to guilt or deception."

Inconclusive! Whaley went to Gil, the technician analyzing the telephone tape. Gil found "no positive similarities between Mark's voice and the phone tape."

Whaley took the recordings to another expert.

In the midst of this, Bill Lufrano, the high school security officer, reported, "Dunkle came by the other day. I said to him, 'Isn't it strange that John Davies never turned up?' and his face dropped. Man, he turned white."

"That's interesting," said Whaley. But Tompkins had cleared Dunkle a long time ago.

The second tape expert found "no similarities" between Mark's voice and the mystery caller's.

Whaley contacted Jim Davies. "Would you encourage

Mark to give me another taped interview for further voice stress analysis?''

Mark blew up. Why should he cooperate? Hell, half the cops didn't even know who John Davies was!

Mark would drive past squad cars and blast his radio until they pulled him over. While they studied his driver's license, he would say, "Recognize the name? Know who John Davies is?''

When friends urged him to talk about his feelings, he fended them off with jokes or anger. When he wasn't drinking, he was sleeping. Here's what Mark knew: If police cared so little about a good and innocent kid like John, who could care for someone as bad as himself?

On March 19, 1983, in Joan's hometown of Kansas City, Kansas, an officer stopped an eighteen-year-old boy for driving a motorcycle without tags. Checking the NCIC, the officer learned that his charge was a missing teenager Ron Luboff from California—the son of Joan's friend and fellow advocate Eileen Luboff.

The news ignited Mark's powder keg of emotion.

"Mark's having a crisis,'' Joan told Whaley. "I think he'll open up if you talk to him now.''

Whaley hurried to the Davies' home with a tape recorder and joined Mark and Joan in their living room.

The boy had the puffy red eyes and hoarse voice of someone who had been crying. "It isn't fair,'' Mark railed. "John's been missing longer than Ron, why can't anybody find John?''

Then Mark paused. "Are you going to arrest me?''

"No, Mark.'' Whaley held his breath, but Mark just spewed forth the usual scenarios about Larry Roche and Jon Dunkle. All old news.

Mark muttered, "I told him LSD is cool. I helped him hide some purple tabs in a thirty-five-millimeter film case that we stuck in that Gallo wine bottle in John's room.

The tabs were gone when John disappeared.'' Mark had tears in his eyes. ''John left while he was high. He was helpless!''

Whaley hadn't heard this before, but he didn't realize Mark had revealed his most painful secret.

''Mark, I need your opinion about this.'' Whaley played the phone tape.

''How shitty,'' Mark said. ''My friends and I used to muffle our voices and do backwards talk like that.'' He couldn't understand the words and didn't know who made the call.

This was not the guilty response Whaley longed to see.

Whaley continued to hit brick walls. In May, when he took case data to Sacramento for the VIA chart, he learned the Santa Cruz skull was not that of John Davies. Department of Justice equipment had deciphered part of the phone tape. ''John is de-e-e-e-ead. John is in *He-e-e-e-e-ellll.*'' To this day the caller remains unidentified.

Left with no new angles, Whaley tackled the old rumor that John had fallen from the balcony of his home and was buried in the backyard. He and Canine Officer Pat Halleran, who would later be an evidence tech in the Lance Turner case, took the BPD dog around the Davies' neighborhood. In an unimproved yard the dog alerted on a raised mound. In it Whaley discovered some small bones. Then he noticed that Halleran was turning red and choking.

''Bee sting,'' gasped Halleran. Whaley rushed him to the emergency room for anaphylactic shock.

The bones Halleran nearly died for turned out to belong to a bird.

In fall 1983, publicity about missing children heated up to support the proposed expansion of the Missing Children's Act. Joan appeared on TV frequently, but at home another crisis was brewing: Jim's photo business failed and he had to file for bankruptcy. His new job with a computer business and Joan's income as a high school principal weren't enough to save their beloved Winding Way dream house. In October 1983, a week before the TV movie about the famous missing/murdered child *Adam* aired, the Davies moved.

By now Whaley followed leads that ranged from far-out to lunatic. He sent a letter and posters to Salt Lake City, where child murderer Arthur Gary Bishop had turned himself in and led police to the graves of several young victims. "As of this time," Whaley wrote, "I have not been able to show that [John Davies] is a runaway and have found no one that has seen or heard from him." Bishop proved to have chosen younger victims, however.

When Whaley heard that in San Anselmo, just north of San Francisco, an informant reported dreams of John Davies living on a mattress in a drain pipe, Whaley sent posters to the San Anselmo police. "I know I'm clutching at straws," he wrote, "but after living with this case for two years I check out all calls."

Chapter Sixteen

Until he was jailed for DUIs toward the end of 1983, Dunkle's odd behavior and occasional violence continued.

In April, recovering from LSD and the bacon fat, he completed the court-ordered Responsible Drivers Program. His instructor noted that Dunkle denied ever having an alcohol problem and blamed his DUI's on friends. Still on probation, Dunkle changed jobs, leaving the gas station position and returning to The Bubble Machine.

One spring afternoon, Dunkle drove his friends John Wolfe and Brian Loftis, then seventeen and eighteen, over winding roads through the redwoods to La Honda, a rustic town in the hills between San Mateo County and the coast. Wolfe noted that, as always, Dunkle knew back roads and drove his Honda Civic like a four-wheel drive, bumping it over dirt tracks or even across fields with no roads at all.

Dunkle chugged up a rough road into a secluded clearing. "This is an old cemetery."

Wolfe didn't like the place. "Let's go to the beach."

But Dunkle was drinking beer and prancing around

acting stupid and immature. "Skeletons are rotting under here." Dunkle giggled. "Murder victims."

"I hate this place," said Wolfe. "Let's go."

"Hey, wait!" Dunkle shouted, all excited. "See this? It's a hunk of flesh with hair on it!"

"God, that's sick!" Wolfe shouted. "Put it down!"

"This is cool!" said Dunkle. "Maybe there's a fresh body somewhere around here."

"I'm gonna puke." Though Wolfe could make ghoulish jokes as much as the next guy, he hated Dunkle's prurient, almost sexual pleasure in death.

When they returned to the car, Dunkle brought his smelly trophy with him. It was days before Wolfe and Loftis could persuade him to take the nauseating thing out of his car.

On July 7, a Highway Patrol officer followed a white Honda Civic that was weaving all over Highway 1 in Half Moon Bay. The driver pulled to the shoulder, but when the patrol car parked behind him, the Honda Civic peeled out again. The officer hit his siren and gave pursuit.

When the driver finally stopped and lurched out, the officer saw blood all over his plaid shirt. Words slurring, Dunkle gave the same explanation he had used with the San Carlos cops when he had blood on his hands: "I tried to change a tire drunk."

On July 16, the boss at The Bubble Machine fired Dunkle. In the personnel file he wrote, "Second customer complaint. He is temperamental and unstable. He gets mean real fast and stays pissed off the rest of the day. He's very touchy and reacts by snapping back."

The next day Wolfe, Loftis, and other friends piled into Dunkle's car to go to the beach. Dunkle said, "I quit that car wash job. It was giving me a lung problem."

"Too bad," said Wolfe. Dunkle's jobs always lasted just long enough for his employers to realize how weird he was.

The friends horsed around and drank beer all day at the beach. At dusk, they crowded back into the car. Dunkle peeled out.

"Jesus, you're all over the damn road!" shouted Wolfe. "You're drunk! Let me drive."

Dunkle turned red and clenched on the wheel. The car lurched over the line. Wolfe checked the rearview mirror, hoping for flashing lights. No such luck.

When Dunkle screeched to a stop in front of Loftis's house in Belmont, the guys couldn't get out fast enough. Loftis walked around to the driver's side and leaned his arms on the open window. "Come in till you sober up."

"Don't tell me what to do!" Dunkle jammed his finger on the automatic lever and the window shot up, trapping Loftis' sleeve. Then he stepped on the gas. The Honda Civic shot forward. Unable to free his arm, Loftis hung from the window and was dragged up the street.

Wolfe jumped on a bicycle and pedaled furiously after the car. "Dunkle! Stop!"

Eighty feet ahead, Loftis suddenly dropped onto the pavement. His sweatshirt flapped from the window as Dunkle careened around a curve.

Furious, Wolfe helped his friend into the house. "Damn it, this time I'm calling the cops!" He and Loftis never associated with Dunkle again.

Sergeant Story, Officer Lisa Thomas, and several other Belmont officers were waiting outside Dunkle's home when he roared up "at a high rate of speed." Story noted that Dunkle seemed to consider taking off, but then saw his parents watching on the front lawn. He slowly stepped out of the car and walked toward the officers, who observed he had "red eyes, a weaving gait and strong smell of alcohol."

"We're going to do some field sobriety tests here," said Story.

"Yeah, yeah."

When Dunkle closed his eyes and stood on one foot, he nearly fell over backward. Then Story clipped a half sheet of paper onto a clipboard, drew a line across its center, and told Dunkle to write the first half of the alphabet on top and the second half on the bottom.

"Fuck you!" screamed the dyslexic Dunkle. He ripped the paper and threw it into Story's face.

The following week, Dunkle was hired as a stockboy in the IRS warehouse in San Mateo. His employer documented that he was "semi-retarded, barely able to read or write. Has a silly grin."

Soon Dunkle was telling his fellow employees that he was a government worker on a secret assignment. Sometimes he suggested he was a sort of double agent for the CIA. "I know all about the law," he said. "You have to be careful around me."

Other times he tried to convert them to Christianity. "I'm a born-again Christian. God talks to me," he said. "One time I'm driving on the freeway and suddenly I feel this urge to drive up on the shoulder. God's voice told me to get out of the road! So I did and that saved me from this accident right behind me."

His mother brought lunches and cookies to him in brown bags.

On July 28, Dunkle pled guilty to the Half Moon Bay DUI and was sentenced to work furlough and one hundred twenty hours of community service. On August 9, he pled guilty to the DUI he got the day he dragged Loftis up the street. No assault charge was filed.

Judge Jensen reviewed Dunkle's past record: eighteen months supervised probation for the November 1981 DUI; the August 1982 hit and run of the man on the Vespa; two

DUIs in July 1983. "Driver's license revoked for three years. A hundred twenty days in county jail."

By November, Dunkle was pleading for parole. In a letter to his new probation officer he wrote that he couldn't sleep, and that he now realized his mistake (spelled, "riilize my mustack"), and that he had a drinking problem. He alleged that he now saw life's responsibilities.

Dunkle's new probation officer was more cynical than the one who had found him sincere and highly motivated. This one found him an oddball who went on binges while in the Responsible Drivers program and who acted like a snitch. The probation officer felt Dunkle's heart hadn't changed—he simply wanted to go home.

Dunkle remained in jail on the work furlough program until the end of December.

Chapter Seventeen

In February 1984, Jim and Joan Davies befriended the family of eleven-year-old Kevin Collins, who had vanished that month from a San Francisco street after basketball practice and became a national symbol of America's missing children. Inspired by Kevin's father, who founded the Kevin Collins Foundation, Jim Davies was ready to become an activist like Joan.

"You get the dreams," he said in his television debut on *Black Renaissance,* a talk program. "Joan recently dreamed that John called her up and . . . the address turned out to be in the middle of the ocean."

After fourteen months, the Department of Justice completed the VIA chart. Sergeant Whaley collected it from Sacramento and invited the Davies in to view its diagrammed leads, sightings, interviews, dead ends, and unresolved clues: Dungeons & Dragons, the LSD rumors, the voice stress tests on Mark, the Larry Roche–Alaska connection, and Jon Dunkle. The John Davies investigation now occupied thirty-six feet of wall space in a cramped police department.

A month later, Whaley's ulcer kicked up when Joan told him, "*Adam* is going to air again. John's picture will appear in the missing children's gallery at the end." Whaley braced himself for another flood of out-of-state leads to which he could not effectively respond.

A bit later, Whaley documented, "Joan spoke on TV about how eneffecient [sic] this Department is. When confronted, she apologized." In fact, what Joan Davies said was, "I'm sorry I have to say things like that."

The tense relationship between Whaley and the Davies mirrored the description in the March 1984 *Newsweek* cover article "Stolen Children." Below a photo of Kevin Collins, the article said that parents of the missing suffered alone and struggled with slow police departments, poor coordination among jurisdictions, and FBI noninvolvement. It noted that parents of the missing always had bitter relationships with the police, as parents wanted action instead of routine and incomprehensible legal processes.

Such publicity influenced passage of the Second National Missing Children's Act, signed into law May 25, 1984. It created the National Center for Missing and Exploited Children—the national clearinghouse so desired by parents of the missing.

On that date, the first annual Missing Children's Day, the Davies, the Collins, and hundreds of others gathered in front of San Francisco City Hall for a Missing Children's Rally. In the Davies' small booth stood a color poster of John with the urgent: MISSING SINCE NOVEMBER 8, 1981.

Around the same time came two hopeful developments in the case: FBI involvement and a significant sighting.

Since fall 1982, the law had required police officers to notify the FBI of all missing children and to call for assistance from the FBI within twenty-four hours if it was assumed that state borders had been crossed or if circumstances suggested abduction.

At that time, Whaley hadn't felt that John's disappearance met that criterion. Even Larry Roche's move to Alaska didn't suggest that John had been abducted. However, the ongoing publicity drew a lot of out of state leads and Whaley couldn't absolutely rule abduction out. Around March of 1984, he began mentioning to Joan Davies that he was "looking for FBI assistance."

By May, Joan grew impatient. FBI agents had entered the Kevin Collins's case within two weeks of his disappearance, and the Collins highly praised their FBI Special Agent Robert Deklinski. Joan asked for help from the Collins Foundation private detective, Mike Murray. He contacted the local FBI office himself. On June 4, Special Agent Deklinski telephoned both Whaley and Joan.

Deklinski was well trained to handle bitter parents and stumped, defensive officers in missing child cases. A tall, mustached man who appeared younger than his forty-some years, the Davies considered him a true professional. Whaley and the Belmont police found him "a nice officer," an expert who behaved like an equal.

On June 4, he listened to Whaley's description of the sixteen latest out-of-state leads, which Whaley had followed up with letters and posters to the appropriate jurisdiction. "My missing Belmont kid isn't exactly a priority to a cop in Indianapolis," Whaley observed. Deklinski found the Larry Roche angle interesting. Whaley said, "I don't know if John's with him or if he saw John killed in a D and D game, and I can't do a damn thing to investigate a kid in Alaska."

"I'd like to help with these out-of-state angles," Deklinski said. "The problem is, the rule is one missing child case per agent, and I'm up to my ears with Kevin Collins. I'll speak to my superiors and get back to you." He let Whaley know he'd be calling the Davies.

''She'll give you an earful about this department,'' Whaley warned.

''Whaley's been saying he'd call you for two months,'' Joan said. Her outline of the case didn't differ factually from Whaley's, but she emphasized points Whaley hadn't, such as ''John would have gone with Jon Dunkle no questions asked.''

Deklinski explained that he had to consult his superiors. ''I'll get back to you soon,'' he said.

Joan had heard that phrase ad nauseam. When Deklinski called back two days later to say let he'd meet soon with Whaley, she was thrilled.

Even when Deklinski notified her in late June that he had to postpone the meeting due to a double murder, Joan maintained her good opinion. ''I can't tell you what it means to me that you are keeping me informed,'' she told him.

Two days later, when a Mr. Paul McLean of upstate New York called the Davies with a strong sighting, the case seemed solved. ''I just left a carnival at Greenwood Lakes, a town up here,'' said McLean. ''I saw a boy who looked so much like your son that I went back to the store to study the poster. This boy has to be your son or his twin.''

His careful scrutiny of the boy and the poster lent credence, as did the fact that this carnival had traveled in California at the time John disappeared.

Joan phoned the Belmont police and was told, ''Sergeant Whaley is out on comp time.''

Joan reported the sighting. ''Please have someone get back to me as soon as possible.''

Three days later, when Braniff Airlines had donated two free standby tickets to New York State, the police hadn't called back. Joan notified the BPD, ''In thirty minutes I will be interviewed by the Channel Four News Team and I will say that the Belmont police have done nothing about this major new lead.''

The chief responded, assuring Joan that the department

"would get right on this." The next day, Belmont officers contacted police in Greenwood Lakes.

Meantime, the Davies had a family conference. Jim and Joan felt that if John had truly run away, he might not want to see his parents.

"I'll go," said Mark.

The next morning, he and a friend from the Collins Foundation headed for upstate New York. The boy, who closely resembled John, ran from them.

On the heels of the Greenwood Lakes fiasco, Whaley spent several days in July staking out Tanforan Shopping Center in San Bruno, a few miles north of Belmont. A shopkeeper had reported seeing John there twice recently. Whaley sipped gourmet coffee and strode among mall rats till his feet and ulcer throbbed. John's lookalike never showed.

At the end of August, Deklinski had time to familiarize himself with the John Davies case. He met with Joan, who gave him a reduced copy of the VIA chart. He observed that she was earnest and driven, maintained control over her anger, and presented information in an orderly way. The woman was an anguished mother, but she behaved like a pro.

The next day, Deklinski met Whaley, studied the thick case file, and walked around the conference room pondering the thirty-six-foot version of the VIA.

So many unanswered questions! Deklinski was hooked. Five days later, he returned to the BPD with official permission to enter the John Davies case.

On September 12 and 13, he and Whaley met with each of the Davies. As Whaley later documented, "Joan aired many complaints about this Department." The interviews covered material deadeningly familiar to Whaley, but fresh to Deklinski. Mark let Deklinski know of the agony police suspicion had caused him and said he couldn't wait to take a lie detector test and clear himself. All the Davies talked a lot about Dunkle. Mark had seen their old friend around town again and this reawakened the family's feeling that it was so extremely odd that "when John disappeared from our lives, so did Jon Dunkle."

"John used to sit with Dunkle in the driveway and listen to tapes on the sound system in Dunkle's car," Joan said. Deklinski thought that significant and Whaley could see why, but as far as he could remember, the Davies had never emphasized this fact before.

Back at the police station, Deklinski and Whaley brainstormed. They would polygraph Mark; Whaley would reinvestigate and if possible polygraph Dunkle; and FBI agents in Alaska would do the same with Larry Roche.

In September, Mark took the polygraph test at FBI headquarters in San Francisco. Deklinski kept Joan informed as the analysis of it progressed. "Not certain yet, but looks good so far." And finally: "He's clear!"

This news solidified Deklinski's special place in the hearts of the Davies.

On October 2, Lance Turner was murdered. Whaley was occupied with the murder investigation exclusively. When he came up for air in the first week of November, he tackled the reinvestigation of John Davies's disappearance and tried to reach Dunkle for an interview. Mrs. Dunkle said her son had recently moved to his sister's home in Sacramento. When Whaley reached Dunkle there, the young man sounded gee-whiz friendly and agreed to meet him the following week.

The day before the appointment, Dunkle canceled. "I got a new job." They rescheduled for mid-November.

On November 8, the third anniversary of John's disappearance, the Davies held a news conference, telling reporters that there were no new developments in the case.

On November 13, Dunkle phoned Whaley to cancel again. "I broke my foot." Whaley agreed to reschedule another week in the future.

The next day, Carlmont High School staff members identified the latest composite drawing of Lance Turner's killer as Jon Dunkle.

Part Three

The Turner/Davies Investigation December 1984– July 1985

Chapter Eighteen

Jon Dunkle didn't leap to the top of the suspect list the minute Carlmont High School people identified him on November 14. Routine background studies brought out suggestive data, but the decisive factor was his behavior. Innocent people don't elude appointments or attempt suicide when contacted for a routine investigation.

In November 1979, Jon Dunkle had phoned the BPD and whispered that marijuana was growing near his home. "Police can call me back *only* at eight-thirty in the morning," he instructed, as if he were a top secret spy, "*only* on Fridays."

In summer1980, Harriet Smith, owner and manager of The Belmont Lapidary, reported that jewelry was missing from her shop and she suspected Dunkle had stolen it. She had hired and fired him three times in a year. "He's violent," she said, "and he was always looking through everything. My employees had to hide their possessions. I think he duplicated my shop keys. He wants to get even with me because I wouldn't give him a job reference for

Pinkerton Security. He's kind of retarded and he might be dangerous."

Detective Sergeant Cinquini had recovered some of Belmont Lapidary's jewelry from a local fence reputed to pay for stolen goods with cocaine. Needing a picture of Dunkle to use in a photo lineup with the fence, Cinquini contacted Pinkerton Security, which had hired Dunkle despite Belmont Lapidary's refusal to give him a reference. Though Pinkerton was putting Dunkle on guard duty at a business and training him in the use of firearms, personnel had no ID photo of him. The fence was unable to identify Dunkle when shown his DMV photo.

During Thanksgiving week of 1980, as the jewelry investigation was petering out, Dunkle went on his wild drive with Mark Davies, hitting speeds of eighty and more. "He wasn't too cooperative at first," said the BPD Daily Watch report, "but he quickly saw the error of his ways. He should be very nice the next time he's stopped."

Dunkle's next DUI in Belmont occurred in July 1983, when John Wolfe reported him for trapping Brian Loftis's sleeve in the car window and dragging him up the street.

Old probation reports revealed the San Carlos DUI in November 1981, one week after John Davies had disappeared. It also showed the Half Moon Bay DUIs, the hit and run of the young man on the Vespa, the revocation of Dunkle's driver's license, and his hundred and twenty days in jail for the accumulated DUIs.

All this was suggestive but no more so than the histories of many other suspects. Belmont abounded with light-haired young males who had assaulted someone with a knife, molested children and/or accumulated DUIs. The investigators knew that the former head of their detective bureau, Sergeant Tompkins, had cleared Dunkle of involvement with the Davies disappearance. It felt like sacrilege to question his judgment, but maybe this one time Tompkins's instincts had failed him. Dunkle's learning disabilities, his liking for younger kids, and his drinking problem all fit the FBI psychological profile. So did the fact that three days after Lance's murder, Dunkle moved from his parents' home in Belmont to his sister's in Sacramento. It was also unusual that a FOR SALE sign suddenly appeared in front of the Belmont home the Dunkle family had occupied since the early 1960s.

Dunkle canceled his November 14 appointment with Sergeant Whaley in the John Davies reinvestigation and rescheduled for the 19th. Now aware of Dunkle's possible connection with Lance Turner, Whaley and Sergeant Don Mattei eagerly prepared themselves.

On November 18, Whaley heard Dunkle's by now familiar voice on the phone. "Jeez, I just can't make it down there."

They set another date, but Whaley had the distinct feeling Dunkle was playing games.

The next day, Lance Turner's grandmother answered the phone in the Turners' home and heard a whispery male voice sobbing, "I'm sorry, I'm sorry! Tell me, should I do it again? Oh, I'm sorry!"

"Who is this?" she cried, but the caller hung up. Shaking and weeping, she notified the police. Sergeant Goulart had a phone trap installed in the Turner house the same day.

When Dunkle canceled with Whaley for the third time on November 24, Sergeant Goulart said, "If he won't come to us, we'll go to him." No other potential suspect had canceled appointments like this. Dunkle was acting like a guilty man.

"Farmer and I will go to Sacramento," said Mattei.

Goulart glanced at him. In his tireless compulsion to avenge Lance's death, Mattei could come on too strong.

"We don't want to scare him off," said Goulart. "Let's let him think we're just tying up loose ends on Davies."

Mattei fumed quietly while Goulart assigned Whaley to visit Dunkle, accompanied by the other John Davies expert, Special Agent Deklinski.

Dunkle agreed to a meeting at his sister's home in Sacramento the morning of December 4. He sounded as eager-beaver, gee-whiz friendly as ever.

At eight a.m., December 4, when Whaley and Deklinski were about a third of the way to Sacramento, Mattei took a call at the BPD. "This is Judy Dunkle. Where's my brother?"

Mattei tensed. "What?"

"He's been missing since yesterday. My parents haven't heard from him and they told me to find out if your department knows anything."

"We'll let you know." Mattei hung up and went ballistic. By now Whaley and Deklinski had driven beyond the range of the Belmont police radio. He had no way to notify them that their suspect had gone AWOL.

At nine, another call came in. It was Dunkle himself. "I can't keep the appointment," he told Mattei, sounding shaky. "I had this accident. There's a hole cut in my stomach."

"Where are you, Jon?"

"I'm hurt! I'm bleeding all over!"

"I'll send help. Are you home?"

"Jeez, my shirt's fucked up, too."

Mattei finally coaxed out the fact that Dunkle had returned to his sister's house. "Take it easy, Jon," Mattei said. "Help's on the way."

Mattei asked the Sacramento Sheriff's Department to do a "welfare check," telling them Dunkle sounded very unstable and might need a 5150, a seventy-two-hour hold for psychiatric evaluation.

Then Mattei slammed down the phone and paced.

"Take it easy," said Goulart, chuckling. "All we can do is wait."

At nine-thirty, Sacramento Sheriff Ray Dick arrived at Judy Dunkle's house. Jon Dunkle told him a disjointed story of getting drunk and lost in nearby Goethe Park the night before and falling onto a piece of chrome. Dick noted a single shallow cut, one to one and a half inches wide on Dunkle's abdomen. Looking up from Dunkle's belly, Dick saw a folding Buck knife on a nearby table. He picked it up, wondering if he should confiscate it. But though Dunkle acted a bit drunk and agitated, he didn't appear to meet the criteria for a 5150, which was to be "a danger to self or others." It seemed he had just gotten staggering drunk. Unaware that Belmont police were madly searching for Lance Turner's murder weapon, a knife with a blade one to one and a half inches wide, Sheriff Dick returned it to Dunkle.

Whaley and Deklinski pulled up in front of Judy Dunkle's modest ranch-style house and saw the Sacramento sheriff outside. They learned of the welfare check and the shallow stomach wound, but not that Dick had seen the Buck knife. Weeks later, when they found out, it had disappeared.

Whaley and Deklinski found Dunkle sitting on a couch in the living room, his clothes bloody and caked with dirt. Dunkle smiled up at the officers like a shy child eager to please the grown-ups. Whaley felt a thrill of recognition: Dunkle *was* the guy in the composite drawing. His hair wasn't blond, as the earliest descriptions had suggested, but under hypnosis Heidi had decided the unknown person's hair was light brown. Sun-bleached strands glinted all through Dunkle's hair, probably because of so many hours of bike riding. But it wasn't just the hair, it was his overall look, the shape of his face and eyes, even his expression, that so uncannily matched the drawing.

Concealing his excitement, Whaley asked, "You okay, Jon?"

Grinning, Dunkle pulled up his shirt, exposing a gash

crusted with blood. The wound didn't appear life threatening, but Whaley would bet anything that it resulted from a clumsy suicide attempt. To question an injured or suicidal suspect invited accusations of police brutality. "Come on, Jon," said Whaley, "we'll take you to the emergency room."

Dunkle went to change his filthy clothes. "What's going on with him?" Deklinski asked Judy.

"He's been getting mad a lot lately," she admitted.

"Ever get violent?"

"Not usually, but he gets upset easily and walks out." The officers figured this indicated that Dunkle was stressed about meeting them.

Judy told them that the day before she had found a note from her brother when she came home from work. It said he was going to Goethe Park to watch people fish. "He goes there a lot," she said. "It has miles and miles of bike trails in the woods along the American River." She had heard no more from him till he stumbled into the house about nine a.m., splotched with dirt, beer, and blood.

"Did he used to be friends with the Davies?" asked Deklinski.

"I remember one Thanksgiving Mark Davies got him drunk and he was arrested for drunk driving."

Asked if her brother preferred friends younger than himself, she said that in high school he liked people his own age, but after graduating, he liked younger ones.

"Let's see, he moved in here with you when?" asked Whaley.

"He was staying with our parents in Belmont, and I visited the last weekend of September. Mom called me up around October 4 and told me Jon was coming to live with me."

Whaley carefully didn't change expression, but he knew Deklinski too caught the significance of Dunkle's move to Sacramento three days after Lance Turner's murder. And the *mother* arranged the move? Whaley also noted that Judy had "an odd affect," showing little emotion. Other officers who met her later told each other she acted like a person who'd had a lobotomy.

Dunkle emerged from his room, looking tired, boyish and so small that Whaley wondered if his growth had been somehow stunted. It was hard to picture him committing extreme violence.

On the ride to Kaiser Emergency, and during the long wait there to see a doctor, Dunkle smiled and chattered with Whaley and Deklinski as if delighted with their attention.

After the doctor treated the wound, he reported to Whaley and Deklinski, "It goes in about a centimeter."

"Pretty shallow," said Whaley; some of Lance's wounds had penetrated five inches. "It's not from some piece of chrome, either," the doctor added. "It's clearly a knife wound." The doctor, like Sheriff Dick, did not find Dunkle suicidal and saw no reason to 5150 him.

Back in the car, Deklinski asked Dunkle to show them where he got lost the night before. Dunkle directed them to Goethe Park. "I got drunk watching the fishermen," Dunkle said, "and then it got foggy and dark and I couldn't figure out how to get home."

Deklinski and Whaley glanced around. The thick trees gave the illusion that they were deep in a forest, but they heard the traffic on nearby streets. At night, lights from surrounding neighborhoods must be visible. Dunkle had already chattered about biking in this park all the time. It was impossible to believe he could lose his way here.

"I got all wet and cold, and then I fell on a strip of chrome that was sticking up from the ground. It really hurt. Then I went into some shack I found, and I made a fire in a coffee can and I slept on a tumbleweed." He made a show of searching up and down some trails. "I can't figure out where that shack is now."

It was after four p.m. by the time Whaley and Deklinski

brought Dunkle home. Now, finally, they could question him.

They began with general subjects like his old crowd of friends and their hangouts. He said John Wolfe introduced him to the abandoned Hassler Hospital, nicknamed "the Morgue," in Edgewood Park sometime in 1980. "One time, man, it was so cool, the guard up there threw a keg party. There were all these girls there in clown costumes."

"The *guard* threw the party?"

"Yeah. There were people there drinking and smoking pot." Much later police learned from Mark Davies that once he and Dunkle and others actually had stumbled upon such a party at Hassler.

Dunkle agreed with the information they had about the white Honda Civic his father gave him in January 1981. For a second his constant grin faltered. "My car's gone now. My father sold it."

"Because you lost your license, right?"

"My friends' fault. John Wolfe and them got me drunk." Finally they eased onto the subject of John Davies. "Last time I saw him was that Halloween," said Dunkle, though he had told Tompkins he'd visited the Davies home the 4th or 5th of November, just before John's November 8th disappearance.

"We hear you had a great sound system in your Honda and you used to let John Davies sit in the driveway with you and listen to music," said Deklinski.

Dunkle gave them deeply sincere eye contact. "John never listened to music with me in my car."

"You never sat with him in the driveway?" Deklinski pushed.

"No, I never did."

"Mark says you used to come by and throw pebbles at his window late at night so he'd come out and party with you."

Grin and head shake. "I never threw pebbles at Mark's window."

"You never took him and John Davies out drinking?"

"I never went drinking with Mark Davies."

Whaley pressed him. "Come on, Jon, Mark was with you when you got that DUI in 1980, and you tell me you never drank with him?"

"I didn't drink with him after that." He denied ever being close to the Davies family or taking Mark and John to "the Morgue" or Edgewood Park.

When they tested him with the old LSD rumors about John Davies, Dunkle said, "Yeah, I heard he used LSD. Mark told me. I wish I could help you, but I really don't know anything about what happened to John. I wish I did."

Toward the end of the session, Whaley slid in some questions about Dunkle's whereabouts on the day Lance Turner was murdered. "Let's see," said Dunkle. "That day I went job hunting. I went out at twelve-thirty and I caught the 7F bus at Ralston and El Camino and got off at the Greyhound station in Redwood City at Brewster, and I applied for jobs at all those stores down there at the Boardwalk Shopping Center."

"Which stores?"

"Toys 'Я' Us. The Big 5. Mervyn's. Some jewelry store. All those places. Then I caught the 5L bus back to Carlmont Shopping Center and I walked up Alameda and got home at four-thirty. My mom was there when I came in."

"Mm-hm," said Whaley, mildly interested that Dunkle presented such robotically precise geographical details. It interested him more that between four-thirty and five was about the time Dunkle would have gotten home if he had killed Lance.

Before they left, Deklinski asked for the bloody shirt so they could get his blood type. "Sure," Dunkle said, and handed it over. Still grinning, he posed while Whaley photographed him with the Polaroid camera.

"You know, Jon, we'd like to polygraph you, just to tie things up here."

"I have to ask my father about that."

Later in the car, Deklinski said, "Can you believe he told us with a straight face he never went drinking with Mark Davies? It's *very* significant that he denies that John Davies ever listened to music with him in that car."

Whaley's stomach was churning. "God, I can still see that Cheshire Cat grin of his. We've spent a day with a serial killer."

Chapter Nineteen

Back in Belmont, Sergeants Goulart and Mattei agreed with Whaley: Dunkle's lies, strange behavior, and fear of the polygraph screamed that he was guilty.

But the work was just beginning. Although learning disabled and odd, their suspect had been smart enough to leave no physical evidence: no murder weapon; no discarded, bloody clothes; no shoes to compare to the trace of a shoe print; no IDs from the partial fingerprints on the Bud Tall can; and no usable saliva samples on the Marlboro butts. Even if witnesses identified Dunkle positively as the stranger in the smoking tree, that proved only that he had been in the area, not that he killed Lance Turner.

If experts are available, go to the experts. Goulart called the FBI profilers back.

The FBI studies of serial rapists and serial killers were conducted not only to build insight into the criminal personality, but to lead to new, "proactive" methods for manipulating such criminals to reveal themselves and confess.

The FBI told Goulart that, based on the profile, investigators should play on the killer's remorse and anxiety. This was the Christmas season, so the papers should carry emotional articles about Lance and his grief-stricken parents, along with descriptions of the killer's characteristics. Officers should mail these articles and the composite that most resembled Dunkle to the sister with whom he was living, and they should send a Christmas card signed *Lance Turner* to Dunkle himself.

Also to increase Dunkle's stress, surveillance of him in Sacramento should be stepped up and done overtly. Ten days before the December 4 session with Dunkle, Goulart had asked the California Department of Justice to help with intermittent surveillance of Dunkle in Sacramento. The twenty-two police officers and FBI agents living in Dunkle's neighborhood were highly motivated to monitor this child killer in their midst. "He acts paranoid," some reported. No wonder. They were learning Dunkle's work hours, his favorite bars, his habit of disappearing all day on bicycle trips. Those unwitnessed bike rides made everyone nervous, but so far no Sacramento kids were missing.

Meanwhile, in order to create maximum anxiety for "The Suspect" in an interrogation, investigators needed to develop strong background information about his character and history so they could exploit his inconsistencies and confront his lies. They needed to know all they could about his personality in order to plan how best to break him down.

Among themselves, Goulart, Chief Sanderson, and the DA agreed that it would be okay to shake Dunkle up some, but they didn't want to scare him into running. They would release some information about the psychological profile, but would zealously guard the secret that they had identified a suspect. They wanted him easy to find when they were prepared to question him further.

Thus, San Francisco and San Mateo county newspapers reported that Lance Turner's unknown killer was a male in his late teens to early twenties who lived near the place of the murder. He had a problem with drugs and alcohol, including criminal charges, and would have increased his substance abuse after the crime. People close to him would notice something was wrong. He might be remorseful. There was a strong likelihood that he had left the Bay Area. The articles stated that while the DA wanted to release the whole profile to reporters, Chief Sanderson would not permit this—a statement that should raise Dunkle's anxiety about the undisclosed details.

Goulart did not ask the papers to run articles about the Turners, but they did so spontaneously. When Lance's schoolmates raised money and purchased an electronic scoreboard in his name for the school, the dedication ceremony made good copy. Another article emphasized how sad Christmas was for the Turner family, adding that Ralston students had conducted a Christmas toy drive for needy children in Lance's name, and a drawing of his face would appear on the cover of the Belmont Oaks League yearbook.

Just after Christmas, the papers published several Ralston students' school essays about what Lance Turner's murder meant to them. They spoke of their grief, their fear now of walking alone, the moment of silence at the first soccer game after the murder, their pity for the family.

Mattei and Farmer dug into Dunkle's background, questioning his friends, probation officers, teachers, employers, neighbors, anyone who could fill them in on his character and behavior. When Mattei asked Carlmont High School for Dunkle's records, he ran into a roadblock. The administration refused on the grounds of confidentiality until he returned with a subpoena. Then the vice principal handed over a single page: Dunkle's transcript. It didn't reveal much except that he had earned an inordinate amount of credits for being a student clerk. The school never released the psychological and other assessments of Dunkle that California special education laws required them to have. Fortunately, school staff spoke openly to Mattei in interviews.

Bit by bit, the officers brought details to Goulart that matched Dunkle to the FBI profile.

The profile had predicted that Lance Turner's killer lived "with a family member on whom he is dependent" and that he would leave the Belmont area as soon as he found a plausible reason. Dunkle always lived with one family member or another. After getting out of jail in spring 1984, he had ridden his bike over three hundred miles in the summer heat to stay with his grandfather, returning to his parents' home in the fall. Three days after Lance's murder, Dunkle's mother notified Dunkle's sister that he was coming to live with her.

The profile scored another bulls-eye by calling the killer an "underachiever with an average to low IQ." Though his former educational counselor, Robert Kauk, told Mattei Dunkle had a 130 IQ in areas that didn't require reading or language, most peers and employers considered him semiliterate, almost retarded. A school psychologist explained that Dunkle couldn't organize tasks and needed clear, one-step instructions—a training method most employers don't have the time or patience to use. The police heard many anecdotes about Dunkle's fury and tears when he had trouble performing in school and at jobs.

Thus, as the profile predicted, Dunkle qualified only for menial jobs and never could keep them long. Farmer traced Dunkle's history from Toys "Я" Us, to the Belmont Lapidary, from which he had stolen jewelry, Pinkerton's Security, which fired him for being absent on the job, The Bubble Machine, where he had yelled at customers, and the IRS warehouse, where he wore a "silly grin," claimed to have secret connections with the CIA, and tried to convert people to Christianity. Now he held a low-level job at a

Carl's Jr. fast food restaurant in Sacramento, where he had already displayed his temper by throwing a hot spatula across the room.

The profile said Lance's killer was "not a shrewd or cunning individual." It was tricky for the investigators to figure if this applied to Dunkle or not. A school psychologist said Dunkle "was immature and simpleminded, yet in a way he was cunning."

Bill Lufrano, the high school security officer, reported, "He seemed like a goody-good but he had a deceptive front. He was involved in stuff—drug dealing, stealing, maybe more. He was in a crowd that was AC/DC [sexually] and bordered on crime." This information matched the way Dunkle's former friends described him. He presented a sweet, innocent, needy persona to teachers and friends' parents—the Davies, for example—but with peers he got drunk and stoned, showed off stolen drugs and jewelry, and was sporadically violent. Kauk said Dunkle had a "poor sense of reality." But was he cunning?

Questions about how Dunkle's mind worked were to puzzle law enforcement, and later, psychiatrists, for many years.

He had other qualities that matched the profile, too. It said the "subject" had problems with interpersonal relationships, no "positive sexual relationships in his own peer group," was not confident with males or females his own age, was considered "an oddball" in high school and later by those who knew him casually. John Wolfe's older brother Don told Farmer on the phone from Chico State College, "I hate Dunkle. He's a little weird jerk. He drinks and drives crazy and does stupid things to attract attention. He's slow. No one liked him in school. He tried to impress people, but he was an outcast."

A girl who had been in Special Education with Jimmy Davies and Jon Dunkle reported, "We all knew he was weird. He never had a girlfriend." Since many boys turned to her for sex, Dunkle's friends once set up a date between him and her so she could give him lessons. It was a fiasco.

Robert Kauk said, "He's a very frustrated person. He couldn't make it with peers, so he had a fascination for younger kids and found refuge in adults. He used to brag about taking Ralston kids drinking up in the hills. He found his power around younger kids."

Interviewing Dunkle's former friends made it obvious to the investigators that the boys had put up with Dunkle in return for transportation and alcohol. His friends matured while he didn't. First Jimmy Davies and Don Wolfe outgrew him, then their younger brothers Mark Davies and John Wolfe. Dunkle had been twenty-one when he turned to fifteen-year-old John Davies for friendship. On October 2 at the smoking tree Dunkle hung out with twelve-year-olds.

No one knew of any sexual relationships in Dunkle's life. Bill Lufrano said Dunkle "got along with dykes, but would fight if a male rejected him or put him down." Kauk observed that "he wasn't typically masculine, but he showed no outward signs of homosexuality."

As a senior, Dunkle had become obsessed with a younger male student who dropped out of school. Dunkle drove the boy around all the time and hung out at the garage where he worked. The investigators questioned this boy several times, but unlike Dunkle's other former friends, he refused to talk about the relationship or Dunkle's behavior. Officers couldn't figure out if he had only been friends with a suspected murderer, was hiding a former sexual relationship, or had been somehow traumatized.

Dunkle's alcohol abuse also matched the profile. All of his old buddies described his drinking problem. Mark Davies said Dunkle was "a psychological drunk," meaning he lost his head after just a few beers. Asked about Dunkle's preferred brands, Mark named Henry Weinhardt Ale, but the other boys said Budweiser. Mark Davies and John Wolfe described wild rides when Dunkle drove drunk.

As the profile also predicted, Dunkle habitually wore a

Buck knife on his belt, and had kept another knife in the glove compartment when he had his Honda Civic. Dunkle owned a knife whose blade was likely to have the same measurements as Lance Turner's wounds.

Matching Dunkle's personality traits to the profile was exciting and fascinating. But though this helped prove to Goulart they had the right man, it didn't provide evidence leading to an arrest. For that, Goulart and his men went hunting for more traditional facts: history of violence, MO, alibi, identification, physical evidence.

John Wolfe showed Farmer and, later Deklinski, the deep scar in the web of his thumb. "That's from the time he charged me with a kitchen knife." Wolfe and Loftis told how Dunkle dragged Loftis alongside his car at high speed. Neither the knife attack nor the assault on Loftis had been previously reported to police, only the drunken driving.

Then the detectives visited Monti Hansen and learned about the New Year's Eve when Dunkle attacked Monti with a two-by-four. When Monti got to the part about seeing Dunkle put away a big knife in the rack in the kitchen, he insisted, "Dunkle was planning to knock me out and then kill me with that knife." Privately, the officers agreed. The MO was very similar to the FBI speculation that the killer hit Lance in the head with a rock to disable him before stabbing him. It appeared Monti's throwing bricks at Dunkle, and chasing him off, had saved his own life. Monti was probably right, too, in suspecting Dunkle intended to harm Monti's ten-year-old brother who lay sleeping in the house.

Farmer investigated Dunkle's alibi for October 2, the day of Lance's murder. Visiting all the businesses where Dunkle claimed he applied for jobs that day, Farmer showed managers and personnel staff Dunkle's picture. One recognized him, but said the application was done in November, not October; another said he applied October 1, not 2, and had appeared retarded and unable to hold a job. None of the others remembered him at all. Farmer and Mattei performed the tedious task of looked through stacks of pending job applications at each store. Dunkle hadn't applied on October 2 or any other time. His alibi was completely blown.

Through the DMV Goulart traced Dunkle's white Honda Civic. The new owner permitted Goulart to search it inside and out. On the front seat on the passenger side he found a large brown stain. Old blood? The owner confirmed that the stain was there when he bought the car.

Goulart photographed and scraped the stain, wondering if he'd found the first physical evidence in the Davies case. He turned it over to the lab, not daring to hope it could possibly determine blood type from such an old sample.

Mattei set up a new photo lineup. Three of the smoking tree girls immediately picked out the Polaroid photo Whaley had taken of Dunkle two weeks earlier in Sacramento.

When the fourth girl came in three days later, she mentioned that the others had told her about their visit. "Oh, no!" said Mattei, quickly covering the pictures. "You can't talk about these lineups. It could taint an identification." He phoned the DA.

"Did they describe the photo to her that they picked out?" asked the DA.

"She says not."

"OK, you can go ahead then."

She studied the group of boys' faces and zeroed in on Dunkle's. "Him," she said. "I'm ninety-eight percent certain."

Dunkle becoming the major Lance Turner suspect changed the Davies from thorns in the department's side to valuable resources. Hostile ones, though. However, by now they weren't speaking to the BPD. They spoke only to Special Agent Deklinski.

Because the department was keeping Dunkle's status a secret, when Deklinski met with the Davies in mid-December, he didn't reveal that their old friend was now believed to have murdered both their son and Lance Turner.

In individual sessions with each of them, Deklinski reviewed the now familiar details about Jon Dunkle and his relationship with them. Mark offered up a new and useful detail. The Yes tape Carlos heard John playing on his last night had been missing ever since the disappearance.

Deklinski nodded, excited. The missing tape fit perfectly with the scenario that John Davies slipped out with Dunkle, stocking-footed because he expected just to sit in the car and listen to his new album on Dunkle's tape deck. Dunkle then took off with John.

Deklinski came away with great material to add to the Davies and Turner prongs of the investigation. As he left, Joan said, "We've been telling police for three years that John would have gone out with Dunkle no questions asked, and you're the only one who ever took us seriously."

Deklinski could not let Joan know yet how seriously the whole department took Dunkle now.

Throughout December, while investigators doggedly built their mountain of damning information, Dunkle continued to behave like a guilty man, trying to keep track of their activities as the FBI predicted the culprit would. He phoned Whaley and claimed (untruthfully) that Jimmy Davies used to go to homosexual drug parties. Later, he had a similar conversation with Mattei. He bragged to Loftis and other Belmont friends that he was under FBI investigation. He phoned staff at Carlmont High School, telling them he was a murder suspect and then inviting them out to lunch. Now terrified of him, the school secretary immediately notified police.

On December 17, Goulart presented a judge with an affidavit for a search warrant, painstakingly outlining the investigation and laying out the reasons to suspect Jon Dunkle had made the mysterious phone call to the Turner family on November 19. He requested a search warrant for the list of long-distance toll calls made from Judy Dunkle's home in Sacramento between October 5, the day Dunkle moved there, through December 4, when Whaley and Deklinski met with him.

The judge granted the search, but the telephone record came up empty.

Dunkle had won this round, but Goulart had more weapons lined up. He sat down with his detectives, Deklinski, and an FBI adviser and planned a confrontation.

Chapter Twenty

Goulart stood in the open doorway and surveyed the motel room. Pizza containers stuffed the wastebasket. Suitcases and clothes crowded together in the open closet. Gift wrap littered the floor beneath the small Christmas tree.

If Dunkle consented to enter this room, he'd get the impression the cops had been watching him from here for a week. Their dedication to solving Lance Turner's murder should hit him immediately. Blond, lightly freckled, innocent, Lance smiled out from an enlarged picture on the wall. His soccer jersey with its big number ten was draped over a dresser. Manila folders spilled police reports and the psychological profile onto a table next to the Bud Tall can from beneath the smoking tree and the bloody rock from the path near Lance's body. Blowups of partial fingerprints, photos from the crime scene and copies of the final composite drawing were scattered on dressers.

This was a stage set, carefully designed for maximum psychological impact on the suspect. The FBI advisers had told Goulart and the investigative team to arrange the room this way so that their quarry would know these officers meant business and wouldn't let up till they won a confession.

Goulart's gaze fell onto the tape recorder. It was plugged in and loaded with a fresh tape. Other equipment was hidden, like the Department of Justice device to transmit sound to the DA and officers in the adjoining room. "Hear me in there?" he said in a normal voice.

Detective Farmer and Special Agent Deklinski thumped the wall.

Goulart and Deklinski had fought a few rounds over the tape recorder. Goulart always taped interrogations. Doing so produced an accurate record, and besides, he hated to interrupt spontaneous talk with note taking. But Deklinski insisted that his portion of today's anticipated interrogation must not be recorded. due to FBI regulations. Goulart had even called Washington, D.C., to demand an exception, but the local FBI bosses held firm. Deklinski must take notes only.

Goulart shut the door behind him and joined DA Chuck Smith and Sergeant Mattei in their unmarked car. All three wore jeans and sweatshirts rather than uniforms and badges. It was two-thirty, and the FBI had advised them to pick up Dunkle in midafternoon when he was likely still to be sober. A few minutes ago, Mattei had telephoned Dunkle's sister, who said her brother was at Sacramento's Sunrise Shopping Center. Smith started the car. They were going hunting.

"Here goes," said Mattei as they approached the shopping center. He was burning to squeeze a confession out of this creep. His only worry was whether he could stay patient enough to continue following the methods the FBI specialists had suggested.

The impressive room setup was one of the many "proactive" ploys they had instructed Goulart and the team to follow. The specialists told Goulart and his team that since Lance's killer was likely to be remorseful and terrified of being caught, they should play on these emotions, both in the interrogation and for weeks beforehand. The next interrogation should occur between Christmas and New Year's, so Goulart chose today, December 27. Since Dunkle had panicked before the previous interview, which had been formally scheduled far in advance, the investigators should take him by surprise this time. Their initial approach should be friendly and nonthreatening, hence the jeans and sweatshirts, and they should question him in a neutral place instead of his sister's home or a police station.

Now they slowly drove the car past the Sunrise Mall shops. "There he is!" cried Mattei. Dunkle had just locked up his bicycle and was ambling into a department store. Mattei jumped out and followed, while Smith quickly parked.

Dunkle was halfway up the escalator when Mattei set his foot on the bottom step.

"Don!" he heard someone call. He looked over his shoulder. Right behind him stood his cousin and the cousin's whole family. "Honey," the cousin was saying, "look who's here. Hey, Don, what's up?"

Mattei blurted, "I can't talk now!" and charged up the escalator.

At the top was a floor of women's goods. Mattei glanced quickly around. He couldn't believe his luck. Dunkle stood just a few feet away, peering through a glass counter at some women's gold jewelry.

Mattei forced himself to act calm. "Hi, Jon. Remember me? Don Mattei, BPD?"

"Oh, yeah. Hi." Dunkle grinned up at him as if running into a Belmont cop in a Sacramento mall was a normal event.

"Some officers and I, and the DA and FBI agent Deklinski would like to talk with you for a little while. Okay?"

"I guess," said Dunkle, smiling past Mattei at Goulart, who was appearing, breathless, on the rising escalator. "I don't have anything else to do."

"We'll drive you over to our motel. Is that all right?"

"Sure." Dunkle showed no emotion other than chatterboxy, golly-gee friendliness, even when they walked him up to the motel and opened the door onto their staged scene. He just looked around at the Bud can, the bloody rock, the pictures of Lance, and stepped inside.

According to plan, Goulart and Mattei tackled Dunkle first. They'd prepared themselves intensively for this moment, listening to the FBI advisers and studying the latest articles about interrogation techniques. A November 1984 *Police Science* article had taught them that interrogation must be a well-coordinated, psychosocial attack designed to wrest information from a subject unwilling to provide it.

The article explained in all seriousness that torture was an ineffective questioning technique because it built up the subject's resistance rather than tearing it down, and if the interrogator lost control of himself, he would lose the subject's respect.

In the sociopsychological approach, the interrogator was to place the subject in a "one-down" position, using classic techniques such as calling the subject by his first name, setting ground rules immediately, and creating a sense of isolation. The interrogators should use trial and error till they found the approaches that elicited the best response from the subject. They could try empathy to develop the subject's sense of trust. If that failed, they could switch back to building the subject's anxiety.

For a person like Dunkle, whose life pattern was to blame others for his wrongdoings, they must "make submission tolerable" by offering excuses like, "You probably didn't mean to do it. Alcohol makes you get mad, doesn't it," or, "Maybe Lance asked for it, the way he was acting." They could also hint that if Jon confessed, he would receive psychiatric help. They must promise nothing, though; to do so would cross the line into enticement or coercion and invalidate the confession.

Goulart read Dunkle his rights and Dunkle consented to talk with them. Goulart and Mattei began by reviewing "inconsistencies" from the December 4 contact. "You said you got drunk and lost in Goethe Park and cut your stomach when you fell on a piece of chrome."

"Yeah." Prodded by their questions, Dunkle said he hadn't been able to show Whaley and Deklinski the exact place where he fell onto the chrome because he couldn't find it.

Goulart said, "Mattei and I searched that whole area and we found the two sheds you described. They're in a Girl Scout camp. But there was no tumbleweed there like you said you slept on." They had, however, found beer cans and a cup with blood in it.

"The tumbleweed was there that night."

Mattei prodded, "There's houses and streets and lights all around that park. How could you not find your way out? That doesn't make sense."

"I was fucked up," Dunkle answered, with the facial expression the men remembered Whaley calling "the Cheshire cat grin."

"How'd you cut your stomach?"

"I told the other guys. I was drunk and I fell on a piece of automobile chrome that was sticking up from the ground."

"We searched that whole area. There was no piece of chrome."

"Maybe I fell someplace else."

Goulart confronted him harder. "The emergency room doctor said that wound came from a hunting-type knife with a blade one to one and a half inches wide." He didn't add that this measurement matched Lance Turner's wounds.

"He's not a real doctor. He's some foreign student."

"Come on, Jon. You were scared to talk to Whaley and

Deklinski and you stabbed yourself with your hunting knife."

Still smiling, Dunkle shook his head. "That asshole doctor doesn't know."

"Your friends tell us you have a folding hunting knife. You cut your stomach with it."

"I don't have a hunting knife. I used to have a little pocket-type knife, metal with black sides. I bought it for forty-eight dollars. But I lost it fishing with my uncle." When they asked how to get in touch with his uncle, he said, "Oh, he died on October tenth."

"When did you lose the knife?"

"September twenty-seventh."

Mattei and Goulart met each other's eyes. Dunkle was not only denying the hunting knife that numerous people said he always wore on his belt, but he was cleverly denying possession of any knife at all prior to Lance Turner's murder. Still unaware that Sheriff Dick of Sacramento had seen a hunting knife on the table in Dunkle's home on December 4, they could confront Dunkle only with his friends' reports. He calmly continued to call them wrong. He gave them permission to search both his sister's Sacramento house and his parents' home in Belmont for the knife. Later, they did so and found nothing.

They shifted into another apparent lie, the one he told when he called up Whaley on December 6. "You told Whaley about a party you went to where there was male stripping and guys watching each other pee and stuff like that."

"Yeah. Jimmy Davies took me there. It was on Heritage Court."

"We've been unable to confirm that any such party ever took place."

Shrug and grin. "People will lie to you about it."

"*You* lied about it."

"Jimmy Davies and some other guys used to have those drug and homosexual parties."

They asked him about his movements during the last several months. "Oh, I was back and forth between Belmont and Sacramento after I got out of jail." Finally they squeezed more specific details from him. He said that in June he had bicycled to Mount Shasta, where his grandfather ran a motel. He helped out there, then returned to Belmont, where job hunting was bad. He went hunting and fishing with his uncle in September. He said he had applied for a job at Jacco Electric on October 1, which was about the only statement he had made on December 4 that police could confirm.

Frustrated, they shifted to his drinking problems. "I don't have a drinking problem," he stated.

"Jeez, Jon," said Goulart, "you've been arrested four damn times for drunk driving. You've been in court-ordered alcohol treatment."

"My friends got me drunk. Other times I got arrested because of unusual happenings."

"Like the time you dragged Loftis with your car?"

"He didn't get hurt or nothing."

"Four DUIs, alcohol treatment, and six months in jail, and you say you don't have an alcohol problem?" prodded Mattei.

"I don't have a drinking problem," Dunkle said. "I just have a drunk driving problem."

Mattei wasn't amused. He switched to Dunkle's skewed take on traditional religions. "I grew up Baptist," Dunkle said, "but it wasn't right for me. Then I was born-again and I went to Salem, Oregon, with the Youth for Christ Mission."

"We hear you have visions."

"Yeah, I used to think they all came true. My quest started when I was a security guard at San Francisco Airport." Mattei and Goulart exchanged another glance. Imagine this kook being an armed guard! "One day they told us to watch for a man coming in who shot his wife and kids. A voice came to me. It knocked me down! It told me to get the hell out of there! So I walked off the job and went home. On the bus that day was when I met Eric, the one who told me of the Born Again Way and I was filled with the Spirit.''

Dunkle told them he believed he could see into the future and that in 1981 the voice came to him as he was driving on the freeway and told him to move into the center to avoid an accident. ''I did, and just then some cars crashed right behind me!''

''You swerved and caused the accident yourself,'' said Goulart.

''The voice saved me.''

They switched back to his violence against old friends. ''We hear you beat up this kid Monti Hansen with a two-by-four one New Year's Eve.''

''I never hit him with any board.''

''There's a whole police report and a hospital report that says you did. He says you planned to kill him with a kitchen knife.''

''He's crazy. I wouldn't hit anyone with a board. I was fucked up that night and I just told Monti I had a problem and he said, 'Get the fuck out of here.' Then I had a blackout. Only one I ever had.''

The officers were more frustrated than fascinated by the mental processes Dunkle was exposing. He'd committed a murderous attack on Monti, yet appeared to see himself as the misunderstood and unkindly treated party.

''We checked on your job applications from October second, Jon. No bus drivers saw you on the bus at the times you said, or any other time that day. And you didn't apply at any of the places you said you did.''

''Those guys just lost the papers. I was at that jeweler's talking about amethyst earrings, too.''

''He says you were there in November, not October.''

Dunkle seemed unshaken. ''He's wrong,'' he said, the grin still in place. ''It was October second.''

They tried to push him about what he did that day.

He didn't budge, just kept smirking and insisting he had applied for jobs.

Circling closer to the subjects of John Davies and Lance Turner, Goulart and Mattei confronted him with the reports that he sought younger friends. Grinning, he said, "No, that's not me."

"You buddied up with John Davies, who was six years younger."

"I wasn't ever friends with John Davies. Sometimes I went out with Mark."

"How about those little twelve-year-old girls you hung out with at Water Dog the day Lance died?"

"I didn't talk to any twelve-year-olds. The last time I was at Water Dog was June, when I got off work furlough."

Mattei slapped a photo of fingerprints onto the table beside the Bud Tall can. "These are the prints from this can. You left it at the smoking tree just before you killed Lance." In reality, the fragmented prints from the beer can couldn't be identified, but the BPD and FBI had agreed to bluff Dunkle with them.

Dunkle looked at them, apparently still calm. "I wasn't there that day. I left home at twelve-thirty to go job hunting." He again specified which bus stops he waited at and which routes he took. "I came in the front door at home at four-thirty and my mother saw me come in."

They confronted him with the composite drawing that matched him almost photographically. They told him that several people had identified him from the picture and said he had been at the smoking tree. They reminded him that his alibi was full of shit and pointed out that the way he had really spent October 2 was to get drunk at Water Dog, flirt with twelve-year-old girls and kill Lance Turner.

Dunkle didn't even act nervous. He kept answering, "You're wrong. Those people lied to you. I wasn't there."

By now, Goulart and Mattei were steaming. As Goulart admitted afterward, long, subtle questioning wasn't in their repertoire. They'd always been basic cops, accustomed to wrongdoers who quickly broke down when confronted with their lies. But this Dunkle just kept grinning and denying, grinning and denying.

"We know you killed Lance!" thundered Goulart.

"I wasn't even there."

"You killed him so he wouldn't tell people you're a fag!"

At last the smirk faltered. "I'm not a fag," Dunkle said sulkily.

"You hang out with young boys, you never even made it with a girl," shouted Goulart. He moved close, invading Dunkle's physical space, a tall, thick-chested, full-mustached man, overpoweringly masculine. "You're a damn fag!" he bellowed.

Dunkle's mouth turned down as if he were ready to cry.

All three jumped when the phone rang. Goulart lifted the receiver. "I'm taking over," said DA Smith.

Mattei documented, "Chuck Smith then relieved us and took a new approach, in a less aggressive manner and with the style of an attorney." Offering Dunkle a soda, Smith methodically covered the same ground. Dunkle didn't crack. Smith called next door. It was time for Deklinski to give it a try.

Deklinski and Farmer entered the room, surprised that after so much grilling Dunkle would consent to speak with them. Farmer noted the constant smirk Dunkle wore and concluded, "He's enjoying this. He feels no remorse at all. He thinks he's real important now."

Farmer watched Deklinski go through the now significant details of the Davies angle.

Dunkle denied he'd ever listened to music with John in his car in the Davies' driveway.

"Several people tell me they saw you do this many times, Jon."

"I don't remember ever doing it."

When Dunkle denied he'd ever thrown pebbles against

any friends' windows, least of all John Davies's, Deklinski said, "Many people, including parents of some of your friends, say that you did."

"I don't remember ever doing that."

That set the pattern: Dunkle denied ever drinking with Mark or John Davies at night, then fell back on memory loss. He denied ever going to the Morgue with them, then couldn't remember if he had or not. He denied having the Yes tape missing from John Davies' room, then said he couldn't remember if he'd ever had such a tape. He denied ever owning a Buck knife.

Farmer, whose natural style was more casual and nonconfrontational than Goulart's or Mattei's, tried the empathy and excuse approach. "I'm sure you didn't mean to do it, if you did do something to John Davies. I can see how a guy might lose control sometimes if he's drinking."

The look Dunkle cast up at Farmer, the youngest and most good-looking member of this group of cops, was nearly flirtatious. He still gave nothing away, though.

Five hours had passed. Defeated, Mattei and Goulart drove Dunkle back to his bike at Sunrise Mall.

Chapter Twenty-one

"He's the best liar I ever met." Goulart angrily jerked the car into the late-day Sacramento traffic. Catching this creep was going to take longer and be a hell of a lot harder than Goulart had anticipated. Dunkle might have learning disabilities, but he was proving to be an expert at denial.

The few clues investigators had picked up about Mrs. Dunkle didn't help Farmer and Mattei know what to expect when they knocked on her front door the next day.

They knew that when Dunkle last held a local job she dropped off bag lunches there for him. As he was twenty-three, did this suggest a loving mother or one so overprotective she couldn't allow her son to be an adult?

From police reports they knew too that, in 1969 at least, this hovering mother was a battered wife, though that term hadn't existed then. During the summer of that year, when Jon was nine, police had been called to the home several times because Mr. Dunkle was terrorizing the family.

The responding officers had documented the incidences and left. In 1969, police duties did not include interfering with family problems or protecting abused women and children.

The Dunkle's divorce became final in 1969, but apparently they continued to have a relationship. One day in 1970, when she learned young Jon, then age ten, had been smoking, Mrs. Dunkle told him his father would spank him. That evening, the father reported the boy missing, though a few hours later he notified police that his runaway son had returned.

In 1971, Mr. and Mrs. Dunkle remarried. The wife had followed a pattern familiar and frustrating to police, who saw battered women return to dangerous men every day. Or perhaps things had changed; no more calls came to the BPD about domestic violence in the Dunkle home.

Middle-aged, subdued, dowdy Mrs. Dunkle opened the door to greet Mattei and Farmer. Perhaps because the house was up for sale, it was spotless. Mattei admired the gleaming hardwood floors and immaculate furniture. When she showed them Dunkle's room, it too was very tidy, though Mattei quirked a cynical eyebrow at the Bible on the nightstand. There was something else off about this room, too. The narrow twin bed had a spread with a childish design, and the walls held no posters of subjects like girls, rock musicians, or cars. This was not the room of a young adult. It reflected a child whose mother still brought lunch and cookies to him.

Returning to the living room, Mattei said, "Here's what my department has on your son." He set a photo of Dunkle onto the coffee table beside the final composite drawing and told her that many people had identified Dunkle as the person at the smoking tree the day of Lance Turner's murder.

"He doesn't look anything like that portrait," she said.

Mattei studied her. He felt that, for a police drawing, the composite's resemblance to Jon Dunkle was remarkable. He forged ahead, explaining that police believed Lance was murdered between 4:20 and 4:40. He drew one of his meticulous diagrams to illustrate where people saw Dunkle shortly before and after, emphasizing that these sightings occurred within a few hundred feet of the spot where Lance had died.

"It was someone else they saw," said the mother. "My son is very gentle. He would never hurt anyone that way."

Mattei reminded her that her gentle son had attacked Monti Hansen with a two-by-four and dragged Brian Loftis up the street with his car. She disagreed that these were violent acts. "Boys fight sometimes, that's all."

Mattei persevered. "We have disproved your son's alibi that he was job hunting the day Lance was killed. He wasn't at any of the places he said he was. His only remaining alibi is you."

"I saw him come in that day," she said. "It was four-thirty when he got home. Soon after that my husband arrived."

Mattei's heart sank. Rather than stopping Dunkle, the family was circling its wagons protectively around him. "What time did you leave work?" Mattei asked.

"About three-fifty." She worked at the Sears store in the Tanforan Shopping Center, in San Bruno.

Though Mattei pressed her, she remained subdued, but didn't budge in her statement.

Heading back to the station, where they had an appointment to meet with Mr. Dunkle, Mattei said, "Can you believe that? She'd rather lie for him than save kids' lives."

"Well," said Farmer, "it's natural. Blood is thicker than—you know. Maybe she really believes he's innocent." She was a mother, after all; how could she face that her son could murder a child?

It would take Mattei nearly three weeks to fight the Sears personnel office for permission to see Mrs. Dunkle's time card. While waiting, he drove various routes between Tanforan and Belmont, learning that the drive generally took about 20 minutes. The time card confirmed that she had left when she said she had, proving she could well have been home at 4:30. But by then Mattei and the others felt certain Jon Dunkle hadn't been. They believed the mother saw him come in around five on October 2. The next day, when Lance's murder hit the media, she must have figured out her son's involvement, because on October 4 she telephoned her daughter in Sacramento to say Jon would move there immediately.

Though they would never be able to prove it, Goulart and his men believed that from her actions Mrs. Dunkle suspected her son was involved.

Mr. Dunkle left early from his job as a barber in a San Francisco hotel to meet Mattei and Farmer at the BPD. They didn't expect much help from him. This was the man, after all, whose pattern of blaming others for his son's problems was well known. On the probation questionnaire when Dunkle requested early release from jail, the father wrote, "His main problem are peer pressure and I'm sure time will take care of it." When police questioned Dunkle a few days after John Davies disappeared, the father shouted at Jim Davies, "Quit siccing the cops on my son! You taught him to drink, you get him drunk, it's your fault!"

Mr. Dunkle's barely concealed hostility deepened during Mattei's presentation of the evidence. When Mattei reached the part about Jon's jail term for DUIs, Mr. Dunkle said, "My son doesn't have a drinking problem."

"How do you explain all those drunk driving arrests, then?"

"He doesn't drink much anymore. He doesn't have a drinking problem."

"Uh-huh." Mattei spoke of the drinking parties Dunkle used to go on with other boys, driving to Edgewood Park and the old hospital they called the Morgue.

"My boy never went out late at night," said Mr. Dunkle.

"Once he was in bed, he stayed there. I would have heard him if he went out, and he didn't."

"All his old buddies say he did."

"Everyone is trying to set him up, blame him for something he didn't do."

"You're saying he isn't capable of violence?" Mattei described the attacks on friends.

"My son doesn't have a violent temper," Mr. Dunkle said.

On and on they struggled. Mattei listed the many known facts that Dunkle had denied the day before in Sacramento.

Then, making it a point not "to get in the man's face," Farmer gently asked, "If he's innocent, why do you suppose he has lied to us about things we know are facts?"

"I don't know about it. My son has always been a good boy."

Any lingering doubts the investigators may have secretly harbored about Dunkle's guilt ended a week later when Goulart spoke again with Sheriff Ray Dick, the officer who had conducted the welfare check on Dunkle after the stomach injury on December 4. Now Dick mentioned that a Buck knife had been lying on the table while he spoke with Dunkle.

"Oh, *God!"* Goulart beat his fist on his desk. "That was the damn murder weapon!"

His men had searched the Dunkle's home in Belmont and the sister's in Sacramento last week. The knife was long gone.

Since neither the suspect nor his parents showed any cracks in their denials, Goulart decided to pressure them through the media again. Until now he had closely guarded the information that a prime suspect even existed. Now he lifted the lid on the search warrant affidavit he had filed three weeks earlier in order to see Dunkle's sister's phone bill.

All the Bay Area newspapers revealed the details covered in the affidavit including "the suspect's" similarities to the composite drawing and the psychological profile. They stated that he was the main suspect in both Lance's murder and John Davies's disappearance.

The reporters presented Dunkle's complaints that the investigation was a "pain in the neck" and his well-practiced denials. He was quoted as saying the police were ruining his life with false accusations and trying to force him to confess to acts he did not commit.

Two reporters identified Dunkle by name, which Goulart hadn't intended. "Shit," he said. "Now for sure he's going to get an attorney and quit talking to us."

But the next day, January 10, Dunkle smiled when Farmer and Mattei visited him again in Sacramento. Goulart had decided to pull himself out of direct contact and see whether Farmer's laid-back, nonthreatening style might dent Dunkle's armor.

Farmer saw Dunkle as having "a boyish, skinny look to his physique, as if his development stopped early." He had also noticed in the last session that sometimes Dunkle acted slow and childish, and other times seemed pretty sharp. All in all, Farmer decided the best approach was to treat Dunkle like an insecure kid.

Farmer showed Dunkle the video camera they had brought. "Jon, we'd like to film this visit, okay?"

Dunkle grinned up at the tall, handsome detective. "Sure."

"Want to see how it works?" Farmer handed the video camera to Dunkle and let him play with the controls. Then, with Mattei filming, the session formally began. After some preliminary talk, Farmer pulled out ink, a small roller, and fingerprint cards.

"We'd like to get some better prints," Farmer said. "You ever use one of these? See, I spread out the ink like this and press each finger in it and then roll the finger slowly onto the card. Want to try it?'' Dunkle experimented with rolling a set of Farmer's prints into the squares on the sheet.

''Wow,'' said Farmer, ''you're better at this than I am!'' Dunkle grinned up at him like a shy child starved for recognition.

Later, when Farmer said, ''Jon, how about walking for us while we run this thing?'' Dunkle cheerfully obliged, laughing and turning around on command.

Still, hunger for Farmer's approval didn't bring Dunkle any closer to admitting inconvenient facts. He smilingly persisted in the same denials, and when confronted with the fact that they now knew he had possessed a Buck knife when Sheriff Dick checked him out on December 4, he calmly said Dick must be mistaken.

''You know, Jon,'' said Farmer, ''we still have this problem where we say some things are true and you say they're not. You could prove you're telling the truth if you'd take a lie detector test.''

''My dad says lie detectors are tools of entrapment.''

''Tell you what, Jon,'' said Farmer affably. ''We can offer you a choice: a lie detector or a psychiatrist.''

''A police shrink?''

''Yeah. We have this really nice shrink who's interested in talking to you.'' Farmer returned to the strategy of the December 27 session and suggested that if Dunkle did have some kind of problem, perhaps the psychiatrist could help him.

''Maybe,'' said Dunkle.

Back at the police station, Farmer and Mattei showed the video to one of the smoking tree girls (only one, in case later a defense attorney claimed that showing her a video of a single suspect would taint her as a witness).

''Oh, wow!'' she said. ''It's him for sure!''

* * *

The police "shrink" Farmer offered to Dunkle did not belong to the Belmont Police Department or the DA's office. He was a gift from Bill Russell.

Dr. Hugh Ridelhuber was in his fifties, with a distinguished career that included serving as a psychiatrist for the Stanford Children's Health Council and later as director of mental health in San Mateo County. He also had worked a long time with attorneys in child custody cases and in some criminal cases, usually for the defense. He and Bill Russell had become friends while working on cases of alleged child sexual abuse. His unusual training had included studies in parapsychology and, more to the point, a stint at the National Center of Truth Verification, where among other things he learned how to use a voice stress analyzer. The issue of how to distinguish truth from falsehood had long fascinated him.

Ridelhuber reviewed the police records, listened to the taped interviews, and watched the videotape of Dunkle with Farmer. Then he gave his impressions to Bill Russell and Goulart.

"He couldn't bear to talk about the Davies. Why block on innocent questions like, 'What was John Davies like?' "

To Ridelhuber, this was more than plain lying. He explained that denial was an internal avoidance of fact, as well as an outward lie. When something is unbearable, a person will block it out. Ridelhuber listed Dunkle's psychopathic traits for the police and made suggestions on how to handle him.

Ridelhuber had cringed when he heard the tape on which Goulart and Mattei loudly called Dunkle a fag in the December 27 interrogation. Not only did this macho style differ markedly from his own, Ridelhuber saw it as ineffective. Insults and aggression had only increased Dunkle's resistance.

Ridelhuber suggested that a less forceful and more indirect questioning style be tried. He added that they should try an older woman interviewer. Dunkle had a history of being drawn to older women, with whom it was permissible to cry. Ridelhuber reminded the police that Dunkle "may also have homosexual fears and conflicts, so may find a male interviewer threatening," which would strengthen his denial with them. Open-ended questions might gain more information than blunt, confrontational, specific ones.

Ridelhuber's ending statements echoed Farmer's insights about Dunkle. Ridelhuber wrote, "I believe he is getting some significant satisfaction from the attention he is receiving from the police and his now having achieved some degree of status from the crime as compared with his otherwise bleak and insignificant life. This factor . . . may lead him to want to tell the whole story and thereby confess."

Chapter Twenty-two

On January 30, twenty days after Dr. Ridelhuber explained the ways Dunkle was a psychopath, a young woman named Lisa Davis started her new job at the Rancho Cordova Carl's Jr. A plain girl, she arrived in a loose sweatshirt and non-name-brand jeans. Her brown hair hung straight and lanky. No makeup softened her sullen, sad face, and she snapped gum like a disenfranchised teenager.

After Lisa watched some training films, the worker she would be replacing took her into the kitchen area. "Hey, Jon," Brenda called, "guess what? They hired one of my best friends from high school."

Dunkle smiled up from the bag of frozen French fries he was opening.

"So, Jon, you'll be orienting her. Help her out, okay?"

Lisa looked around the kitchen nervously, her insecurity showing.

"Don't worry," said Dunkle. "I'll teach you everything you need to know. Know what this is? A deep fat fryer!"

As they worked side by side, Lisa saw that Dunkle was

showing off and lording it over her, obviously with great enjoyment. He reminded her of how little kids act big for others on the playground. When he misread the instructions on a food package, she let it pass rather than pop his bubble of delighted self-importance.

"Hey, come with the rest of us to Brenda's farewell party at the Wits End," Dunkle said at the end of the shift.

"Okay." When Lisa joined them in the neighborhood bar, she told Dunkle she'd seen his mountain bike locked up outside. "It's a good one," she said.

"You ride?"

She shrugged. "Some."

"I biked all the way to Shasta last summer," Dunkle bragged. "I had fun playing chicken with truck drivers." He made *vroom, vroom, screech* noises. "I made them think I had a gun, but I just had a knife."

He talked a lot about his grandfather. "I worked in his motel in Shasta. He told me secrets about his maid. He bugged her room. Then it got dangerous because I knew too much, so he paid me to leave."

"Wow, how weird," said Lisa, her eyes going big.

When the group complained about work, Dunkle confided, "I asked to be fired from one job. I got sick of working at The Bubble Machine and I thought, why not live on unemployment?" He giggled. "Then I worked at the IRS. I was in charge of three gay guys and I was spying on the auditors. Man, I could've got the IRS in big trouble if I wanted!"

Clearly Dunkle was feeling the beer. He nudged Lisa. "Hey, see that?" He snickered, pointing at a poster on the wall. "The cops think that guy is me."

"What did he do?"

"Oh, he killed a twelve-year-old kid in Belmont."

"No shit," said Lisa.

"Yeah, it's in the papers a lot. See, I was at Water Dog Lake, drunk, the Friday night before the murder, and I found a knife at the pier."

"That's why they think you did the murder?"

He shrugged. "They're trying to make me take a lie detector test. Cops trick you with those things. They're tools of harassment." He made sure she understood what an important suspect he was: "There's cops from Belmont, they come up here and stay in a motel just so they can watch me. This one, Goulart, he's an asshole. This other guy, Whaley, he's okay, but he works with this FBI agent who suspects me of killing another kid, John Davies, because he was kidnapped and I was at his house the night before he disappeared."

"God."

"There's Mafia in Belmont. The cops should take a look at those guys."

"But isn't Belmont one of those rich goody-good towns?"

Dunkle nodded. "Lots of Italians. Mafia. See, I know stuff most people don't know."

When the group poured out of the Wits End, Dunkle mounted his bicycle, popped a wheelie for Lisa's benefit, waved happily, and sped away. When she was sure he wouldn't return, Lisa walked down the dark street to a parked car. Sergeant Goulart leaned over from the driver's side to open the passenger door.

Inside, Lisa peeled off the transmitter taped to her abdomen. She was bursting with excitement. "God, can you believe the luck? He talked about Lance my first time out!"

Two weeks earlier Sergeant Goulart had approached Officer Lisa Thomas at the BPD Coke machine. When she realized he needed an officer to go undercover in the Dunkle investigation, she leaped at it. Only the second female ever hired as an officer in the BPD and barely more than a rookie, Lisa felt she needed to prove herself. To her, the detectives were a closed inner circle. After the first day of the Lance Turner investigation, when she helped question Ralston School kids, her only role in the case had been to be the female cop required to be present when male detectives repeatedly interviewed the smoking tree girls.

Now she immediately saw that in some ways she was a natural to work with Dunkle. She knew Sacramento well, having spent her miserable high school years and her unsuccessful marriage in the neighborhood where he now lived. While working her way through police science courses, she'd cooked fast food next door to the Rancho Cordova Carl's Jr. that employed Dunkle now. She was twenty-four, the same age as Dunkle, and small enough to be nonthreatening and could portray an immaturity level that matched that of the smoking tree girls'.

Goulart admitted the team's first choice was to use a young male officer, but Dunkle already knew the ones willing or able to try it. The other choice would have been a middle-aged female, since Ridelhuber pointed out that Dunkle confided in older women. Unfortunately, the BPD's other female officer had the right age but the wrong personality.

Goulart had learned that Dunkle "took a liking" to a young female employee at Carl's Jr. named Brenda, and he realized Lisa might suit. With some consultation with Ridelhuber and the FBI, the detectives brainstormed about the character Lisa should portray. Because Dunkle apparently wasn't able to have good relationships with peers and thus turned to younger people, Lisa needed to appear nearly as immature and airheaded as the smoking tree girls. She mustn't be as provocative, though. A sexually available female his own age would scare him off. Lisa must desexualize herself with baggy clothes, plain hair, and lack of makeup. To make Dunkle feel confident around her, she must come across as a low self-esteem loser. She must be able to hold her own in a bar.

She would wear a wire at all times. Goulart and Farmer would trade off backup duty; she was to be alone with

Dunkle only when one of them was nearby and listening. Still, she had to be prepared to take care of herself if things went wrong. She must always carry a concealed weapon. No one knew whether Dunkle might be as dangerous to a young woman as he was to boys.

Returning to the name she'd used before marriage and divorce, she entered Dunkle's life as her old self, Lisa Davis, ugly duckling.

The first day's excitement let down fast. The next couple of weeks would bring the work and routine the investigators had originally expected. While Lisa's relationship with Dunkle would progress rapidly, the closest he would come to talking about the case would be to complain constantly about police harassment.

Dunkle bounced around cheerfully at work, enjoying his role as Lisa's teacher. He loved giving her orders. Once when Lisa was slicing strips from a slab of lard, Dunkle said, "No, here's how to do that." He gripped the knife like a weapon and stabbed.

Debriefing her on the second night, Goulart said, "The manager says our boy's acting giddy, like a kid in love. Good work."

On the fourth day, Dunkle and Lisa took a smoking break together outside. "There's lots of undercover cars around here," Dunkle said. "The cops watch me all the time."

Lisa took a long drag on her cigarette, conscious of the transmitter taped to her abdomen. "I don't see any cops," she said.

He pointed to a car cruising slowly past, its driver peering at signs. "That asshole right there. You'd better watch out, Lisa, he might think you're my girlfriend."

"Yeah, a killer's girlfriend," she joked. Inside she wanted to laugh; the person cruising past wasn't an officer. "I don't like cops," she said. "They took my driver's license away once."

He giggled. "Hey, me, too! What did you do, get fucked up?"

"Maybe."

"Hey, me, too!"

When they returned to the kitchen, the manager asked Lisa to scrape the grill. She snapped gum and raised her eyes to heaven for Dunkle's benefit, then searched for the scraper. "Hey, Jon, you know where it is?"

"It's been gone for months."

She knew that was a lie, as she'd seen it herself earlier that day. At the end of the shift, when she emptied the trash, the scraper fell out. That night Goulart asked the manager about missing tools and learned that since Dunkle had come to work, several knives and a meat ax had disappeared. Accustomed to petty theft by employees, the manager didn't see the implications that leaped to Goulart's mind. "Watch yourself," Goulart warned Lisa.

"God, Jim," she said, "it's really hard to believe he might be dangerous. He's like some overgrown kid."

Goulart shook his head. "Never let your guard down."

The next day, as Dunkle and Lisa walked together to his sister's house, Dunkle waved and grinned at the surprised driver of a passing car. "Another undercover cop," Dunkle explained. "They're trying to pressure me to confess to things I didn't do."

When they reached the house, Dunkle checked the mail. "Gotta see if the cops sent me any clippings today."

"God, they send you stuff in the mail?" Though he kept identifying ordinary citizens as undercover cops, Dunkle was right that the BPD was trying to pressure him. What Lisa couldn't figure out was whether it did anything, except make him feel important.

"The papers lie," he said. "They quote me wrong. That's all part of the pressure." His eyes suddenly narrowed. "Hey, Lisa, you're not a cop, are you?"

Two blocks away, Goulart gripped the ignition key to his car.

Lisa turned down her mouth and gave Dunkle a wounded dog look. "God, Jon," she said, allowing her eyes to fill.

"Just kidding," he said.

Later, they wandered over to the Wits End, where they shared a pitcher of beer and challenged each other to pool. When Lisa slid behind him on the way to the ladies' room, he bumped her rear with the cue stick. "Oh, sorry," he said, his teasing grin showing that he'd just made his first pass at her. He had all the finesse of a backward thirteen-year-old.

When they said good-bye and rode bikes in opposite directions away from the bar, Lisa Thomas as usual joined Goulart in a coffee shop for debriefing. Then she returned to the motel and typed her daily report, sometimes searching the taped conversations for sections she needed to transcribe word for word.

Finally she fell into bed. Like most nights after being with Dunkle, she couldn't fall asleep till she watched the most boring program she could find on late night TV.

Dunkle was infatuated enough to take Lisa home to have dinner with his sister. He introduced Lisa as "my girlfriend" and Lisa laughed as if flattered and embarrassed. Judy Dunkle struck Lisa as very shy, depressed, and intensely guarded. She also saw, over the course of many evenings, that Judy was devoted to Jon.

During dinner, Dunkle regaled Lisa with more tales of police harassment. "There's cops watching me all over this neighborhood," he said, correctly. He giggled. "Kids run when they see me coming."

Judy said, "How can they believe Jon committed that murder? He'd never do a thing like that."

"Right," said Lisa. Across the table Dunkle grinned boyishly at her. He had such sweetness about him. He didn't look like a killer at all.

"After dinner let's play Monopoly," he said.

Lisa felt a sharp pain low on her abdomen. " 'Scuse me," she said, heading for the bathroom. She locked the door and pulled up her shirt. The problem of how to store extra batteries had hassled her from the beginning. It didn't work to hide one in her boot and she didn't dare slip one into a pocket, so she had taken to wrapping one in tissue and taping it on her body. Tonight she'd simply taped a bare one to her skin and her sweat was corroding it. She wrapped it in some tissue and taped it back on.

Judy had laid out the Monopoly game. "We can't stay up too late," she warned. "We're going to church with Mom and Dad in the morning."

The adrenaline high Lisa had been on since day one dropped away, leaving her drained and sad and uncertain. *He's just a goofy kid who plays Monopoly on Saturday night and goes to church with his family. What the hell am I doing here?*

The pain on her abdomen sharpened. After forty-five minutes of throwing dice and moving her Monopoly piece around the board, she headed back into the bathroom.

The battery had continued to leak through the Kleenex and had eaten a hole into her skin. She had to tuck it into the side of her boot and try not to limp the rest of the evening.

Lisa never went to a doctor about the injury and it left a permanent scar.

Lisa and Dunkle loaded their bike baskets with food, Coca-Cola, and Jack Daniel's, and rode into Goethe Park—Golfe Park, as Dunkle called it. Lisa had told Goulart the route Dunkle planned to take, but now Dunkle shouted over his shoulder, "I know a different way." Bypassing the bridge which Lisa had told Goulart to use, Dunkle led her down a narrow bike trail along the water and headed deep into an area where no car could follow. Was he cleverly evading the corps of imaginary cops tailing him? Or did he want to get her alone because he'd blown her cover?

Sweat trickled around the tape on the uninjured side of her abdomen. What if he groped under her sweatshirt and found the mike? If necessary, she would protect herself.

One reason the detectives let her go undercover was that she'd proven herself. While she was still a rookie, her male partner had been knocked down and disarmed by a man threatening to shoot his wife. When the man held his gun on her partner, Lisa pulled her own weapon and shouted, "Drop it!"

The man glanced over. "Yeah, I'm scared, babe." He turned back toward her partner, finger tightening on the trigger. Lisa fired. The man's gun skidded across the floor and he dropped, clutching his thigh. "You bitch!" he screamed.

When the paramedics came, he complained, "A Goddamn *woman* shot me."

She told no one about the nightmares afterward, or the way her visual memory made the man's black gun appear bright blue. It disgusted and confused her how the shooting raised her status in the macho BPD. She had proven to her fellow officers that she had balls.

Now she mentally practiced reaching into her boot and swinging up with the switchblade taped to her ankle.

Dunkle stopped at a grassy, tree-filled spot along the river. They broke out the picnic baskets, popped open a couple of Cokes, and poured in some Jack Daniel's. Dunkle leaned back, propped up on an elbow.

"I'd like to pipe bomb Belmont's cop cars. Can you picture it? Blow them right up."

Lisa laughed.

"You know," he said, "it's fun to fuck with the FBI. They questioned me in a motel room, pictures of Lance Turner on the walls and everything. First I told them yes, then I told them no." He laughed. "They don't know what to think."

"Hey, that's pretty smart. Keep them guessing."

"Who wants to talk to cops anyway?" said Dunkle. "I'd rather talk to a shrink." He finished his Coke and wiped the can carefully before crumpling it. "I always clean my cans now," he said, "ever since they found that Bud can with my fingerprints on it at Water Dog." He pulled another out of the basket, topped it off generously with whiskey, and made jokes about robbing houses.

A few days later, Dunkle pulled Lisa to the door of the Carl's Jr. kitchen. "That damn Goulart is here again."

She hid, acting scared. "I don't want him to see me. He questioned me about you the other day." Goulart had walked in several times the past two weeks to keep up pressure on Dunkle. Once Dunkle had fallen apart. He gave Lisa conflicting orders and then threw a tantrum when the manager told him to wash dishes. "Fuckin' cops are going to make me lose my job!" he'd fumed.

This time, though, he told Lisa, "Watch this."

Dunkle walked over to Goulart's table, grinning. "Hey, Whaley left a note on my door. He wants me to come see him. Wanna give me a ride to Belmont?"

The next day, Lisa Thomas acted as Goulart's backup, following him from about a mile back as he drove Dunkle to the Bay Area. She knew Goulart had switched his gun from his right side to his left as a precaution. Over the transmitter she heard Goulart and Dunkle kidding around.

As Goulart approached the Bay Bridge, Lisa heard him say, "Hey, Jon, you could save us all a lot of trouble if you'd just get out here and jump."

Her surprised laughter stopped abruptly. The tracking device had gone dead. She'd lost them. She tried cruising closer, but didn't dare approach too close. Finally, she stopped and kept calling the BPD until she learned that Goulart had arrived safely.

A couple of days later, Goulart told her the time had come for her to push Dunkle harder. They strategized about ways she might do it.

By mid-February, Lisa and Dunkle hung out together during most of their free time, their dates including many nights at the Wits End, movies, dinners, and board games at Judy's house, and long bike hikes away from roads, driving Goulart crazy.

Sex crept into the relationship, but Dunkle's approaches were so juvenile Lisa could easily fend them off. Once he stopped outside a health food store while they rode bikes. "I'm getting some 'minos. You wouldn't understand. It's guy stuff." He bought amino acid tablets. "These improve manhood."

One day, during a picnic when Dunkle kiddingly grabbed for her breast, Lisa said, "Jon, remember I told you I had that terrible experience and I'm really turned off on sex. I have to feel really close to someone before I can get physical." She hinted that to grow closer, she and Dunkle should exchange confidences about their deepest secrets.

Dunkle pushed her for the worst memory of her childhood. She told him her parents had divorced when she was young and she didn't get along with her mother. "When I was about eight, I called my father and asked if I could come live with him. He told me to pack my suitcase and wait on the porch. I sat on the steps until nighttime. He never came."

"Poor little girl. Her daddy never came."

Lisa asked herself what she was doing. She'd given Dunkle the true story of an old, deep hurt, as if he were an actual friend instead of someone she was tricking and manipulating for a confession. Next she'd be telling him about the time in high school that the popular girls took her out to a field and said, "You're ugly and you smell. We don't like you." Then she reminded herself that that was the self she had left behind when she became a police officer, and it was as a covert officer that she pulled herself together and prodded Dunkle for memories of his own.

Dunkle straightened up and lit a cigarette. "Okay, I'll tell you one of my hit-and-run accidents. I was cruising along, had one of the bottles of Jack Daniel's, one of the great big ones, twelve-dollar ones. Friend of mine, we drank it together. We were at the beach. I took him home. I thought shit, I want to cruise, heh. I had my, I had a Sony stereo, seven speakers, blasting away. I was cruising along this park and I ran a stop sign and I went up this hill and pretty soon all I see is a blur, my eyes were all, you know, fucked up. . . . And it was a moped. I pushed this moped twenty-two feet of scrapes up this hill and that means like thirty-five feet I pushed him. The guy got my license plate and pretty soon I hear, *Boom-boom-boom* on my front door and I'm arrested."

"Shit!" she said, her excitement not a pretense. He'd never mentioned one of his crimes before.

At the debriefing that night, Goulart and Lisa Thomas decided she should make up her own hit-and-run story next time. He might loosen up some more.

On their next picnic a few days later, after a few Cokes laced with Jack Daniel's, Lisa said, "I've got this secret, this really bad thing—God, I can't talk about it."

"Hey, come on, this is me you're talking to."

"It's really hard, though."

"Well, hell, I've done stuff, you know. Like, when I was a security guard, I stole gold from the place I was guarding."

"That's just stealing. This is worse. You could almost say it's got kinda to do with what you're being investigated for. Kinda sort of."

Dunkle perked up. "What, you saw a murder? A rape?

You could go to prison as an accessory, you know that? But I'd never let you down. The more you tell me and the more I tell you, the more closer we get." He poured more drinks for both of them.

Lisa said, "I used to have this light green Mustang, and I was out late at night, I was all fucked up, you know—" With many hesitations, she finally said, "It was raining bad, I was on the wrong side of the road, and there was this old lady there, and I ran her over, and I just kept going. The lady died."

"Hey," said Dunkle, "I did the same thing once, except the person didn't die."

Lisa rambled on. "I read in the paper that when they did the autopsy they found green paint flecks on the old lady's nose."

Dunkle burst out laughing. "That's great! Green paint on her nose!"

"Yeah, well, I had to sell my green car right away."

Dunkle talked about the moped hit-and-run again. Lisa yawned. "You already told me this story, Jon."

"Yeah?" He studied her a moment. "OK, what about, what about, oh shit, when did I have a car last? Whenever it was. I was cruisin' along this street and I saw this guy and I looked over to my left and I ran into him. My windshield was busted all over."

"That isn't much. You never did anything as bad as what I did to the old lady."

"You know about Monti?"

"No," said Lisa honestly. The detectives had deliberately withheld information from her so that she wouldn't make the mistake of showing Dunkle she knew things she shouldn't.

"They say I took a two-by-four and bashed him in the head with it. I don't remember. I told my dad the next day when I found out I had a blackout."

Lisa peered at him through cigarette smoke and, thinking fast, came up with a tale to lead into the subject of harming kids. "I'm in trouble for hurting two little girls when I was baby-sitting."

"What did you do? Pick them up and throw them against the TV set?"

"Something like that."

"Hey, all right, that's pretty good. At least I have the right girlfriend." They laughed companionably. Then he said, "Okay, I got one. I was driving up this road, I was so fucking drunk. Nobody knows about this, nobody. I saw some guy walking along, I mean he was fucked up, and I went over to ask him something, so I drove over toward him, I was cruisin', I didn't know how fast I was going, and I ran into him, knocked him cold on the ground. Didn't know what to do, so I stuck him in my car." Dunkle laughed.

Lisa was having trouble following this. "The guy?"

"Yeah, I mean I just picked him up and stuck him in the trunk of my car, which was a hatchback. You know, if I would've got pulled over, they would've saw him. I cranked up my tunes, I didn't want to hear a word or nothing, you know. Cruised along, dumped him somewhere. Next day, it's in the paper—mystery hit-and-run. His whole skull was split open. He was in a coma seventeen days. I lived three blocks from him. Next day I cleaned the car." A giggle. "There was hair stuck to the bumper, so I took off the rubber stripping and I cleaned it and glued it back on. Broke my windshield the same night, but there was no glass where the guy was."

Shit, she thought. He's shining me on with some damn make-believe.

Chapter Twenty-three

Detective Farmer wasn't enjoying the weeks he took Goulart's place on backup duty in Sacramento. Sitting for hours in a cold car and listening to Dunkle's inane, drunken conversation was "the opposite of exciting," a very far cry from the action-filled glamour of police work on TV. On top of that, the Dunkle detail forced him to sacrifice important family time. At home his wife was alone with their new baby girl, their first child, and here he was, mind and body numb in an unmarked unit, too far out of his jurisdiction to even go home when his shift ended.

On the other hand, he never could forget the sight of Lance Turner at the scene or on the autopsy table. If this work would get his killer locked up, it was worth everyone's sacrifices now.

Over the transmitter, Farmer heard Lisa Thomas spin the tale that she and Goulart had cooked up about running over an old woman. As usual she was throwing in just the right embellishments. Green paint flecks on the nose—great! She was a natural.

A few minutes later, Farmer sat up straight. "He was in

a coma seventeen days. The papers called it a mystery hit-and-run. . . ."

"Oh, my God!" Farmer said. "Steve Murphy!" He remembered very well the gravely injured, diabetic sixteen-year-old someone had run over and then left for dead in the Marburger turnaround. It was a miracle the teenager had survived, the attack had been so vicious.

Farmer banged the steering wheel. "Damn!" Dunkle had never even been a suspect.

Dunkle's old Honda Civic took on new significance with the Steve Murphy revelation. Goulart recontacted the new owner, who fortunately continued to be very cooperative. He permitted detectives to dismantle the bumpers and search for remnants of the hair Dunkle described cleaning off after he rammed Steve. Sure enough, a few hairs were embedded on the bumper and car. Goulart painstakingly removed and bagged them and turned them over to the police lab.

The lab results wouldn't be back for several months. Meanwhile, the BPD tabled the Steve Murphy aspect of the investigation. They couldn't risk blowing Lisa's cover.

In early March, Joan Davies opened the front door to Whaley. "Long time no see," she said edgily. She was pretty pissed off with the BPD. In December and January, unaware that the department was conducting an intense investigation of Dunkle, Joan periodically telephoned to ask about the jewelry police had confiscated from her and was annoyed that they took days, even weeks, to return her calls.

"The Belmont Lapidary owner identified some pieces of the jewelry as stolen," Goulart told her when she managed to reach him.

"When will it be returned to me?" She couldn't get her

mind around the concept that Dunkle's gifts to her were stolen property.

"Tell me," Goulart asked, "did Dunkle keep giving you gold after John disappeared?"

"I've been telling you people for three years that when my son disappeared from our lives, so did Jon Dunkle."

From Goulart's point of view, the investigation took priority over maintaining good relations with the victims' families. Margo Turner, Lance's mother, whom the police admired as a near-saint, had innocently shared a piece of privileged information with the media. Goulart could risk no more leaks. He did not enlighten Joan about Dunkle's status as prime suspect.

From the Davies' point of view, it was cruel and offensive that they had to learn this crucial information from reporters. In the second week of January, when the search warrant went public, one had come to the house and asked, "What are your comments about Jon Dunkle being the suspect in your son's disappearance and Lance Turner's murder?"

"Jon Dunkle?" The question didn't fully register. "Well, he's one of several people who police think could possibly be involved in John's disappearance. It's so very frustrating because we obviously want to bring closure to the case after three and a half years."

Joan's imagination had never conquered her resistance to what "being involved in the disappearance" might mean. The worst scenario she could visualize was that Dunkle or someone else abandoned John after an accident that perhaps had something to do with drinking.

The reporter handed over a poster of the final composite drawing. "This is Lance's killer."

Joan hadn't been following the articles about Lance very closely; they were too tragic, too upsetting. To her, the series of publicized composite drawings resembled no one.

The reporter held up a high school photo. "And this is Jon Dunkle."

In the picture, Dunkle cocked his head and smiled up

in the same shy, endearing way he'd done when he used to call Joan "Mom." The person in the composite drawing of Lance Turner's killer held his head the same way. His eyes and smile and mouth suddenly looked too familiar. . . .

Joan burst into tears. "Oh, my God! John is dead! My son is dead and Jon Dunkle killed him!"

Yet once the shock passed, the Davies didn't abandon hope. How could they be sure John was dead if there was no body? In February, Joan signed a release permitting John's photo to appear on milk cartons and grocery bags. This method of publicizing missing children had grown out of the efforts of the Collins Foundation and other organizations the Davies worked with and was sponsored by Assemblyman Gray Davis. She and Jim kept telling reporters and television audiences that nothing was worse than not knowing. Their stock phrases were "As long as there is no body, there is no closure. We still hope John will be found alive."

Now, two months after the newspapers identified Dunkle as the big suspect, Whaley told Joan, "A large brown stain, probably blood, has been found on the passenger side of Dunkle's old Honda Civic. I need John's blood type."

"Blood in Dunkle's car?" A full scenario sprang instantly into her mind: John and Dunkle listen to music in Dunkle's car; Dunkle stabs John; John is dead before Dunkle pulls out of the driveway. Terrible as this image was, it allowed her to believe John died fast and suffered little. She would cling to it in the future, even after new facts told a different story.

"Don't you remember?" she said. "We don't *have* John's blood type."

"There just has to be a way to get it," Whaley said, and he recontacted the Colorado Springs Hospital where John was born, hassled every doctor John ever went to, and pored over medical records. John's blood type turned up nowhere.

A few weeks later, Deklinski met with Jim and Joan. "We

believe Dunkle is involved with the disappearance,'' he said, the first official to formally tell them this. ''We're having trouble getting him.'' He said he was now at liberty to disclose that for six weekends search and rescue teams had been scouring the grounds around the old Hassler Home in Edgewood Park for John's remains. So far they'd found nothing.

''We asked police to search there the first week our son disappeared,'' Jim Davies said bitterly.

The dog searches had begun the day Lisa Thomas started work at Carl's Jr. Sergeant Whaley met with San Mateo County's volunteer Search and Rescue team at an entrance to Edgewood Park. He sat on a Jeep's tailgate with Dorothy Hammond, dog handler and search expert, studying the area's map and guessing at places Dunkle had probably partied with old friends. Suddenly a cold, wet nose pressed his neck. Turning, he was face-to-face with a huge Doberman. ''Oh, Cinnamon,'' said Dorothy, and the highly trained search dog cavorted around them like a puppy. ''She's a pussycat,'' Dorothy said.

After the six weekends of searches, Whaley obtained county permission to dig in the areas the dogs had alerted on. Nothing.

During this period, Farmer reinterviewed Dunkle's old buddy John Wolfe and heard about the ''flesh with hair'' that Dunkle once played with in a wooded area off Whiskey Hill Road in La Honda. Cinnamon sniffed around that whole area, too. Nothing was found there either.

Whaley wrote the searchers a letter of commendation which said in part: ''They are hard workers and do not hesitate when it is necessary for them to follow their dog into a flooded basement, hole in the ground or anyplace else. . . .'' He added, ''Our suspect might also be involved in the death of John Davies. (At this point I am assuming that Davies is dead.)''

Like the Davies, though, Whaley couldn't *act* as if John were dead. Even sharp-nosed Cinnamon had found no trace of him. When the milk carton and grocery bag publicity brought a new wave of sightings, Whaley had to follow them up.

Mattei and Farmer also continued prying information from Dunkle's old friends and contacts. Dunkle's odd tales to Lisa about his grandfather in Shasta were inspired by learning Farmer had visited the old man. The grandfather hadn't bugged the maid's room or paid Dunkle to leave for "knowing too much." He'd hired his grandson to do simple maintenance jobs at the motel. He'd been troubled when Dunkle became obsessed with the children of a guest, watching them for hours in the pool. Dunkle had also constantly followed the maid and her children around. The grandfather mentioned that Dunkle had befriended a local sixteen-year-old boy and went camping with him a few nights. Farmer questioned the boy, who reported the same behavior Dunkle's old friends did. Dunkle drank beer, but couldn't hold it well, and he acted sulky and jealous when the boy joked around with other campers.

Goulart assigned Mattei to travel to Santa Maria, a few hours' drive south, and interview Jeff Dunkle, now out of prison, reputedly "burned out" on drugs and working with the elderly as an attendant.

The day Goulart drove Dunkle to Belmont in mid-February, Dunkle served Whaley coffee and cookies in his parents' home. Whaley had needed to give a lot of reassurance before Dunkle agreed to this meeting. "You'll coerce me with the lie detector," Dunkle had said on the phone. "Or else you'll trick me with truth serum, or you'll lock me up on a 5150."

Yet now Dunkle offered cookies and acted "sweet as sweet, with his eyes kind of twinkling. 'Jerry, I'm really sorry, but I have no idea what happened to John Davies.' "

He now admitted his old friendship with the family. He reminisced about Christmas stockings the Davies gave him, drinking sessions with Mr. Davies, and the DUI he got with Mark as his passenger. He even admitted that John used to sit in the Honda Civic and listen to Dunkle's sound system late at night.

He talked about Jim Davies, Jr. "One time Jimmy asked me if I'd still like him if he was gay. I said no way! I talked to his dad about it and it brought him and me closer." He described Mark and Jimmy teasing John mercilessly, adding a bizarre detail: "Jimmy used to throw forks into John's feet. One got stuck."

With his weird tales of Jimmy going to "gay drug parties" and being cruel to John, was Dunkle trying to divert suspicion from himself, police wondered.

Whaley took Dunkle walking on the Water Dog trails. He videotaped as Dunkle chattered, hoping in vain that later some expert would be able be able to analyze the suspect's body language. Dunkle stopped near the switchback. "I was on this trail," he said, "and I saw a short person walking away."

Whaley looked hard at his suspect, who was mugging with apparent delight for the camera. Did "short person" mean Lance Turner?

The next day, surprising everyone, Dunkle agreed to meet with the "police shrink," Dr. Hugh Ridelhuber.

Dunkle smiled up shyly when Farmer brought Ridelhuber into the conference room. Ridelhuber noted that the whites of Dunkle's eyes showed all the way around his irises. He knew that Eastern considered this phenomenon a sign of the spiritual illness found in killers.

"This room bugged? You taping this?" Dunkle looked around at the walls.

"No, this isn't being taped, Jon," said Ridelhuber truthfully. He led into the interview by presenting himself as someone who could help with emotional problems: for example, if Dunkle was troubled by urges he couldn't control.

Dunkle spoke of the police's suspicions and harassment, lie detectors and truth serum. He disclosed nothing useful in the session, but as it ended, Ridelhuber told him, "I believe there is something inside you, Jon, that causes you to do things you don't want to be doing. I believe this is very troubling to you. If you decide you want to look at those things, I can help you." He slid his business card across the table.

Dunkle looked at it, his lower lip sucked in, his thoughts apparently sad and inward. Ridelhuber waited.

Abruptly, Dunkle jumped up, pocketed the card, and walked out.

Two weeks later, in early March, Jim Davies, Jr., came home on leave from the navy because Mark had signed up for the navy, too. "I'm going to see you off," said Jimmy.

Arriving not long after Whaley had told his parents about blood in Dunkle's car and Deklinski notified them officially that Dunkle probably killed John, Jimmy walked into a maelstrom of emotion.

"The cops think Dunkle killed John? That's crazy," he said. From the beginning, John's disappearance had left Jimmy bemused. In the navy for a year and a half before it happened, he had not experienced the events and agony firsthand and didn't really understand his parents' obsession and rage. The situation made him feel like an outsider with his own family.

"Come on," Mark said, "I'll take you to see Whaley." Since Deklinski had cleared Mark of suspicion with the lie detector test, Mark's attitude toward the police had brightened. Now he dropped by the station every so often to chat with Whaley and cruise around the walls that held the VIA chart.

John Davies was 15 when he disappeared in November 1981. *(Photo courtesy Jim and Joan Davies)*

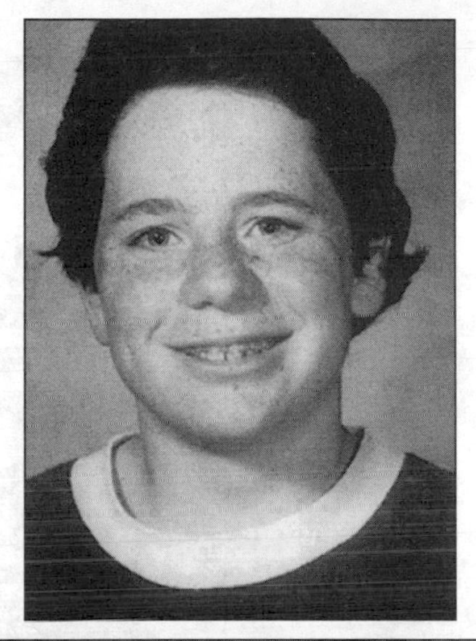

John Davies's Missing Teen poster was displayed at the May 1984 San Francisco rally for the National Missing Children's Act. *(Photo courtesy Jim and Joan Davies)*

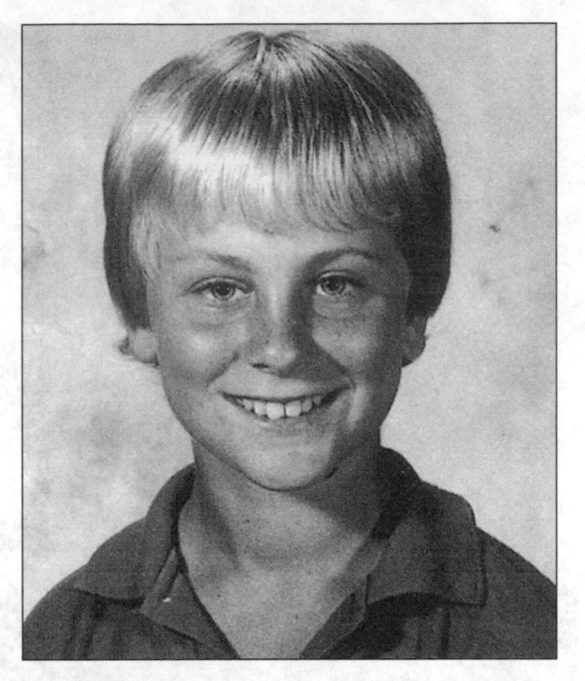

Lance Turner, 12. *(Photo courtesy Margo Turner)*

Sean Dannehl, 12. *(Photo courtesy Guy Dannehl)*

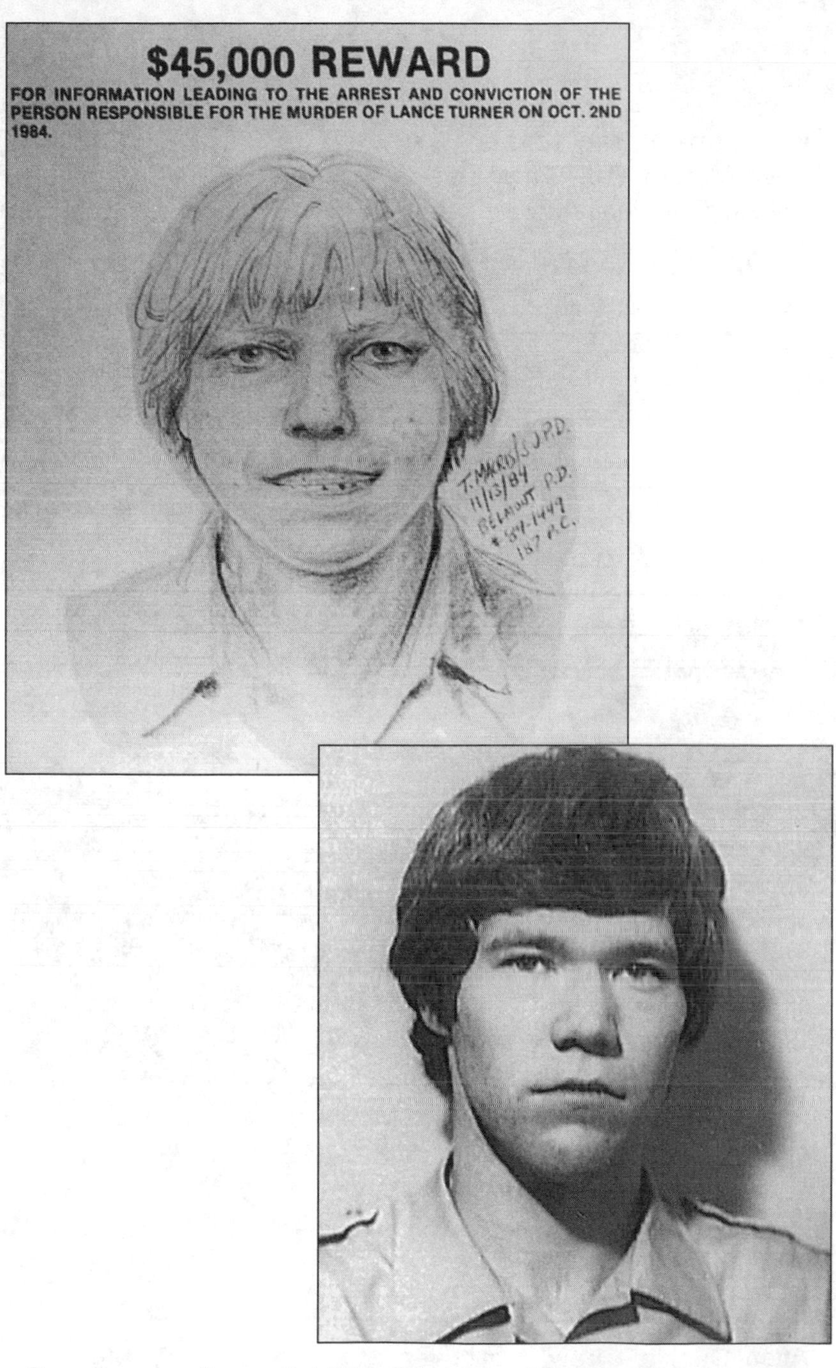

San Jose police artist Tom Macris's drawing of the young man seen at the Smoking Tree near the site of Lance Turner's murder clearly resembles Jon Dunkle.
(Photo courtesy Belmont, California Police Department)

Jon Dunkle ran over Steve Murphy, 16. *(Photo courtesy Steve Murphy)*

After Dunkle threw him over an embankment, Murphy crawled up to the road and collapsed beneath this No Dumping sign. *(Photo courtesy San Mateo County, California Superior Court)*

Lance Turner's battered body found by searchers four hours after he was last seen. *(Photo courtesy San Mateo County, California Superior Court)*

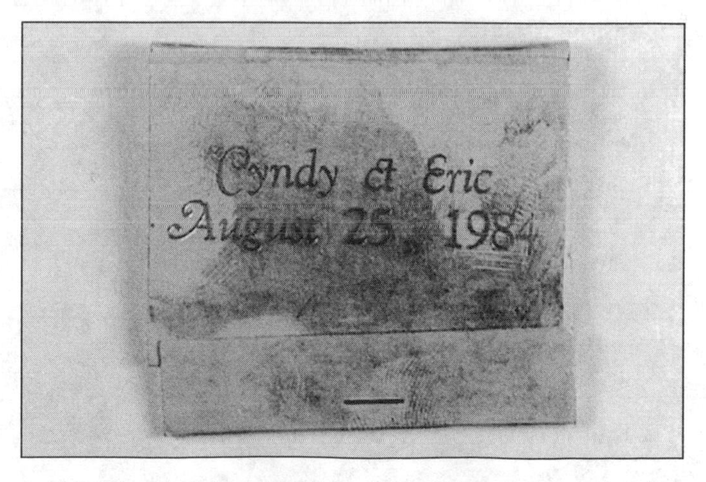

In his confession, Dunkle described the sky-blue matchbook found near the Smoking Tree. It was a piece of evidence the police had not made public. *(Photo courtesy San Mateo County, California Superior Court)*

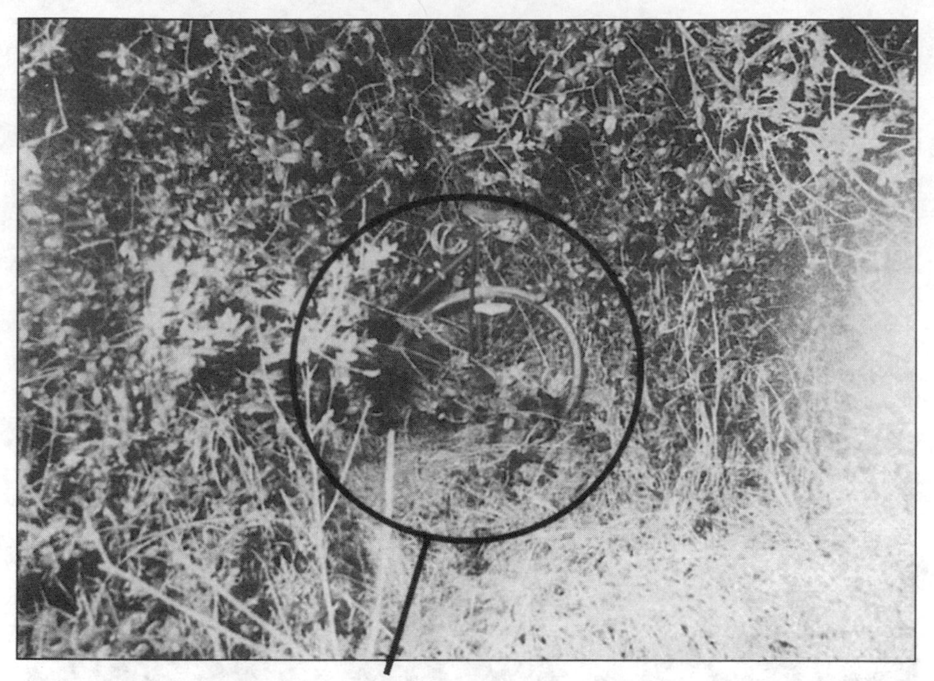

Sean Dannehl's blue bicycle half buried in brush forty-five feet from the trail. His body lay twenty feet farther back. *(Photo courtesy San Mateo County, California Superior Court)*

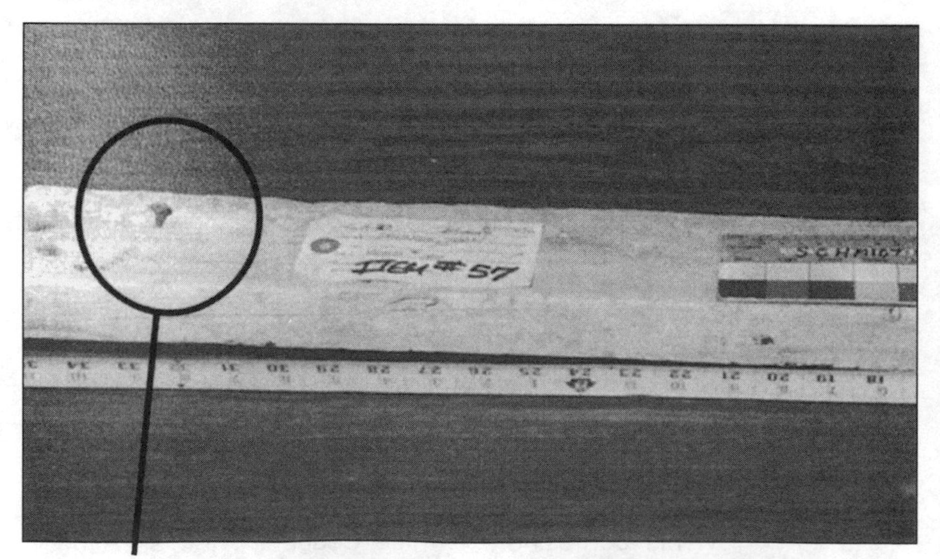

The nail in the 2x4 found at the scene matched an injury to Sean Dannehl's head. *(Photo courtesy San Mateo County, California Superior Court)*

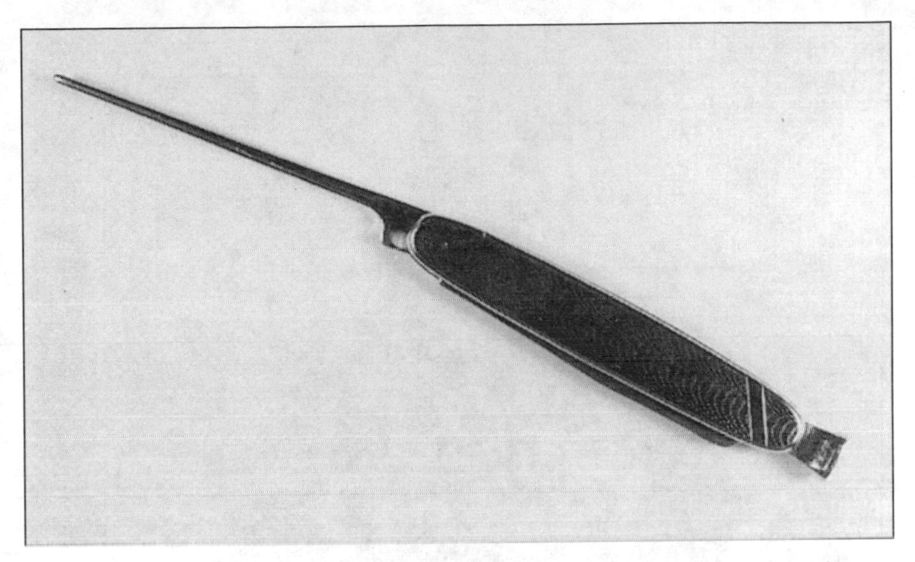

Pipe cleaning knife is a match for the one Dunkle claimed to have lost on the night of Sean Dannehl's murder. *(Photo courtesy San Mateo County, California Superior Court)*

Jon Dunkle, 24. *(Photo courtesy Belmont, California Police Department)*

On December 4, 1984, Dunkle cheerfully posed for police in his sister's home during one of the many interviews they conducted with him. *(Photo courtesy Belmont, California Police Department)*

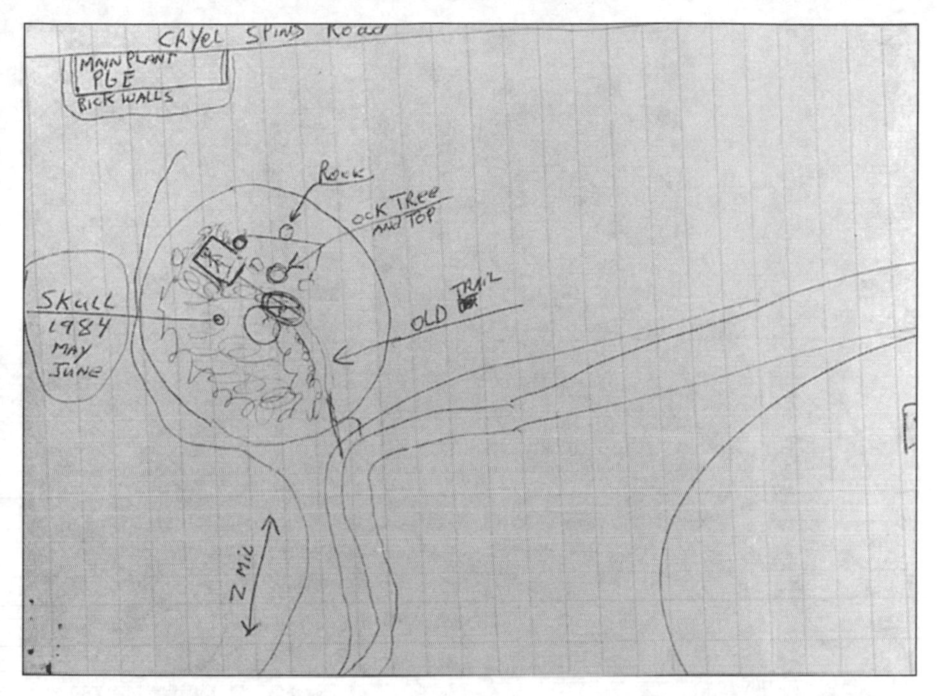

In late September 1986, Dunkle drew maps of murder sites for his cellmate. This one shows the Edgewood Park area where he left John Davies's body. *(Photo courtesy San Mateo County, California Superior Court)*

Edgewood Park area that matches Dunkle's drawing. *(Photo courtesy San Mateo County, California Superior Court)*

Almost five years after he disappeared, the scattered remains of John Davies's body were recovered. *(Photo courtesy San Mateo County, California Superior Court)*

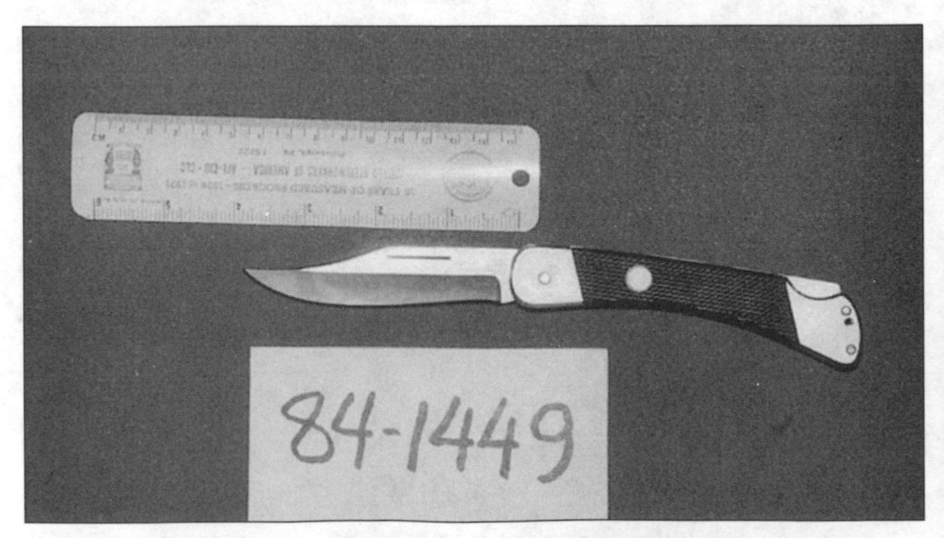

Dunkle led police to the Sacramento flower bed where he'd hidden the Buck knife he'd used to kill Lance Turner. *(Photo courtesy San Mateo County, California Superior Court)*

Former district attorney Bill Russell was a member of Lance Turner's search party and was involved in the entire case against Dunkle. *(Photo courtesy Bill Russell)*

Chief James Goulart and Commander Don Mattei.

San Mateo County District Attorney Steve Wagstaffe.

Psychiatrist Hugh Ridelhuber.

Jimmy sat down with Whaley and cautiously answered questions. He told Whaley Dunkle was a mama's boy, with a mean father who didn't want him to have any friends. Jimmy (wrongly) believed himself to be the person who had taught Dunkle to drink and that the parties he'd taken Dunkle to had introduced him to drugs. He admitted it was he who first introduced Dunkle to his family, a fact he was finding hard to handle now.

Whaley said, "He says you and Mark used to tease John all the time."

"Yeah, well, we went round and round like brothers do, you know. John was the youngest so he got the brunt."

"He says you threw forks into John's feet."

"What?" Jimmy was getting mad. "I never did anything like that. Maybe his brother did that to *him.*"

"He says you once asked him if he'd still like you if you were gay."

Jimmy laughed cynically. "He asked *me.*"

Whaley thought awhile. "You were once his best friend."

"Once."

"How about giving him a call, see if he'll say anything incriminating to you?"

"God, I don't know." Jimmy was the only shy, quiet member of the noisily articulate Davies clan.

"Come on, Jimmy," Mark urged.

Whaley attached a recording device to the phone.

"I don't know what to say," said Jimmy.

Mark poured out suggestions, but Jimmy wasn't Mark. When Dunkle's voice came on, Jimmy greeted him awkwardly.

"Oh, hey, Jim," bubbled Dunkle, "wow, what's up?"

Hearing Dunkle act like everything was normal sent Jimmy into a rage. He blurted out, "If you killed my brother, I'll kill you."

"Oh, God!" cried Mark as Jimmy slammed down the phone and stormed out. "I should've talked to him! I've got the gift of gab!"

A few days later, Mark's friends threw a two-day farewell party for him. Driving home from this brawl the night before he was scheduled to enter the navy, Mark saw flashing lights behind him. "The good news was," he said later, "I just spent a short time in jail. The bad news was I had a DUI. I couldn't go to the navy."

The next day, after fast-talking the recruiters into accepting him for submarine training once he completed his community service sentence, Mark joined AA.

By now Dunkle had confessed the Murphy hit-and-run to Lisa, changed some details of his stories, and seemed to be considering opening up to Ridelhuber. The detectives hoped all this meant he was about to crack. Lisa remained their biggest hope.

Dunkle flirted with confessing throughout March, but then made a move no one had foreseen.

Chapter Twenty-four

A few days after telling Lisa Thomas about his hit-and-runs, Dunkle said, "My dad warned me to be careful around you. He heard there's a female private detective out to get me. Like, how come you never let me come to your place?"

"I told you," she said, thinking fast, "my brother doesn't like me to bring my friends over."

Lisa contacted her ex-husband, who met with Goulart and agreed to pose briefly as her brother so she could bring Dunkle by. "He's pretty hinky about it," Goulart told her. Lisa brought Dunkle over to repair his bike. Polishing his car in the driveway, her ex acted barely civil. "See?" Lisa told Dunkle. "It's better to go to your sister's."

Meanwhile, in Belmont, Goulart was storming. "There's been a leak," he shouted at Bill Russell, "and you damn well better not be the source!"

"Jim, I haven't even told my wife anything." Bill Russell was the only civilian allowed to know about the undercover operation and had met Lisa the day before she started.

He'd been horrified. "This is a disaster," he had said to Ridelhuber. "She's a complete airhead!"

Ridelhuber laughed. "Bill, she's in her role now." Bill's feelings changed instantly. He feared for her in Sacramento as if she were his own daughter. He considered her a heroine. He would never do anything to endanger her.

Eventually, the leak proved to have come from within the department.

"Why did I feel so bad after I talked to you?"

Dr. Ridelhuber was surprised but delighted that Dunkle had phoned. Perhaps the guy really was preparing to unload the secrets that must burden him terribly.

"Well," Ridelhuber said in his gentle Southern voice, "I expect we may have stirred up some troubled feelings you have, Jon."

"Can I talk to you again? Not at the police station. Here in Sacramento."

Thrilled, Ridelhuber agreed to meet him at Carl's Jr. "Then I'll tell you where to go from there," said Dunkle.

Ridelhuber's wife convinced him that it was too dangerous to go on his own to meet Dunkle. When Ridelhuber notified Goulart about it, Goulart was horrified that the psychiatrist would even think of going without backup. "He's been stealing damn meat axes, for God's sake!"

In mid-March, Ridelhuber met Goulart, Farmer, and Belmont's two sharpshooters at a Sacramento shopping mall. They were driving a plain van and carrying rifles with long-distance scopes. As Goulart attached a wire and transmitter to Ridelhuber, he said, "We'll keep you in sight at all times."

Bemused, Ridelhuber nodded. This kind of thing lay outside his experience. Normally he worked for defense attorneys, not for policemen trying to get the goods on a murderer. He considered it his duty as a psychiatrist to build a person up, not to trick him into cracking and confessing, and though not tender toward killers, he used the same deep and compassionate approach with them that he used with less antisocial patients.

When Ridelhuber stepped into Carl's Jr., Dunkle quickly ordered him out to the side parking lot. Soon Dunkle slid into the passenger seat of Ridelhuber's station wagon. "Okay," he said, looking around. "Go straight down to the corner there and hang a left."

Ridelhuber obeyed. Soon he realized that Dunkle was directing him on a zigzag route designed to shake a tail. Glancing in the rearview mirror, Ridelhuber couldn't see the van. "You mean turn left up there at Gerveis?" he asked, hoping the detectives could hear the street name.

Dunkle said, "Yeah," clearly enjoying the power of ordering the psychiatrist around. The whole scenario reminded Ridelhuber of a grade-B spy thriller.

Eventually Dunkle ordered him to pull into an empty lot next to an abandoned warehouse. It was an isolated spot and Ridelhuber still couldn't see the van. He turned in his seat and faced Dunkle. He perceived his patient as a "large, ugly fellow, very strong," and was surprised later to learn that police considered Dunkle stunted and puny. Nearly forty years older than Dunkle, and physically unprepared to fight a man who might use a meat ax as a weapon, Ridelhuber covered his vulnerability with interview techniques and his true fascination with Dunkle's mind.

"I felt bad after I talked with you last time," said Dunkle.

They talked awhile about comparatively nonthreatening subjects, like Dunkle's old buddies and their parties. He spoke of a friend's mother who cursed at him when he threw pebbles against the friend's window. "I was hurt. I didn't think someone's mother would act like that." Ridelhuber knew from police reports, but didn't mention, that Dunkle's father had treated Dunkle's friends that way. He wondered if the episode with the friend's mother happened near the time of one of the murders.

Ridelhuber guided Dunkle to his strange inner life, starting with his story about the time God knocked him down when Dunkle was an airport security worker and was ordered to watch for a serial killer. Dunkle had walked off the job and on the way home met the born-again Christian who led him to join Youth for Christ.

Though Dunkle's point seemed to be that God set it up for him to meet the born-again Christian, Ridelhuber offered another interpretation. "It sounds to me like hearing of a man who killed his wife and children touched a repressed trauma inside of you. The trauma would be very strong for you to be knocked down by it."

Ridelhuber gently but repeatedly brought up the violence in Dunkle's home during childhood, particularly the fights between his father and his brother, and the episodes when his father broke furniture and threatened his mother's life. He reminded Dunkle of reports that as a child Dunkle often ran away from the battles and sought comfort and cookies from concerned neighbors. He spoke to Dunkle about the episode when Dunkle either attacked two boys with a two-by-four or they attacked him, and Dunkle's attack on Monti Hansen with a two-by-four. Ridelhuber sensed that two-by-fours had some deeply significant meaning in Dunkle's mind, linked to a trauma.

Dunkle downplayed his violent history and his feelings about it, yet his next topics seemed symbolically connected with these elements. He told Ridelhuber about leaving or being kicked out of the church camp in Oregon, and though dates weren't mentioned, Ridelhuber remembered from the police record that this had happened about a month before John Davies disappeared. "In the camp, I had a lot of nightmares," confided Dunkle. "Red-eyed demons were fighting with God for my body. They would carry me away."

"You were fighting a monster inside yourself, Jon," interpreted Ridelhuber. "You must have been very afraid that he would take you over." Ridelhuber believed the demons represented Dunkle's repressed rage and his murderous desires.

"But I have a special relationship with God," said Dunkle. "I camped one time with this boy and he wouldn't believe me, so I asked God to give me a sign. The lantern went out. The boy still didn't believe, so I lit the lantern again and it went out again."

Ridelhuber was beginning to wonder if Dunkle had a demonic sub-personality. "You have a relationship with God and also with the Devil," he commented.

Dunkle considered this. "When I came back from Oregon," he said, "one night I went to a party. I went in the bathroom and the room turned 180 degrees around and I came out the other end. The room just turned me right around to the other side."

"Your unconscious was telling you that you could make these 180-degree turns, that the demon could take over." Inwardly, Ridelhuber now had no doubt that Dunkle was very dangerous and would continue to kill. He pushed Dunkle as hard as he dared. "This devil is a part of you that you don't understand and it comes out in violent ways. I believe you have done the things the police say you have done. You need help in order not to do more violence. If you want to talk about the things you have done, I will do all I can to help you understand what's going on inside you and stop doing these things."

Dunkle gazed at him a long time with what Ridelhuber later described as, "these really soft, soft eyes." Ridelhuber waited. Dunkle's longing to confess was palpable.

Suddenly, the moment ended. "Take me home!" Dunkle demanded.

Ridelhuber hesitated. In his office or in a hospital, with staff members nearby, he would continue to push. But out here in an uncontrolled environment—he still had no idea if the police knew where he was—he mustn't take the risk. Getting killed wasn't part of the job description.

Ridelhuber started up the car and followed Dunkle's circuitous directions to Judy Dunkle's house.

Later, he learned that during the whole three-hour interview, the sharpshooters had Dunkle's head in their cross-hairs.

When Dunkle cheerfully told Lisa, "I talked with my police shrink," he gave no clue that he'd come close to cracking. Lisa and he continued their picnics, evenings at the Wits End, and endless board games. Sometimes he fantasized with her about going to Reno to get married. Yet the confidences dried up. Since describing the Steve Murphy hit-and-run he'd confessed to no new crimes.

Toward the end of March, the Department of Justice and Belmont's Chief Sanderson decided the costly undercover operation should shut down. Goulart reluctantly agreed. "We'll give it two more weeks," he said, "then we'll pull her out." It was only later, in retrospect, that they understood that as Dunkle struggled with his intense desire to confess versus his equally intense fear of it, he was edging closer and closer to another kind of blowup. In psychiatric terms, he was getting ready to act out.

On April 2, Dunkle walked into Carl's Jr. and found a new poster of the composite facing the door. "Shit!" Nearly in tears, he ripped it off the wall. He remained agitated through the shift, and afterward, when he and Lisa went to his sister's house, he talked obsessively about the cops.

"Come on, I'll show you something," he said. He took Lisa into his sister's room, where he stored the clippings about the case. "This is John Davies. He's dead and gone."

"He is?"

"And this is Lance." He showed her the same newspaper photo that she looked at every night in her motel room. Lance's face had been helping her to stay motivated.

"Ugly, huh," said Dunkle, laughing. "See this? This is

the oak tree behind the school where those damn girls claim they saw me.''

They went to the Wits End bar, where another poster of the composite awaited. ''It's getting really bad,'' Dunkle complained. ''Bartenders recognize me. They think I'm a killer.''

''The cops are probably trying to make you so mad you'll go out and kill another kid,'' said Lisa.

Dunkle didn't bite. ''I was seeing this police shrink and he says he believes I did it, too. Damn cops went up to Shasta and showed my granddad pictures of the body and the composite. It doesn't look like me at all.''

Lisa noticed that he was really slamming down the beer and not holding it well. ''You know how to break into houses?'' he asked, words slurring. ''You case them so you know when people are gone on vacation. Or else, I was watching this kid play basketball in his yard and then he goes in his house—if we need a key, we can tie the kid up and have him tell us where the key is. He's eight or ten, and they don't remember nothing. Cops don't trust them under eleven, just twelve and older. It was a twelve-year-old who did the damn composite.''

His eyes turned glassy and distant. Suddenly, he had gone far away. She felt like calling, ''Hello-o-o,'' except that he was acting too strange to kid around with.

''We could go into a house,'' Dunkle said, for once not smiling, ''tie the kid up, rip off the house. We could use handcuffs, knock him out. Dead twelve-year-olds can't talk.'' Dunkle looked up at her. ''Hey, Lisa, let me squeeze your boobs.''

''No.''

''I knew you'd say that. I believe in respecting a girl. You're the only girl I really like. I want to go steal you some jewelry.''

Lisa found it weird, the connections he was making. The more he talked about breaking into houses, hurting kids, and stealing jewelry, the hornier he became.

"We could cut the wires to alarm systems before we break in," he went on. "I turned off the alarms when I stole gold from places I used to guard. We have to wear gloves. We'd steal cars, switch license plates." He grabbed her breast.

"Hey, Jon, quit it." He squeezed her breast with one hand while rubbing his other between her legs. He'd never been anywhere near this aggressive. Lisa said, "For God's sake, Jon, go jack off in the bathroom."

He staggered into the men's room, but not long enough, as far as Lisa was concerned. He hadn't cooled down any when he returned. Right away he grabbed her hand and pressed it to his crotch. "Feel my balls."

"Cut it out, Jon."

"I want to fuck you." By now he was so drunk he was nearly lying on the bar. When he stood up, he swayed as if he would fall. He lurched back to the men's room and when he came back, he stared morosely at the composite for a while.

"Let's get the fuck out of here," he said. Lisa followed him outside and they walked together to Goethe Park. Now Dunkle was acting hyper, darting back and forth, spying on a couple in a car, stopping often to pee into bushes. "Come on, Lisa," he called, and entered a side trail into Goethe Park.

From the corner of her eye, Lisa saw Goulart drive past them on the park road and disappear into the darkness. Dunkle led Lisa around the Girl Scout camp trails. "Here's the place I got lost and cut my stomach that time," he said. "See that cabin?"

Lisa noted that he was finding his way without hesitation. He seemed to know the place well. He continued talking rapidly about robbing houses. Lisa held herself on full alert, ready to pull her knife if he made a false move. She knew Goulart wouldn't be able to get to her fast enough if Dunkle attacked her.

A gun blast shattered the quiet.

"God, Jon, what's that?" Lisa cried. Later, she learned it was Goulart's way of flushing her and Dunkle out of the park. "Let's get out of here."

"This way," said Dunkle. He led her to a spot where a residential area backed up to the park. They looked out at a row of dark, fenced backyards. "See that picnic table on that patio? I want to go in and take that bug zapper. Got anything sharp?"

"Sharp?"

"A pin or something so I can open the lock." He walked the length of the fence, stopping to relieve himself yet again.

Lisa ducked her head and muttered into the mike, "We're on El Coralito Drive."

"This gate's open!" Dunkle said in a stage whisper. "I'm going in. You be my lookout."

He crept across the yard, explored around the side of the house and returned to the back, where he tested a sliding glass door. It opened.

Dunkle disappeared into the house.

"It's a 459!" Lisa cried into the mike.

A moment later, Goulart burst out of the park and ran over to her. "Get away from here. Go to the next block, knock on someone's door, and call the sheriff. Don't come back." Lisa rushed off. After calling the sheriff, she ran down dark, empty streets toward the motel.

Goulart stood by the fence. Children's play equipment in the yard told him Dunkle was skulking around a house where children lay sleeping. Goulart was torn. The most direct action would be to go in after him, but the panicked homeowner might shoot them both. The more sensible plan was to grab Dunkle on the way out.

But as the minutes passed, Goulart's anxiety soared. The longer Dunkle stayed inside, the greater the chance that he would hurt someone.

Goulart walked across the yard. As he approached the sliding door, Dunkle came out.

Goulart shined his flashlight directly into Dunkle's face. "You're under arrest, Jon. Lie down."

Dunkle shouted and argued. Goulart grabbed him and forced him to the ground.

"Help!" Dunkle screamed. "I'm being attacked!' "

Goulart wrestled the struggling captive to the doorway, threw him halfway across it, and lay on top of him to hold him down. Now they were both shouting. "I'm being framed!" Dunkle cried shrilly, while Goulart's deeper voice bellowed, "Help! Call the Sheriff!"

Upstairs, Richard Renne sat up in bed, confused. He'd spent the evening socializing with his wife's grandparents, who were now asleep in their motor home in his driveway. Around eleven, he and his wife went to bed. Their habit was to sleep with their bedroom door open so they could hear their nine-year-old son and seven-year-old daughter. But tonight he had shut the door long enough to make love with his wife. Less than three minutes after he opened the door again, he heard shouting.

At first he figured it must be coming from next door. When he realized something was happening at the back of his own house, he told his wife to stay put and walked slowly down the hall. Deliberately he did not put on any lights. He wanted to remain silent and hidden till he checked things out. At each child's room, he paused long enough to hear regular breathing coming from the bed.

As he stepped past his daughter's room, his feet bumped into something bulky and soft. It was her thick quilt. That was very odd. She never dragged her covers around the house.

He felt his way down the stairs. Two men lay struggling in the doorway. The larger one shouted, "I'm an off-duty officer! Call the sheriff!"

Renne switched on a lamp and the big man threw a badge across the floor to him. Renne peered at it suspiciously. Where the hell was Belmont?

While the smaller guy screamed obscenely about the

violation of his rights, Renne called the sheriff. Meanwhile the officer forced handcuffs onto his prisoner and persuaded him to sit on the couch.

When the sheriff's men arrived, Renne listened in bewilderment while Sergeant Goulart explained to him that during a surveillance of Dunkle, he saw him enter Renne's home and remain inside several minutes.

One of the Sacramento officers started telling Goulart off. "What the hell do you think you're doing, arresting suspects in my jurisdiction? No one told me about any damn surveillance."

"Look, it's been cleared with the Department of Justice. Biondi knows all about it. Patrol in your own damn division knows."

While they wrangled about jurisdiction, Renne figured out that the weird-acting prisoner had prowled around the house while he and his wife were making love.

A sheriff turned to Mr. Renne. "Is anything missing or disturbed?"

"My daughter's quilt is lying in the hall upstairs," he said. "God, he must have gone into her room . . . ." As he spoke, he noticed his wife's large sewing shears lying on the living room rug, as if Dunkle had dropped them as he ran for the door. Renne jumped up. Though he'd checked on his children on his way down the hall, he felt suddenly desperate to reassure himself that they were all right, because it sure looked as if Dunkle was clutching those scissors when he pulled the covers off Renne's little girl.

Chapter Twenty-five

Driving home to Belmont the day after the break-in, Lisa couldn't stop crying. For two solid months, she'd lived at full throttle, portraying dumb Lisa Davis on the outside while maintaining red alert as Lisa Thomas on the inside. With the daily debriefings, report writing and tape transcribing, she'd never relaxed except the few times her boyfriend Terry had visited late at night. Dunkle, with his frightening inner self, and his irritating but sometimes likable boyishness, had lived in her consciousness twenty-four hours a day. The abrupt halt of her undercover role left her with a terrible emptiness.

A few days later, Lisa was instructed to make a final contact with Dunkle. He'd been arraigned and was now out on bail pending a preliminary hearing scheduled in May, several weeks away. Lisa reached him by phone at his sister's home. "Hi, Jon."

"Oh, hi," he answered, sounding as gee-whiz friendly as ever.

"I got the hell out of there," she said.

"Yeah, okay."

"I'm going to San Jose. The cops mustn't know about me. I can't stand to go to jail."

"Hey, I lost my job," he said. "Assholes fired me."

"Damn," she said. "I guess I lost my job, too." Ironic words. She knew he had no idea what job she had really lost.

After he chatted a while about biking and job hunting, Lisa repeated, "Remember, keep quiet. Don't you fink on me."

"Hell, no." He showed no emotion over losing her or facing charges.

Dropping the receiver into the cradle ended Lisa's role as Dunkle's girlfriend.

At work she went through the motions, feeling dead inside. She didn't feel good about the commendation she received for the job she'd done with Dunkle. Her life began to fall apart and an ex-con she helped get into drug treatment broke into her home and stole her gun. The department nearly fired her over this.

Lisa couldn't figure out what was wrong with her. Neither she nor the Belmont PD had yet been educated about post-traumatic stress disorder.

Belmont citizens read the expurgated version of Dunkle's break-in and arrest with puzzled excitement. Newspapers presented Lisa as Dunkle's unnamed female companion whose whereabouts were unknown and Goulart as an off-duty Belmont officer tailing Dunkle voluntarily at the time of the break-in.

"How can our cops tail someone in Sacramento?" Belmont folks asked each other. "Is that legal?" The general feeling was that the local police were bending over backward to solve Lance Turner's murder.

But inside the BPD, everyone felt let down. No small city department could have done more than theirs to catch a killer. The hundreds of overtime hours plus the expense of the undercover operation cost the department the modernized computer system scheduled for installation that year. And what did they have to show for all this effort and sacrifice? A still uncorroborated hit-and-run confession, a breaking and entering arrest, and a stalled investigation. Mattei, Farmer, Goulart, and Whaley didn't let go of the case, but from now on their occasional trips to Sacramento to bird-dog Dunkle had to be on their own time.

The detectives kept in touch with the twenty-two officers who lived in Dunkle's Sacramento neighborhood, who continued to spot-check him, monitored by Sacramento homicide detective Bob Bell. Sheriff Ray Dick reported to Whaley that he was developing a rapport with Dunkle's father, who now "indicated that he believed Jon might be involved in Lance Turner's death." Mr. Dunkle had told Dick about a large stain upstairs in his home in Belmont. Unable to eradicate the stain before selling the house, Mr. Dunkle finally carpeted over it.

In May 1985, a month after Dunkle's arrest and release in Sacramento, Mark Davies dropped by the BPD to visit Whaley. Mark and Whaley chatted about Dunkle and Mark half-jokingly suggested, "Hey, I could get him drunk and see if he'd loosen up. I could do my community service sentence as your undercover agent!"

"That's an intriguing idea," said Whaley. "You and he used to be friends, and you certainly have the gift of gab." He began thinking out loud about strategy, hidden mikes, and backup.

When Mark mentioned this exciting plan to his mother, she grabbed the phone and called Whaley.

"How could you even *consider* having Mark work undercover? I've lost one son already! You want Mark to meet him in *bars*? Mark is a *minor*. He's on probation for a DUI! He's in *AA!*"

In July, Mark entered the navy. He had been clean and sober for almost four months, but as soon as he reached submarine training school, still messed up because of his brother's unresolved disappearance, he started "drinking like a fucking fish."

After his release on bail for the burglary charge, Dunkle found himself cut off from his previous activities. Fired from Carl's Jr., he stopped hanging out at the Wits End Bar, too. The officers sporadically keeping watch on him noted that he made some half-hearted job applications and hung out in libraries. He spent many hours bicycling at high speed along highways and on the thirty-five-mile bike trail along the American River Parkway.

Fearing that Dunkle would get supervised probation instead of jail time, Goulart, Dr. Ridelhuber, Sacramento Homicide Chief Ray Biondi, and Detective Bell fed information to the DA. Ridelhuber presented his impressions that Dunkle was a serial killer and urged that he be evaluated by a forensic psychiatrist. Goulart let the DA know that Dunkle was the prime suspect in the Davies disappearance and the Turner murder and had admitted a hit-and-run to Lisa Thomas which could be called attempted vehicular homicide.

The DA postponed the hearing till July 25 in order to gather more data about Dunkle's history of violence. The good news was that Dunkle would be more likely to serve time; the bad news was that he'd be loose for two more months before he had even a preliminary hearing.

On July 2, with three weeks to go until the hearing, Dunkle bicycled with a young man he'd met on an American River trail. Having left San Mateo County because of trouble with police, Dwayne hadn't made many friends yet in Sacramento and went that day with Dunkle out of hardship. He later confided to police that he considered Dunkle "strange" from the moment they met. When Dwayne and Dunkle had compared notes on legal problems in San Mateo County, Dunkle puffed up and bragged, "I'm a suspect in the Lance Turner murder."

Dwayne felt uneasy. "Did you do it?" He'd read a lot about the case.

Dunkle laughed. "No way!" But when he finished the beer he was drinking during this conversation, he crushed the can and explained importantly, "I always do this now because the cops found my fingerprints on a can where Lance was murdered."

After that, Dwayne refused several invitations to go biking with Dunkle, but on July 2 he was too bored to say no. They rode several miles of the trail along the American River. In the 103-degree heat, Dunkle left Dwayne in the dust. Dwayne huffed along, later commenting that for a little guy, Dunkle sure had powerful legs and lungs.

Around five-thirty, they stopped at a picnic table near Sunrise Bridge, where Sunrise Bouelvard crossed the river and linked the Fair Oaks side on the north bank with the Rancho Cordova side on the south. This section of the American River Parkway was Sunrise Park, where by day kids played in inner tubes and paddle boats. Though heavily populated neighborhoods lay within a block on both sides of the river, people who entered the band of trees and trails felt they were in the park of a small country town. Bikes whizzed past on the trail, children shouted at the water's edge, elderly couples walked dogs over the old Fair Oaks footbridge east of Sunrise Boulevard. or over the footbridge off Pennsylvania Ave to the west. For most people, this seemed a safe oasis of peace and happiness.

Dunkle and Dwayne plopped down at a lone picnic table overlooking the river and opened their first beers. Cars roared over the nearby bridge. Soon two of Dwayne's other new acquaintances joined them and the four passed around a joint to go with their beer. Before long Dunkle was giggling uncontrollably. The others exchanged glances. What a lightweight!

Dunkle crushed his beer can and explained to his new audience that he had to hide his prints because he was suspected of killing a twelve-year-old boy in Belmont.

* * *

While Dunkle and his companions were drinking their beers, twelve-year-old Sean Dannehl was getting his mother's permission to bicycle across the Old Fair Oaks footbridge to the Rancho Cordova side. His route would take him two miles down the bike trail along the parkway to Rossmoor Road, and up Rossmoor's residential blocks to Columa Street, where some old friends lived. Sean's mother, Ellen, said he could go as long as he returned before nightfall. Later, she reported she had told Sean, "If it gets dark, have Mike drive you back in the truck." Ellen knew Sean was afraid of the dark and believed he wouldn't ride the trails at night.

Wearing his purple-and-white soccer shirt, black soccer shorts, and white athletic shoes, Sean sped down Bridge Street, rattled loudly across the widely spaced wood slats on Old Fair Oaks Bridge, and careened down to the level trail. Fair Oaks was a new place for him. His mother and her boyfriend, Kip Dammen, had moved there from Rancho Cordova after Sean had left two years earlier to live with his father in Twain Harte, a small town in the foothills of the Sierra Nevada Mountains. His father, Guy Dannehl, had wanted Sean to join him, his wife, Debbie, and their three-month-old baby on their vacation in Tahoe, but Sean pleaded to visit his mother. He'd rarely seen her in two years.

All Sean's soccer, baseball, basketball, swimming, and biking kept him strong and coordinated, and he maneuvered the bike well on the trails despite the cast on his left arm. He'd broken it falling from a rope swing at church camp. When his baseball coach heard about it, he shouted, "Let it be his right arm!" because Sean, a leftie, was the top pitcher for the upcoming Twain Harte Little League All Stars games.

Hot and sweaty, Sean made it to his old friends' home on Coloma and said ceremonious farewells to his surrogate big brother, who was leaving in the morning to join the military. At seven-thirty, Sean Dannehl jumped back onto his blue ten-speed and headed for the Sunrise Park bike trail.

By now two of Dunkle's companions had returned from a trip into a nearby neighborhood to score some speed. Giggling, Dunkle said he felt dizzy. They were getting tired of his disjointed stories about police harassment and composite drawings that didn't look like him.

He pulled an odd knife from his pocket. When he unfolded it, the blade resembled a short ice pick. "It's a pipe-cleaning tool," he explained, scraping his nails with the point. "It was my grandfather's."

The other three decided to dump him. They took off while Dunkle was in the men's room. Alone at the picnic table, Dunkle played with the knife, poking its point into the soft, weathered wood.

Around eight-fifteen, he heard a bike whirring down the nearby trail. He looked up. A good-looking boy wearing soccer clothes was riding toward him.

Part Four

Sean Dannehl
July 1985–
September 1986

Chapter Twenty-six

Seven days later, Sergeant Goulart lay beneath his van in his Belmont driveway, contentedly wrenching and banging away at long-needed repairs. This was his first vacation in two years and he was easing into using his mind and body on tasks that had nothing to do with detective work.

A pair of polished shoes and neatly uniformed legs stepped into his range of vision. Goulart scooted out from under the van. "What's happened?" he asked the patrol officer, a rookie who looked as if he still belonged in high school.

"They want me to drive you to headquarters, sir."

Detective Farmer met him at the station. "They found that missing boy in Sacramento," he said. "Dunkle's done it again."

When Sean Dannehl hadn't made it home to Fair Oaks by eight-thirty p.m. on July 2, and his mother, Ellen, learned he'd left his friends in Rancho Cordova an hour before, she'd enlisted a neighbor's help. The woman walked down toward the Fair Oaks side of Sunrise Bridge and noticed a crowd near a brush fire. "He's just watching the fire!" she thought, but she couldn't find him.

At ten, Ellen left her boyfriend Kip Dammen by the phone and walked the bike trail herself. Dense night had replaced dusk, and she worried about how Sean feared the dark.

Near midnight, Kip Dammen hit the trail with a bike and flashlight while Ellen called the police. At two a.m., an officer came by and told her, "Nothing can be done officially till the boy's been gone twenty-four hours."

Ellen tearfully repeated to the skeptical sheriff that Sean had no reason to run away. "Kip and I had a fight this morning," she admitted, "but it didn't involve Sean. He's a reliable boy. He wouldn't just take off."

Checking their records, the police quickly discovered that the boy could have had reason to do just that. The previous fall, NARCs had confiscated masses of drug paraphernalia from the apartment and arrested Ellen and Kip.

Ellen, Kip and friends spent July 3 and 4, a record heat wave, showing Sean's picture to passersby at the Sunrise Park trail and the nearby mall. Ellen had contacted the Kevin Collins Foundation, which helped put together the flyers and obtained quick financial help from local businesses.

No one recalled seeing Sean, and Sean's friends reported having no idea where he was, though two told police they thought he'd run away and that they might have seen him.

The media was slow to pick up on the disappearance because at the time newspapers were daily devoting full pages to "grisly discoveries" in the Calaveras County cabin where Charles Ng and Leonard Lake had allegedly tortured and killed many victims. Sean didn't make the TV news till the evening of July 4.

A friend of Guy Dannehl, Sean's father, saw the broadcast and called Dannehl's pastor. Knowing the Dannehls were vacationing with relatives in Tahoe, the pastor asked the Sacramento sheriff's office for Ellen's phone number. From her, he learned how to reach Dannehl.

At first Guy Dannehl wasn't worried. His son was independent and resourceful; he had to be, to survive what Dannehl considered Ellen's "complete disarray" of a lifestyle. Before Ellen had moved to the Sacramento area, Sean had traveled alone at ages nine and ten by bus from Ellen's place in Wyoming to visit his dad in California. People instantly liked Sean, who was both outgoing and sensitive. He was bright, too, an honor student. He could handle himself.

That's what Dannehl thought until the next morning, when he and his wife, Debbie, saw the Sunrise Park and Trail. Then he knew something terrible had happened.

He and Debbie met with two Youth Services officers. Debbie told them that Ellen ran a looser household than Sean's church-going home with its rules and expectations in Twain Harte. "Sean can probably wrap Ellen around his little finger," she told police; she herself would not have allowed him to ride at dusk and had trained Sean never to go places alone. Asked if she thought Sean would run away, she answered that perhaps he had because of "the environment" in Ellen's home.

Dannehl disagreed. "Sean's pretty easygoing," he said. "He's well-behaved. He's never run away. He isn't the rebellious type." To him it was obvious that if Sean wanted out, all he had to do was phone the family in Tahoe and they'd come get him. "But the officers just wouldn't hear me," Dannehl said later.

He spent the next two days in Sunrise Park, passing out flyers, asking questions and searching.

The same day the Dannehls arrived, July 5, the missing child report filtered its way up to Homicide Chief Ray Biondi, who along with Detective Sergeant Robert Bell, had worked with Goulart and Farmer on Lisa Thomas's undercover operation. "Go check on Dunkle," Biondi ordered Bell. "There's a Fair Oaks boy missing."

Bell instantly saw the significance of the geography: three easy miles of bike trail connected Sunrise Park with Goethe Park, where Dunkle took Thomas the night of the break-in, and the Rancho Cordova neighborhood where Dunkle lived with his sister lay directly across the river from the missing boy's apartment in Fair Oaks.

Before interviewing Dunkle, Bell talked with Whaley in Belmont, so it didn't surprise him when Dunkle greeted him with no apparent anxiety. Before the session ended, Bell understood Whaley's remark about Dunkle's "Cheshire cat grin."

Bell asked about July 2 and Dunkle cheerfully replied that every Monday through Thursday he rose at five-thirty a.m. and caught a bus—he specified number and route—to Sacramento City College, where he was taking a computer class. Bell listened carefully as Dunkle described his afternoon bike hike and evening beers in Sunrise Park with Dwayne.

"I didn't get home till after ten that night," Dunkle said. "I got a flat tire by Cordova school. I walked my bike the rest of the way." He smiled engagingly.

Bell nodded. Dunkle had placed himself in the same area as Sean, denied seeing the boy and provided no verifiable alibi for the crucial hours between eight and ten.

As Dunkle wore only shorts, Bell could see that apart from an abrasion on his ankle, he had no recent bruises or scrapes. If Dunkle had killed Sean, his body carried no record of a struggle.

"I may need to speak to you again," Bell said as he left.

"Sure. Any time."

It was the beginning of a long and complex relationship.

Bell went directly from Dunkle's to Dwayne's place. Dwayne confirmed that they'd been together on July 2 until around 7:45. He described how Dunkle always talked about being a murder suspect and made a big deal over crushing beer cans to destroy fingerprints. He added that Dunkle had recently invited him to go camping but, "I thought he could be gay and I didn't want to be alone with him. . . . He made me kind of nervous."

When Bell questioned Judy Dunkle, she verified that her brother arrived home around ten at night on July 2. She'd expected him at four and had been so worried that she phoned their parents.

Bell advised Biondi that despite reports that Sean had been sighted, sheriffs must conduct a serious search.

On July 6, three and a half days into Sean's disappearance, Lieutenant Biondi set up a command post edging Sunrise Park. Detectives, officers on horseback and motorcycles, and fifty work-furlough inmates searched from Goethe Park to Sunrise Bridge, while a helicopter crisscrossed above. They called it off in the early afternoon when the temperature reached 106. In four hours, the searchers had found nothing, but the search finally earned Sean a headline in the July 7 *Sacramento Bee*.

The Sacramento County Sheriffs' Department spokesman, Sergeant Roger Dickson, withheld the information that a suspected child killer and Sean had probably been on the trail at the same time. Stating that the department considered Sean a probable runaway, he reported that two boys had told investigators that Sean spoke of running away and had allegedly been sighted at a fireworks display.

Dickson explained the department policy that required officers to pull out all the stops for missing kids under the age of twelve. He said that "individuals," even runaways, in this age group were less capable of caring for themselves out in the world than teenagers were. He added that about 170 juveniles a month, most over age twelve, were reported missing in Sacramento County and that their average disappearance time was three days. Kids often camped in the park, snuck home for food and clothes, and went back out again, he said.

Ellen told reporters that she'd ridden bikes with Sean

till she was satisfied that despite his cast he could maneuver well. He'd left for his friends' home in broad daylight and, because he feared the dark, she'd trusted him to return home before nightfall. No one considered the park dangerous, she said.

She insisted that his disappearance was very unlike him and described him as a good, uncomplaining boy with good manners and a kind nature. She said she would make a "personal appeal" to the boys who reported he'd run away, asking that if they knew where Sean was, to tell him not to be afraid to come home. No one would be angry. They just wanted him home and safe.

Guy Dannehl continued his own search when the inmates, horseback officers, and motorcycle cops quit. He tried to put himself in the mind of a boy. "What would he be doing here? Why would he stop, where would he go?" There were lots of woodsy hiding places along the river, but Guy didn't believe for a second that he'd find his son in a tree house or cave.

"It was a real bear of a day," Dannehl testified later, "just terribly hot. . . . So I am out there, looking in the bushes, trying to, you know, think, 'Well, if somebody hurt him or something, they might have thrown him in the bushes here. Because I didn't think he was a runaway or anything.' " At a parking lot near Sunrise Bridge, he bent over a drinking fountain. As he splashed his face and felt the unrelenting sun on his back, Dannehl knew, "If he's been here since he turned up missing, there's no doubt he's dead."

Traffic was heavy on nearby Sunrise Bridge. Dannehl walked down toward it, looking intently at brush and trees. Close to where the trail went beneath the bridge, he stopped. Well back from the path, the low branches of a huge granddaddy oak tree spread like an umbrella over dense undergrowth. Dannehl figured no one could maneuver through such heavy brush. He turned back.

The next day, Dannehl returned to Tahoe. The park

was too big for him to search by himself, and he felt certain he was too late to save his son.

But he had come within sixty feet of finding him.

After the sheriffs' search, Sean's case was kicked from Homicide back into the Sheriffs' Department Youth Services Division. The sheriffs' amateur radio program, SHARP, recruited volunteers to elicit information about sightings. They showed three-by-four photos of Sean to people in parks, convenience stores, apartment complexes, and other places, all day July 7. Nothing came of it.

Around 7:45 the next evening, July 8, when Sean had been missing exactly six days, two young men—Kirk Bowden and Jeffrey Whisman—were riding bikes on the Sunrise Trail. Nearing Sunrise Bridge, Kirk noticed a blue bicycle about forty-five feet off the trail, half buried in the brush. He crashed his way through the scrub till he could see that it was a boy's ten-speed. About twenty feet farther back, through low hanging oak branches, Kirk thought he saw the outline of a person. He stepped closer. Who could sleep in that prickly brush?

He saw two bare legs, knees up. At the same moment, he caught a foul odor.

Kirk hit the path running.

At eight-fifteen, local sheriff Worley and fellow officers met Bowden and Whisman in the Lower Sunrise parking lot, noting that both were shaking and distraught.

"There's a dead body over there!" Bowden pointed down the trail where twenty or more people crowded around.

Worley hurried to the area. "This is a crime scene," he barked. "Move back to the pavement."

He squinted. Around forty feet off the trail, low boughs hung over the brush like an awning. Worley dropped to his knees and crawled slowly through the undergrowth. Directly beneath the limbs he found a small clearing.

Describing the scene later, he wrote, "I was able to see what appeared to be a Negro male. The subject was lying on his back with his legs spread outward and his feet close to his buttocks, so that his knees were in the air. It appeared that the subject was possibly asleep. I called out and got no response. I approached to within an arm's length of the subject and tapped on the left knee. . . . The outer skin felt soft and flexible and shifted. . . . I realized that he was not asleep, but dead."

Noting that the naked body had a cast on the left arm, he thought of Sean Dannehl, but the skin color confused him. When the evidence techs and homicide investigators arrived, they asked the coroner's office to send someone to examine the body *in situ* and tell them if this boy could be Caucasian. While they waited, the officers roped off the crime scene and the surrounding area to create inner and outer perimeters. Officers were posted to guard exits and document all comings and goings.

After the crime scene and body had been photographed and videotaped as found, investigators and evidence techs hacked their way into the site from another angle, taking pictures as they went and searching for footprints and other evidence beneath the dense brush. Near the nude body, they saw clothes stacked together. Beside the left hand lay a huge two-by-four with a protruding nail.

The coroner, Dr. Robert Anthony, knelt about forty-five minutes in the brush to examine the victim. He noted that the body was in an advanced state of decomposition and was infested with tiny maggots. Disgusting to the lay person, the maggots would be useful to investigators. Forensic pathologists would be able analyze the stages of maturity and number of generations, which would help determine the time of death and whether the boy had been killed where he lay or brought there later.

Dr. Anthony told investigators that the intense heat had dried and darkened the skin. The facial structure was probably Caucasian. "This could well be the boy everyone's been looking for," he said.

Officers documented that they went to speak with "Sean's parents." They meant Ellen and Kip.

In Tahoe, Guy and Debbie Dannehl had just entered the family's vacation apartment when Debbie's aunt, uncle, and cousin, who lived nearby, beat on the door. "Turn on Channel 3!" they shouted. "They found Sean!"

The scene appeared: A live broadcast showed uniformed sheriffs working around a spotlit, huge oak tree near Sunrise Bridge. Dannehl recognized the umbrellalike branches instantly.

Behind him, Debbie felt overwhelmed with disbelief. Holding their three-month-old daughter, she began a slow fall. Her aunt rushed over and grabbed the baby.

Earlier that day, regretting that she'd allowed Sean to visit his mother against Dannehl's express wishes, Debbie had said that when Sean returned, they should go after sole custody and adopt him. Now Sean was dead and though Debbie believed he was all right, that he was in Heaven, as time passed, she couldn't stop feeling his death was somehow her fault.

Chapter Twenty-seven

As Goulart would repeat to his furious officers and later to reporters, he did not feel Sean Dannehl's murder reflected badly on the BPD. "We did so extremely much to get Dunkle," he said later, "so much more than most departments would ever do. Each of us has been involved since day one. We're more personally involved than if each of us handled one piece of it and then moved on."

Yet they hadn't gotten Dunkle, and none doubted that this new Sacramento murder was his work. It was a devastating blow. The best defense against their frustration and rage was to be task oriented. "There's gotta be physical evidence this time," Goulart told his detectives. "It doesn't matter if Sacramento gets the credit. We'll help them nail him." He sent Farmer to assist the detectives there.

Goulart's practical attitude did little for Lisa Thomas. When a phone call woke her with the news about Dannehl, she buried her face in her pillow. On the surface, she knew that she and the department had done all they could to get Dunkle. Deep down, though, she couldn't escape the agonizing belief that Sean had died because she failed.

* * *

While Farmer was en route, two Sacramento County detectives witnessed the autopsy. Though the body remained officially unidentified pending dental comparisons, everyone knew this five-foot-two-inch body with the cast on its arm and the soccer clothes at his side was Sean Dannehl.

Dr. Robert Anthony conducted the autopsy, a painstaking three-and-a-half-hour task because of the decomposition. He documented that the body's partially mummified condition indicated that the victim had been dead and exposed to the elements for several days. Decomposition prevented him from determining if there was injury to the neck or if sexual molestation had occurred. He made other significant findings, though.

In the right frontal section of the skull was a small circular puncture wound. He couldn't determine its depth, but saw that it entered the frontal lobe. "That's the part that houses the personality," he told the detectives.

Detective Machen peered at the wound. "The two-by-four with the nail?"

"That would be consistent with this injury."

He also found puncture wounds in the left chest and between the fourth and fifth ribs. Their shape and depth suggested an instrument like an ice pick.

"The blow to the head probably knocked him unconscious," Dr. Anthony said, "but here's the cause of death." He pointed out several deep wounds in the boy's heart.

Location and time of death remained unanswered questions. As Homicide Chief Biondi told reporters, Sean might have been killed elsewhere and later dumped at the Sunrise Park site, or he could have been killed there. Biondi admitted that possibly the searchers just hadn't found him.

BPD Detective Farmer's first task in Sacramento was to

collect data to help pathologists calculate answers to these questions. The "data" were larvae from where Sean's body had been, plus ground and air temperatures from various hours and heights.

Farmer found that the midday temperature two feet off the ground was 122 degrees. He could see how the body became "mummified," if it lay there in that heat for six days. Most likely, Sean had died where he was found.

Finished with scut work, Farmer brainstormed with Sacramento investigators about similarities between Sean's murder and Lance Turner's. Both boys were light haired, unusually good-looking twelve-year-olds, wore soccer clothes at the time of the attack, and were found in brush off trails in wooded suburban parks near water. Both were left on their backs and had multiple stab wounds. Witnesses placed Dunkle near both scenes, drinking and smoking pot, just before the victims disappeared. Both murders occurred on a Tuesday that was the second day of the month.

The few differences carried chilling significance. Lance was found fully clothed. Sean was naked, and the investigators believed that if it weren't for the decomposition, they'd have found evidence of sexual attack.

Lance's head injury had been superficial, while Sean's penetrated the brain and probably knocked him unconscious. Lance put up a big fight and had many more stab wounds than Sean. Sean appeared not to have fought at all, had fewer wounds than Lance, but more injuries to the heart.

Thus, as Farmer documented, "if these two cases have a common assailant, this assailant has become more proficient in incapacitating and killing the victims." Also, his sexual motivation was becoming more overt.

While the investigators brainstormed, the California Senate Judiciary Committee was conducting a hearing in Sacramento about proposed missing children's bills. Since the National Missing Children's Act had become law fourteen months earlier, grass roots organizations in many states pushed for parallel state laws. In California, groups like the Kevin Collins Foundation, the Vanished Children's Alliance, and others were supported by Assemblyman Gray Davis–D, who conducted that day's hearing. After parents of a long-missing child told of police neglect and lack of help in publicizing and searching for their child, the star speaker stepped up.

John Walsh, father of the famous Adam, leader of the national movement and now a board member of the National Center for Missing and Exploited Children, gripped the edges of the podium, surrounded by posters and grocery bags featuring missing children's pictures, and told the audience that because California hadn't set up a statewide clearinghouse of missing children or legislated strong penalties for child molesters, it was inviting child predators to come.

Then he mentioned Sean Dannehl, whose body had just been found. He said that law enforcement didn't take suspected runaways as seriously as known victims of abductions, yet Sean's case demonstrated that suspected runaways were also at very high risk.

Though Dunkle was the prime suspect in Sean Dannehl's murder, the investigators, of course, had to look at others. The background study of Sean's family and friends forced them to focus on his stepfather, Kip Dammen. There were rumors that Dammen had knocked Ellen down, that she was often seen with black eyes, that he jammed a shotgun into her face and threatened to "blow her head off." People described constant comings and goings from the apartment, which officers confirmed from their own records.

It was also rumored that Dammen had broken Sean's

arm, but investigators knew that it happened when he fell from a rope swing in church camp.

Dammen denied ever beating Sean. "I just yelled at him and told him to shut up." He described Sean as a "Mama's boy, very quiet and mellow."

Dammen had apparently been home with Ellen during the period that Sean was riding through the park. Investigators doubted he was their man.

After Sean was found, police reinterviewed Ellen. She identified the blue ten-speed and the soccer clothes, but when questioned about her activities before and after the murder, she closed her eyes. "I'm having such a bad time right now that I can't remember."

Guy and Debbie Dannehl met with Bell and Biondi. Dannehl identified Sean's clothing, but did not have to view the body. He arranged with a family friend, a mortician, to do that. When Sean's body was released, the Victims' Assistance Program funded the funeral in Twain Harte. Sean was buried in a beautiful, wooded cemetery.

Since there was no composite drawing of a suspect, investigators weren't deluged with the multitude of leads to clear as Belmont had been, but they did have some. People slept in Sunrise Park, as a few did in the Water Dog Lake area and they had to be checked. Officers also checked the alibis of locally known molesters and collected the park rangers' card file of problem people to check and clear.

Meantime, the public was alarmed about danger in the parks, and news articles spoke of the frequent muggings and rapes there. As had happened in Belmont when Lance Turner died in the Water Dog Lake preserve, Sacramento County citizens demanded patrols and protection along the American River Parkway.

Meantime, Sergeant Bell was pursuing Dunkle, hard.

Chapter Twenty-eight

"We have a twelve-year-old boy murdered," Bell told Dunkle the morning after Sean Dannehl was found. "The circumstances are very similar to the Lance Turner case. I have to either eliminate you or establish you as a suspect. I don't plan to get into the same situation as Belmont. I'm clearing this up fast."

"Okay." Dunkle was his usual chipper self when Bell and his partner drove him to headquarters and took him straight to an interrogation room. Homicide Chief Ray Biondi joined in the questioning.

Though Dunkle wasn't under arrest, Bell took the precaution of reading him his rights. "You have the right to remain silent. . . ."

Dunkle parroted, " 'Anything you say can and will be held against you in a court of law,' " and signed the waiver form.

"I've been talking to Dwayne," said Bell. "He says you told him you were a murder suspect."

Dunkle shrugged. "We both have legal problems in San Mateo."

Bell took him through the timelines of July 2—the bike ride with Dwayne, the early evening partying with the other guys at the picnic table by Sunrise Trail. Dunkle obligingly drew a picture of the table's location and where everyone sat.

"How much did you drink?"

"Four beers." Dwayne had told Bell it was between four and six.

"You guys had a few joints, too," said Bell. Dwayne had opened up to Bell when told of Sean's murder.

"I took three hits."

"What time did the guys leave?"

Dunkle wasn't clear. "Dwayne left awhile and came back, and then they all left." Finally Dunkle said, as if giving them a gift, "Okay, I'll level with you."

"Uh-huh."

"Dwayne snorted two lines of cocaine and then he got some money from the guys so he could go buy more."

"Mm-hm," said Bell. Dwayne had said the drug was "crank" (speed), not cocaine.

"So he went away," said Dunkle, "and when he came back, they all left around eight-fifteen. I left at eight-thirty, in the other direction." He repeated his story that he was late getting home because his tire had a flat by Cordova School.

"What was wrong with the tire?"

"It had a slow leak."

Bell circled closer. "I hear you had a knife that night."

Dunkle didn't seem upset. "I usually carry Coca-Cola knives," he said helpfully, "but that night I had a pipe-cleaning tool. It was my grandfather's." He agreed that it had a blade similar to an ice pick's, and another blade with a flat round end meant for tamping down tobacco in a pipe bowl.

"Let's see," said Bell.

"I don't know where it is. I think I lost it." Pressed, Dunkle said maybe the knife was in the bag on his bike, or maybe it fell from his pocket when he tried to fix his tire by the school.

Lieutenant Biondi joined the questioning. "All this time we've been talking, you haven't asked us anything about the crime."

"I just know what was in the papers," said Dunkle. "They said the kid ran away from home because of a fight with his mother. Some teenagers saw him in Goethe Park."

Biondi said, "Usually innocent people ask about time and place so they can clear themselves."

"I don't want to know about this crime. You know why. Those guys had pictures of Lance everywhere."

Bell glanced at Biondi. Sounded like the FBI technique of using the pictures and items from Lance Turner's crime scene in the BPD's big interrogation had made an impact. At the same time, was Dunkle thinking that since he hadn't cracked in that heavy session, he'd have no trouble holding out in this one?

Biondi said, "The Belmont psychiatrist, Ridelhuber, said the killer would feel remorse. I think you can't face what you've done."

Dunkle just smiled.

The questioning circled through the same details a few more times. Bell brought up another subject with which Belmont had not succeeded. "Listen, Jon, how about clearing yourself with a polygraph?"

"My attorney says I shouldn't do that. They're only ninety-eight percent accurate. You could switch wires around and screw me up. If I take one of those tests, the FBI and Belmont will be here to harass me."

Biondi challenged him. "How much longer are you going to kill kids without getting help?"

"You're starting to sound like someone," Dunkle replied. Bell recognized the allusion to Goulart, who had blown up and called Dunkle a killer and a fag.

Bell asked in a concerned, fatherly tone, "Why is it that everywhere you go, dead children turn up?"

"They just harassed me about Lance. I'm a born-again Christian. God talks to me."

"You were sighted with a little boy in the park," bluffed Biondi.

"That's wrong. It wasn't me."

"Why did you hurt Sean?"

"I didn't. I never saw him."

Biondi and Bell tried the same method that the FBI had taught the BPD: They offered a face-saving way to confess. "Maybe it was an accident when you hurt him. Maybe he did something that caused you to lose control."

Dunkle smiled. "Sorry. I wasn't there." Bell could see why Goulart had lost his temper.

Biondi looked into Dunkle's eyes. "Whatever reason you had, we're willing to listen to it now. Do you understand?"

Dunkle stood up. "It's ridiculous." He glanced at his watch. "I need to leave now."

"Wait," said Bell. "I want permission to search your home."

Dunkle smiled. "It's okay with me, but I have to ask my sister. It's, uh, her time of the month. It might embarrass her if you find her dirty clothes."

This was among the weirdest excuses Bell had ever heard for avoiding a house search. Deadpan, he answered, "I'll ask her permission, too."

Judy Dunkle was disgusted with the police. "I'm afraid to ever let my brother out of my sight, because if anything happens when he's not home, next thing you know, the police are here trying to make him responsible. All the police do is twist everything we say. The Belmont police were the worst. Turn everything around against him. They brought him into a room and mentally roughed him around. They made him look at gory photos and kept telling him they knew he did it. And they put that picture of him in the paper. Jon's very bitter about that. They just got his name because of some prints on some can that could have been left there any time."

Still, she signed the Consent to Search form.

Bell and Reed immediately explored Dunkle's room, praying that during the six days since the murder he hadn't disposed of everything useful to them. They searched through the sheets and beneath the mattress of his double bed, dug around in his dresser drawers and hamper, and examined the clothes and shoes on the floor of his accordion-door closet. They found several pornographic magazines. Dunkle had scribbled red over pictures of naked women. Bell wondered how a psychiatrist would interpret this. Cutting and blood evidently turned Dunkle on, and the crude drawings of blood coming from women's sexual organs brought back Dunkle's remark about his sister's "time of the month," as if he equated menstruation with injury.

On the closet floor, Bell found a pair of Sears shorts whose crotch was wrinkled and crusted with semen. "What happened here?"

"I had a wet dream."

Bell collected the shorts and their matching yellow-knit pullover. Though the clothes had no apparent bloodstains, the semen was very suggestive. The act of murder gives some killers prolonged orgasms.

Bell and Reed couldn't find the knife. Dunkle helpfully looked through drawers and under the bed for it. "No," he said sweetly, "I don't know where it went."

He showed them his ten-speed bike in the garage. Not very happily, he allowed them to confiscate it.

Dunkle returned to the station, where he permitted them to take head and pubic hair along with blood and saliva. Then he met Detective Arnold Petty, the Sacramento County polygraph expert. Petty showed Dunkle how the machine worked and let him play around with it. "See, Jon," said Petty, "we really can't tamper with it."

"Yeah," said Dunkle. He never did agree to the test and

investigators believed they knew why. It was usually the guilty who feared the polygraph.

The next day, July 10, Bell took Dunkle to Cordova School. "Okay, you worked on the tire right here. Where could the knife have fallen out of your pocket?"

Seemingly eager to help, Dunkle joined him in searching the underbrush there and by the picnic table by Sunrise Trail. The next day, a fellow detective went over the same places with a metal detector. He had no luck either.

During these searches with Dunkle, Bell was careful not to indicate where the body was found. He had officers staking out that area at night, hoping in vain that Dunkle might return to it.

"Okay, Jon, let's see if we can find a knife like yours in a store," Bell finally suggested.

Dunkle appeared delighted, as if this were a kid's shopping trip with a kindly uncle. They tried several sporting goods stores, and pipe and tobacco shops. "There, Bob," said Dunkle.

Bell took it from the display counter and pulled out two blades, one like a pick and the other with a flattened end for tamping tobacco.

"Just like mine." Dunkle looked up at Bell for approval.

"Great!" said Bell. He purchased the knife and drove Dunkle home.

"See you later, Bob," said Dunkle.

"Right." Bell's style combined authority with fatherliness, and the more he worked with Dunkle, the more he felt what so many before him had—Dunkle's childlike neediness. There was definitely a lovable side to the guy, though underneath he must be twisted, cruel, and violent. Dunkle made it clear that he hated most of the Belmont police, yet liked and respected Bell. At the same time, Bell understood that Dunkle wanted to stay close to him in order to know how the investigation was progressing.

Bell would keep working with him. Perhaps Dunkle would eventually trust him enough to tell him the truth.

* * *

Dr. Anthony turned the pipe tool over in his hands. "Yes," he said. "This is the type of blade I envisioned while conducting the autopsy."

Bell took it to Dwayne, who reacted much the same. "Yeah, that's almost exactly like Dunkle's, only his had a brass tip on the tamper and it was pretty old and worn looking." Dwayne added, "You know, I phoned Dunkle the morning after we were together. I thought the guys and I were pretty rude just to leave him that way in the park. Anyway, Jon said to me real loud that he left at eight-thirty. Then, after you guys questioned him, he called and told me I was his alibi. Man, I was shocked."

Dunkle was sailing close to the wind now, telling friends to alibi him and handing over a replica of the murder weapon.

Three days later, Dunkle phoned Bell. "Hey, what should I do? This Mike Murray guy wants to come talk to me."

Bell played dumb. Murray, the investigator for the Kevin Collins Foundation, had asked Bell's permission to go drinking with Dunkle and talk about the Davies disappearance.

"I don't want to see him," said Dunkle.

"It's up to you, Jon," said Bell, who found it interesting that Dunkle would confide in him.

"Hey, Bob," Dunkle added, "on my bike, you know, you might find a little blood. Paul fell against it and scraped his ankle."

"Okay. Thanks, Jon."

Paul confirmed the blood story. "Yeah, I had to wash my ankle off in the river, and when I got home I put peroxide on it."

Bell and Biondi examined the bike. Dunkle had told

the truth about a slow leak, and the bike bag contained no useful evidence. Bell returned the bike, telling Dunkle that if the department had done any damage, he could file a claim with the county.

On July 25, three weeks after Sean Dannehl's murder, Dunkle attended a hearing on the only crime police could prove—the burglary at the Renne home. The judge set the trial date for May 1986. Ten months down the road.

Despite Bell's vow, the Sacramento homicide detectives were facing the BPD's fate of knowing their perpetrator and having no proof. Still, they weren't quite ready to fold up the investigation. They had one more trick up their sleeves.

In mid-August, a rough-looking street person clumped down Judy Dunkle's walkway. He wore dirty jeans, an open vest, and large shades. His beard tangled with his chest hair. He stuffed a smudged envelope addressed to Jon Dunkle into the mail slot. The note said, "Jon, it took me a while but I found you. I live on the river. The cops are bugging me. I saw what you did. I know about the board and I haven't told the cops. I'll be calling or writing again. Get rid of this." It was signed, "Ron Cross."

Four days later, "Ron Cross" reached Dunkle by phone. "Hey, man," he said gruffly, "get my note?"

"Yeah."

"I saw you hit him with that board."

Dunkle said nothing.

Cross went on, "If you don't want me to tell the cops, you got to pay me, man."

"Yeah?"

"Meet me where you left him, two nights from now, eight o'clock, got that? So we can deal."

"Uh-huh," said Dunkle.

Bell's extension rang and rang. Another detective picked up. "Sorry, Jon," he told Dunkle, "Sergeant Bell is on vacation." Grinning, he notified Biondi that the plan was working. Undercover officer Ron Goesch was getting Dunkle rattled.

Bell testified later, "We recognized that when Jon was able to talk to me that he was able to calm down a little bit, that he wasn't as nervous or as scared if he knew what was going on, because I would inform him on some of the aspects. . . . Without me there, he didn't know what was going on and therefore his anxiety would be able to build." With Bell out of touch and a scary guy threatening Dunkle with the detail of the board, a detail never given to the press, Dunkle might go to the murder site to look for the two-by-four or incriminate himself when he talked to "Ron Cross."

Bell spent his so-called vacation in a tree above the spot where Sean had lain, but Dunkle never showed.

A few days later, Lieutenant Biondi called Dunkle in and played him a tape recording. "My name is Ron Cross," said Goesch's rough voice. "I live down on the river. . . ."

"It's not true," Dunkle said when Cross described him attacking Dannehl.

"Let me show you the video," said Biondi. On film, with his dirty clothes and scruffy beard, Cross made a convincing park resident.

"I seen him grab up that board," Cross said, "it had a nail in it, and he hit that kid in the head and knocked him down. . . ."

When the video ended, Dunkle said nothing.

"An eyewitness, Jon," said Biondi.

Dunkle, whom Biondi knew to "always have an explanation for everything," just shook his head.

When Bell again made himself available, Dunkle phoned him constantly. "This guy who claims he's a witness, he keeps calling me. I need protection."

After days of this, Dunkle came into Bell's office. "I'm scared of that crazy guy."

"What did he see, Jon?"

Dunkle dropped his eyes a while. "Bob," he said quietly, "what if I did see that kid? Suppose I saw him being attacked and he was screaming and I didn't help him? Would I be in trouble?"

Hiding his surge of hope, Bell asked, "Are you talking about the Good Samaritan law, like would you be held responsible if someone died because you took no action?"

Dunkle nodded.

"Well, Jon, that's not the case here," said Bell. "We just want to know the truth. We want to know what happened to Sean." Bell sat quietly while Dunkle gazed at him for a long, poignant moment.

Then the mask slipped back over Dunkle's features. He stood up. "I was just wondering," he said, and walked out.

Chapter Twenty-nine

Dunkle's voice crackled over the transmitter. "Cops watch me all the time. That white van back there's probably doing surveillance on me right now."

Goulart lifted his foot from the accelerator and slowly dropped back. A car eased in front of him, the driver's eyes meeting his briefly. In this last-ditch undercover effort, Goulart wasn't tracking Lisa Thomas and Dunkle alone.

Two months had passed since Dunkle had almost confessed to Bell. Now Sacramento and Belmont officers had resurrected Lisa Thomas's role as Dunkle's girlfriend. The past couple of days she'd been visiting him, and today, in her car instead of riding bikes down trails inaccessible to backup vehicles, she and Dunkle headed up Highway 50, following the American River beyond Sacramento to the Folsom Lake Recreation Area. The plan called for her to aggravate him during the picnic in hopes that he'd blurt out something incriminating.

"Here's the place," Goulart heard Dunkle say. "Turn here."

Goulart couldn't see them after they took the exit, but

knew the officer ahead of him would watch them in the recreation area.

Then an arm slammed flashing lights on the roof of the unmarked car ahead. Others did the same. Goulart's backup team peeled away toward a bank robbery in progress.

By now, Lisa was walking up a trail with Dunkle and Goulart didn't know where. He pulled into a parking lot by the lake, listening and sweating, unable to alert her of the danger.

"Don't fink on me, Jon," said Lisa's voice over the transmitter. "They're going to arrest me for being with you that night. I'm scared to go to jail."

Goulart heard no response from Dunkle. Probably he was shrugging it off. "You're the one who went into that house," Lisa went on. "You gotta tell them I didn't have nothing to do with it."

"Quit talking about the case!"

Lisa escalated. "They already questioned me about your other crimes and I didn't tell about you running over that guy on purpose."

"I never did that."

"You said he was in a coma seventeen days or something."

"You have it wrong."

Lisa pushed harder. "What about that boy that got murdered right where you and I used to go biking? Just like Lance."

"Cops just harass me about that shit."

"If you fink on me, I'll tell everything."

"I never told you nothing!"

Goulart tensed. Dunkle always packed at least one knife.

Lisa Thomas kept reaming Dunkle out. Goulart sure wished he could see Dunkle's eyes.

Rustling noises told him Thomas and Dunkle were cleaning up the picnic mess. Now they were walking. Goulart moved his van up a shaded side road. Dunkle and Thomas emerged from one of the trails and when they reached the car, Dunkle took the driver's side. The car roared down the road. Goulart followed at a safe distance. Lisa and Dunkle hadn't stopped arguing, and Dunkle hit fifty, then sixty, jerking the car all over the lane.

The original plan had called for a sheriff to stop them on the highway and arrest Lisa for her role in the break-in. Alone now, Goulart winged it, following the car and frantically radioing the sheriff's department. As Goulart parked near Dunkle's house, two sheriffs' cars appeared and uniformed officers rushed out of them toward Lisa.

"Lisa Davis, you are under arrest."

Lisa screamed, "Help me, Jon!" Dunkle didn't respond. "You fucking faggot," she shouted. "*Do* something!" She burst into tears.

The gallant Dunkle vanished into the house.

Lisa documented that her mock arrest was "to terminate my relationship with Jon Dunkle," but it accomplished more than that. Dunkle would believe that his furious ex-girlfriend was spilling everything he'd ever said. Now investigators could confront him with the Steve Murphy hit-and-run, and at the right moment they could reveal that she'd been working undercover and had his story on tape.

In March of 1985, when Dunkle had first described the hit-and-run to Lisa, Belmont police had told Steve Murphy they knew who'd hurt him, but that they could reveal no more until a sensitive undercover case ended. Toward the end of October, Steve Murphy sat beside his mother, Deanna Baldwin, in Goulart's office and heard Lisa Thomas's tape.

"I was driving up this road," said a drunken male voice. "I was so fucking drunk, nobody knows about this, nobody. . . . I ran into him, knocked him cold on the ground. Didn't know what to do, so I stuck him in my car.

[Laughter]. . . . Cruised along, dumped him somewhere. I saw it in the paper the next day. He was in a coma seventeen days." The voice described taking the front bumper off his car to wash away hair and blood. "I mean, my car was clean as a whistle."

Three rough years had passed since Steve Murphy had crawled up the ravine into the Marburger turnaround, covered with blood and nearly dead from injuries and shock. Losing his spleen and one kidney made his diabetes more brittle and weakened his resistance to illness and infection. He lost his driver's license after blacking out at the wheel from an insulin reaction. Illness cost him several jobs. As he aged, diabetes would damage his remaining kidney. Dunkle had shortened Murphy's life span.

Now Steve had a focus for his rage. "Lance Turner's *murderer* ran me over?" Steve devoted some satisfying hours to mentally beating the bastard to a bloody pulp. He and his stepfather hoped they'd someday witness the execution.

Concerned about Steve's anger, Mrs. Baldwin phoned the Victim Assistance Office. She'd called them shortly after he was hurt, but was told that because the perpetrator was unknown, Victim Assistance couldn't provide counseling. Now she said, "We found out who did it and my son is still having problems."

Victim Assistance refused to provide counseling. "The crime occurred too long ago."

Mrs. Baldwin slammed the phone down. She knew that Presidential committees had studied the needs of victims, yet there was still no real help, financial or emotional.

She decided to help Steve in a different way. She asked Goulart if he knew a good lawyer. When he suggested Bill Russell, he set in motion a chain of events that influenced the final outcome of the murder cases.

* * *

Though the detectives had more on Dunkle in the Murphy case than the others, they faced the usual obstacles in gathering corroborating physical evidence.

Goulart submitted samples of Murphy's hair and blood for comparison with the old hair and dried blood from Dunkle's Honda Civic. Eventually the lab said the hair didn't match unless Murphy's had darkened in the last three years, and the blood from the front seat was too old and deteriorated for analysis.

Goulart located the body shop that Dunkle's father's insurance had paid for repairs after the hit-and-run. The manager would not release the repair records.

The emergency room doctor who had treated Murphy now claimed, "He could have fallen from a cliff," though his original note in the medical chart specified that the injuries "were consistent with Motor Vehicle Accident."

Whaley and Goulart met with Mark Davies, who was home on his first leave from the navy. Mark confirmed that the isolated, woodsy Marburger turnaround where Dunkle dumped Steve Murphy was a popular teenage party spot well known to Dunkle.

Bell and Whaley, wearing wires, met with Dunkle at a Sacramento fast food place to question him about his hit-and-runs. "I had two accidents in Half Moon Bay," he said. "I ran into a lumber truck and a piece of lumber came through my windshield. Another time I ran off the road and banged up my right front fender and blew a tire. I cut my finger changing the tire and bled on the bumper and fender."

This clever (and possibly true) explanation for blood on his bumper and car seat failed to impress the detectives. Bell confronted Dunkle with what he'd told Lisa Thomas about the hit-and-run.

"I made that up to impress her," said Dunkle.

"It's quite a coincidence that you happened to have all the facts right," said Bell.

Dunkle clamped his lips tight and, as Bell later documented, "he refused to say more."

A couple of weeks later, Whaley met with Dunkle's parents in their new home a few towns north of Belmont. He documented their response to his question of whether their son had mentioned the hit-and-run or explained the damage to his car: "They were very irate and spent a long time venting their anger toward this department. . . . Mrs. Dunkle asked when the hit-and-run occurred and then said, 'I'll think of where he was.' It appears she will come up with an alibi for that date as she did with the date of our homicide 10/2/84 [Lance]."

Mr. Dunkle said probably the famous alleged serial killer Charles Ng ran over Steve Murphy and murdered Lance.

The three-year statute of limitations for the Murphy hit-and-run was running out. In a frantic, last-minute scramble, the DA filed the charges on November 5, 1985, the exact three-year anniversary of the crime.

Three weeks later, Bill Russell filed a civil suit against Dunkle in Steve Murphy's behalf.

Bill Russell welcomed the Murphy case. At last he could give practical assistance to one of Dunkle's victims.

Collecting data for the lawsuit, Russell took a deposition from Mr. Dunkle, who stated he'd always had a "casual" relationship with his younger son, Jon, and wasn't especially aware of his comings and goings. He said he'd never paid much attention to bumps and dents on the boy's car, though he and his insurance funded the frequent repairs. He denied that his son had a drinking problem.

Bill Russell considered Jon Dunkle his father's creation. Mr. Dunkle had always blamed others for Jon's troubles and discounted the seriousness of the known crimes: Others got the boy drunk through peer pressure; it was the school's fault that Dunkle could barely read; and the Monti Hansen assault was just a fight. Bill Russell believed the father's attitude directly encouraged the son's antisocial behavior and that at the unconscious level, Jon was carrying out his father's urges.

In his petition, Russell charged Mr. Dunkle with Negligent Entrustment: "Jon Dunkle was supplied with a vehicle by people who knew he was unfit to drive and had a history of driving drunk." Russell also charged that Jon and Mr. Dunkle "spoiled evidence," Jon by cleaning the car after the hit-and-run, and Mr. Dunkle by paying for body work which altered the damage.

The complaints Russell made against Dunkle himself included not only deliberately running into Steve Murphy and abandoning him in the ravine, but also "assaulting and battering Steve with hands and feet," which Steve's original medical record suggested and which Steve himself had reported in the emergency room before losing consciousness and memory. Studying photos and descriptions of Steve's head wound convinced Russell that Dunkle had struck Steve with a tire iron.

Publicity about the Steve Murphy lawsuit made an impact on some of Dunkle's victims' families.

When the story broke, Guy Dannehl realized that the "suspect" Bell and Biondi had mentioned to him was Dunkle, whom Dannehl already knew was the Lance Turner suspect. Dannehl had lived in Redwood City, near Belmont, with his wife and Sean when Lance was killed. They'd moved to Twain Harte in early 1985, and Dannehl still worked in the Bay Area during the week. He'd been extremely aware of the Lance Turner case, but it hadn't occurred to him there could be any connection. Now, learning that the undercover operation had been dropped, yet Dunkle had been wandering around loose without twenty-four hour surveillance, sent Dannehl into a fury.

"They were playing Russian roulette with a kid's life," he said later. "It was just a matter of time before Dunkle killed again, and my poor kid was stuck in it all."

For Joan Davies, too, the articles brought new information about the investigation. All the Davies knew about the

Sacramento part was from Whaley, who had told them the BPD was working on Dunkle with Sacramento and that Dunkle was "playing games and acting strange."

Learning about the lawsuit was one of the first good things that had happened to the Davies in relation to the case for a long time. In July, when the Charles Ng/Leonard Lake serial murder case broke, the Department of Justice had again requested John's dental X rays. One of the torture-murder victims in the cabin was an unidentified teen male.

Then Whaley had notified Joan that a local psychic believed John's remains lay "in the Bishop and Bartlett Road area," close to Marburger Turnaround. With the now familiar mixture of hope and dread, Joan had replied, "My boys used to play up there, and we met Dunkle in the church on Bishop." But Whaley's dog search turned up a single sock and a bone, neither of which belonged to John Davies.

To be thorough, Whaley had purchased infrared photos from a 1982 geographical survey of the area. He hoped to see "hot spots" that indicated decaying remains, but some photos were taken from too high up and the rest revealed nothing.

Meantime, the Davies had suffered setbacks both with the FBI and with the missing children's movement. Their hero, Special Agent Deklinski, was promoted, and his replacement, Special Agent Lamar, showed little interest in John's case.

The nation's massive publicity and panic about missing children during 1985 suddenly shifted to a backlash when a trio of *Denver Post* reporters learned that ninety percent of missing children were not stranger abductions, but were runaways or parental abductions. They also lowered the estimated number of annual missing children from 1.5 million to 32,000. The public felt duped, and advocates like the Davies found their cause suddenly denigrated in the papers as a yuppie fad.

Now Joan reread an article about the Steve Murphy case and Bill Russell's legal action. She dialed his phone number. "Mr. Russell? I might have information about Jon Dunkle's character that would help your lawsuit."

Chapter Thirty

During his many visits to the BPD, Bill Russell had heard how difficult the Davies were. Officers said, "I'm a parent myself, I can understand what they're going through, but . . ." Then would come stories of Jim's abusive phone calls and Jim and Joan telling national television audiences, "The police did nothing to help us when our son disappeared."

Yet the large, blunt couple Russell met at the end of 1985 weren't irrational hotheads. They simmered with rage and Jim ranted and cursed, but they also possessed intelligence, strength and, surprisingly, humor. They presented coherent information and supported it with clippings, videotapes, and a log of dates and names. They described their son's character frankly and without sentimentality: "He was very smart, but very naive. Kids at Serra High called him a fag." They did not allow suspicion or rage to distort their stories about Dunkle.

Davies's statements that Whaley had often heard struck Russell as fresh and significant. Jim said bitterly, "John never went further than the driveway in stocking feet. His only shoes were Goddamn still in his room. He left his jacket and wallet and pet calculator, for God's sake. But Tompkins didn't respect our knowledge as parents."

Joan said, "I told him that I knew my son was either dead or he'd be gone a long, long time, and all he said was, 'When he gets cold and hungry he'll come home.' " Joan's angry eyes remained tearless. She produced a bundle of clippings about the first weeks of the disappearance. Russell scanned police quotes saying John was a probable runaway. He could understand the Davies' anger.

Jim thrust a tape into the VCR. "It's kind of a weird film," he warned. Russell immediately saw that whoever had made it lacked a steady hand. The camera bobbed its way down the San Francisco street from which Kevin Collins had vanished. A voice-over in Japanese accompanied the visual.

"We'll work with anyone," Joan said with an ironic smile.

Joan produced for Russell her notes about the psychic who had told them John was alive, but in bad company. She repeated the bitter story of the mystery telephone call and pointed to log entries supporting her complaints about police.

Russell felt the Davies had every right to be angry. He agreed that the police should have suspected John didn't run away. Dunkle's boyish smile and innocent act had fooled Tompkins the first week. In Russell's opinion, Dunkle was the blown suspect in the Davies case.

Russell leaned forward. "Jon Dunkle killed your son," he said, "and I'm going to get him."

"Wow!" Joan said, and told him she was thrilled because he was the first person to be this frank with them.

Russell began to grasp the depth of the split between the Davies and the BPD. Unlike police, he believed the Davies could be trusted to behave like professionals and to guard information. He filled them in on the Sacramento investigation and the Murphy case.

He saw that with their knowledge of Dunkle, the Davies were the investigation's wasted resource.

As Bill Russell was making friends with the Davies, a change was taking place in the BPD that would make it easier for him to mend fences between the family and the investigators.

When Chief Floyd Sanderson took over the department in 1981, he set up a practice common to small departments and established three-year rotations among officers' positions. Following this system, Sanderson pulled Sergeant Jerry Whaley from the juvenile officer slot toward the end of 1985, and put him back on patrol.

Whaley was devastated. He argued that the juvenile officer should be exempt: He had made himself a specialist, attending workshops, learning to interview sexually abused children and prepare them for court, and becoming unwittingly an expert on the politics of missing children.

Sergeant Don Mattei, formerly recreation specialist "Rock," and currently the detective most obsessed with Lance Turner, won the juvenile officer position. The day he took over, he found seventy open cases on Whaley's desk.

Mattei had kept the John Davies case and now, when Bill Russell visited the department, he planted seeds with him. "Gee, Don, the Davies know an awful lot about Jon Dunkle," Russell would say. "They could be useful allies." He did the same with the Davies: "The new juvenile officer would be a good person for you to get to know."

Gradually Russell's efforts began to pay off. One day Joan told him, "I phoned Sergeant Mattei. He's a real professional. He returned my call immediately."

"Oh, that's excellent!" Russell said. He kept it up, though he had no idea how useful this burying of the hatchet would prove to be.

* * *

In Sacramento, the DA's office was preparing for Dunkle's upcoming burglary trial. Forensic psychiatrists listened to tapes from Lisa Thomas's undercover work and Bell's and Biondi's sessions with Dunkle. Like Ridelhuber before them, the psychiatrists concluded that Dunkle was a psychopath, probably suffered homosexual panic, and was likely to continue committing acts of violence.

Sacramento officers continued their sporadic open surveillance of Dunkle. Once Dunkle spotted two cops watching him, burst into tears and darted into a busy street. A few weeks later, the Sacramento 911 received a frantic call. "They're out to get me!" Dunkle cried. "These teenagers on my street, they want to kill me!" The sheriff who went to the house noted that Dunkle was drunk and acting "paranoid."

In March 1986, while Russell forged ahead on the Steve Murphy lawsuit and detectives crossed their fingers about the upcoming Dunkle burglary trial, Jim and Joan attended the First National Missing Children Conference in Chicago, organized by the National Center. They attended workshops on the aftermath of a disappearance, emotional needs of families of the missing, and how to start a nonprofit organization, which inspired Jim to launch a California foundation called PACE—Parents Against Child Exploitation.

Joan gave a keynote address. "If this tragedy could happen to my family," she said, "if we could be the victims, then it could happen to any of you. I would like to emphasize *any.*" She described the morning John wasn't in his room. "The burden of the search became ours. . . . Simple questions about how and where to get posters printed, how to get John's picture into the newspapers were major decisions that we faced. . . .We ask that police officers talk to us, return our phone calls. . . . Tell us the truth. We can handle it!"

She had advice for reporters, too: "Get your story, but question us gently, think before you ask. We are already traumatized enough. To not be believed, to be treated as second-class citizens, and viewed with suspicion only adds another burden to our already broken hearts."

In mid-April, Dunkle appeared in court with public defender Paul Irish and pled "No contest" to the felony burglary of the Renne home. Mr. Irish argued that because it was a minor crime that resulted in minimal loss and no bodily harm, Dunkle should be released on straight probation.

Prosecutor Bill Portanova refused. Sacramento and Belmont detectives, along with Ridelhuber and Sacramento forensic psychiatrists, had made sure he knew how dangerous Dunkle was. Portanova demanded the maximum possible prison sentence.

To allow time for a thorough presentence investigation, Judge Long postponed the sentencing phase of the trial to May 7, then to May 16.

Bill Russell urged the Davies to write to Judge Long about Dunkle. He also helped the BPD feed all the useful information about Dunkle's past DUIs, hit-and-runs, and violent acts to the probation officer conducting the presentence investigation.

Joan's letter to Judge Long said, in part:

> I believe that Jon Dunkle is the murderer of our son, John. . . .
>
> We became alarmed in late 1980 as Jon Dunkle began drinking heavily. We encouraged him to come to our house when he was drunk, no matter what the hour, rather than cruise the streets. On several occasions he passed out on our living room couch or floor

> rather than go home where he claimed he was beaten by his father. . . . I sincerely believe he is a threat to public safety at this point. . . . I am greatly concerned that some justice be done to make up for the incomplete job that was done four and a half years ago.

The sentencing hearing was attended by a Belmont contingent that included Bill Russell, Jim and Joan Davies, Margo Turner, Steve Murphy, Thomas Mahnke (the victim of the first hit-and-run), Sergeants Goulart and Mattei, and Lisa Thomas. Unaware of the trial, Guy and Debbie Dannehl did not attend.

Judge Long ruled that the court should not hear testimony about the murders of Lance Turner and Sean Dannehl or the disappearance of John Davies, since these were "uncharged crimes," but he allowed testimony about the hit-and-runs because it was known that Dunkle had committed them.

After the court heard testimony about Dunkle's past convictions, probation, and jail time, Thomas Owen Mahnke took the stand and described driving his moped and being mowed down by Dunkle in August 1982

Then Steve Murphy testified about how he'd found himself injured and abandoned in the Marburger turnaround and how the damage had affected his life. As he spoke, Steve cast glances at Dunkle, amazed that the person who had done him such terrible harm was just a nerdy little shit, a despicable nothing.

Lisa Thomas took the stand, long hair curling around the shoulders of her feminine jacket. Lipstick and blush softened her features. Dunkle showed no particular emotion at seeing her, but his mother muttered urgently to defense attorney, Paul Irish. Later Lisa learned that Mrs. Dunkle had said, "That's not the same girl! That's an actress!" Ugly Duckling Lisa Davis had won her way back to swanhood.

Thomas testified that she'd been wired when Dunkle

described both hit-and-runs to her. The tapes of both chilling monologues were played.

The defense zeroed in on the fact that Thomas had been drinking on these occasions. She admitted that when Dunkle talked about ramming Mahnke's moped, she and he had each drunk an eight-ounce glass of Jack Daniel's and Coke.

Judge Long leaned toward her. "So in your opinion, you were holdin' the liquor pretty good?"

"Yes," said Thomas.

Then she described the night Dunkle got drunk with her at the Wits End Bar, made passes and talked about tying up and killing twelve-year-olds, walked with her through Goethe Park till he found the open gate of the Renne yard, then slipped through the sliding-glass door into their home.

Mrs. Dunkle watched her with furious eyes.

In closing arguments, Mr. Irish pointed out that the Mahnke incident was minor and the Murphy case was flawed by the problem with the statute of limitations. He mentioned the "mitigating circumstance" that Dunkle was under the influence of alcohol at the time he entered the Renne home and that he neither harmed anyone nor stole anything of value. He requested probation.

DA Bill Portanova had an easier job than the defense. He argued that Dunkle had a proven history of alcohol abuse and of increasingly violent acts. "He's exhibited a pattern of denial throughout the offense," he said. He pointed out that Dunkle had been given probation twice before and had violated it.

Judge Long told the court that in determining the sentence he was considering two main factors. First, "The victims in this crime were particularly vulnerable. They were asleep in their own home at night and they should have the reasonable expectation of being safe and secure in their own home." He said that the seven-year-old girl's quilt found lying in the hall and the scissors dropped on the living room floor "might indicate an intention of bodily harm."

The other factor was the hit-and-runs. "In a very wicked and rude manner, you ran down and injured and maimed another human being who will suffer the rest of his life. . . . I believe that is a cowardly act."

Judge Long agreed with the prosecution that Dunkle's history of denying responsibility and violating probation indicated the need for the maximum sentence now. He sentenced Dunkle to six years in state prison.

It was a bittersweet victory. On the courthouse steps, Lance Turner's mother told reporters she was glad about the six years, yet felt no true satisfaction because this had not been a murder trial. She hoped the sentence would save another child's life and said she believed that if Dunkle were ever tried for a murder, it wouldn't be for Lance's.

Near her, the Belmont contingent was embracing and smiling, a sight that caused Mr. Dunkle to redden as he stepped outside the courthouse. Bill Russell enjoyed a moment of revenge: He raised his camera and captured that rage-swollen face.

Chapter Thirty-one

The day after sentencing, Jon Dunkle stepped into an interview room in the Sacramento County Jail and greeted his visitors with apparent joy.

Seeing that familiar grin and shy ducking of the head, Joan Davies felt a second of confusion. Her heart so wanted him to be the sweet, needy boy who used to call her ''Mom'' and bring her gifts. Almost immediately, though, his body language and facial expression told her he had killed her son.

Jim's hearty hello barely masked his anger. Joan felt Dunkle had to be sensing Jim's rage, too.

''Thanks for agreeing to see us,'' Jim said.

They sat down as if nothing odd was happening, though law enforcement almost never permits a victim's relatives to visit a suspect. They could not only disrupt the investigation, they might smuggle in a weapon, kill their child's killer, and receive considerable public sympathy for doing so.

This meeting resulted from weeks of Bill Russell's hatchet-burying efforts. Early in his relationship with the

Davies, Joan had said, "I wonder if Dunkle would open up to me and Jim." Rather than brushing off this idea, Bill Russell found it exciting.

Russell and Dr. Hugh Ridelhuber had been researching psychopaths. During one phone call to an expert, Russell received an unwanted lecture about the insanity defense. "Hire a couple doctors to testify to his underlying paranoid schizophrenia and psychotic episodes—" the specialist began.

"I'm not defending him," Russell shouted, "I want to convict the son of a bitch!"

Several times Russell heard the theory that, contrary to the popular belief that psychopaths have no conscience, they appear to have a buried core of guilt and remorse and expend much energy concealing these emotions from themselves and others. They struggle with the urge to confess and nearly always will eventually "leak." Guarding their secret crimes and living in constant fear of discovery is exhausting—confession may bring huge relief.

For someone like Dunkle, it would also bring attention and importance. As Ridelhuber had written in his report to the BPD, "I believe he is getting some significant satisfaction from the attention he is receiving from the police and *his now having achieved some degree of status from the crime as compared with his otherwise bleak and insignificant life.* This factor . . . may lead him to want to tell the whole story and thereby confess."

Ridelhuber also believed that Jim and Joan Davies were in a unique position for playing on Dunkle's emotions. Dunkle's denial of having even been friends with John Davies suggested that John's murder caused him intense shame or guilt. He noted that serial killers stalk strangers for a reason. They need to see their victims as depersonalized objects onto which they can project fantasies and rituals. But John Davies and his family had been dear friends. Killing John was the deepest possible betrayal of people who loved Dunkle and whom he probably had loved back, in his limited way. Ridelhuber felt that the Davies could well shake emotion loose in Dunkle.

Bill Russell had presented these arguments to the BPD and set up a meeting between the Davies, himself, and the BPD. Then Mattei had coordinated with Bell and Biondi in Sacramento. Now Jim and Joan were sitting, wearing wires, in a jail room with Dunkle.

Joan said, "You know that we want to talk about John."

"I don't know why everyone thinks I know what happened to him. If I knew, I'd tell you."

"Well, we always wondered why you never came around after John disappeared, when our other friends were distributing posters and helping us search."

"I did come over. Your mother told me off."

"That was after a week or more of our friends helping us distribute posters," said Jim. "My mother was upset with you for staying away when we needed you so badly."

Dunkle shook his head. "I put up hundreds of posters. You go around telling police I never helped, but I did."

Joan interceded gently. "That just isn't so. We keep saying that when our son vanished from our lives, so did Jon Dunkle, because we never saw you again, and you wouldn't return our calls."

"You don't remember it right, Joan."

Jim bolted from the room.

"I guess Jim's upset," said Dunkle.

"Well, it's hard for us to believe you don't know anything about what happened to John." She tried to make him comprehend this agony. "Suppose he's out there wandering around and doesn't know who he is. We worry that's what happened."

She paused to collect herself. "I know in my heart that he's probably already dead. I want him to have a Christian burial. I'd like Pastor Bob to do the service and I want you to come to the service with us. We really want to put this behind us and get on with our lives."

"Gosh, Joan, you know I'd help you if I could."

She shifted to a more neutral, though still calculated topic. "Remember that time when we all went to Billy Graham and you and Jim and Mark were saved?" Ridelhuber had suggested that the Davies play on Dunkle's religion.

"Yeah. That was neat."

"Do you have a Bible with you?"

"Uh-huh."

"The minister and his wife are concerned about you," Joan said, and launched into other memories of church events the Davies and Dunkle had shared.

Three hours into the conversation, Joan returned once more to the real subject. "We've had a very difficult time the last five years, emotionally and financially." She told him all that Mark had gone through, as well as Jim and herself. Though Joan rarely cried in front of others, she found herself breaking into tears now as she begged Dunkle to help her.

Dunkle's eyes dampened. He gave Joan the same wounded look that she'd heard Ridelhuber describe. She held her breath as she waited.

He broke eye contact. "I can't help you, Joan."

When she reached the office where Jim, Bill Russell, and investigators waited for her, she slumped exhausted in a chair. "It didn't work," she said, though she'd be damned if she'd break down in front of all these people.

Russell said, "You were great! Don't give up! Let's see what Dunkle does next. He's going to leak to someone, I know it."

A month later, the Belmont Police Department's three-year rotation policy caught up with Sergeant Goulart. He had led the Dunkle investigation since it started, but now, in June 1986, he was back on patrol. He felt deeply frustrated and let down. He knew Dunkle was a serial killer and it maddened him that he couldn't nail the guy. He explained to reporters who covered his transition back to patrol that cops can't "manufacture" evidence; if it wasn't there, it wasn't there.

He believed the evidence would never surface.

The same reporters reached Dunkle's mother, who told them how sad it was that the police would try to set her son up and blame him for their unsolvable case. She insisted that instead of focusing on her son, they should try to find the killer who was still out loose somewhere.

Inside the BPD, the case wasn't closed as far as Sergeant Mattei was concerned. He kept track of Dunkle's activities in prison, and communicated regularly with corrections officials, hoping that Dunkle would crack. Mattei had good reason to hope for this: Ever since the Davies' visit, the severely dyslexic Dunkle had been pouring out letters to them.

In the first letter he professed to be very glad the Davies had talked with him the night before and that he and they had expressed their feelings to each other. His spelling, phrasing, and oddly placed capital letters betrayed his extreme dyslexia. "Really glad" came out "Rilly glad"; "expressing feelings" was "to know what youre fillins are with the fillin we expressed."

Then he launched into a harangue about Joan's letter to Judge Long, saying it was untrue. He claimed he'd stopped coming to the Davies' home because her mother told him off and made him feel rejected. He also denied having a drinking problem, though he admitted he enjoyed drinking and did it "with ever one there at your Home." He said the boys hid their drinking from Joan and that when she found out about it, she told them not to party there ("part there") any more. "Hush Hush!"

This seems to refer to the events surrounding Dunkle's drunk-driving arrest with Mark in November 1980.

The letter went on to deny that he'd ever stayed at the Davies' to avoid his father's violence: "My Dad never

Beaten me.'' He said that was a lie he told in order to stay at the Davies' and have someone to party with.

He offered obscure information, saying he began lying to people in February 1980 because he was "troubled." He said his family did not reject him and he'd felt lucky to have two families, "one where I could get away with anything and [then] go home and be a good kid."

Befriending the Davies had caused him to live a double life, he was claiming. By blaming his drinking and badness on the atmosphere in the Davies' home, Dunkle was following the lifelong pattern of blaming others for his behavior. Joan knew this, but the accusation still cut deeply. She and Jim had allowed the kids to drink at home to prevent their driving home drunk from other places and had hoped that this way they'd have some control over what went on.

Dunkle's letter shifted to the subject of John and how sad it made him that they would treat him as if he knew where John was and if he were alive or dead.

He spoke of his contacts with Dr. Hugh Ridelhuber, claiming he'd thought that speaking with the psychiatrist would clear him of suspicion. He expressed fury that Ridelhuber "was trying to feel me out" and "told me I did it." Dunkle called this brainwashing and said that the psychiatrist "is a rill prick!"

Dunkle wasn't wrong in believing that the psychiatrist had tried to influence him to confess, but Ridelhuber felt he had reflected Dunkle's pain and inner sickness back and forced Dunkle to acknowledge these in himself.

Dunkle signed off the first letter urging the Davies to pray for an answer because Jesus would hear their prayers. The hypocrisy infuriated Jim Davies.

After this, Dunkle wrote once or twice a day. Joan visualized him spending hours on his narrow bunk, fighting to express his twisted thoughts through the block of his severe reading and writing disabilities. Though none of the letters disclosed John's whereabouts, they revealed Dunkle's paranoia and psychopathy. Several themes appeared in nearly every letter.

Dunkle blamed the media and the BPD for influencing the Davies' suspicions of him of killing John, and resented the Davies' habit of speaking to the press. He kept writing, "You should have come to me sooner!" which was self-serving: The Davies had tried over and over again for years to speak to Dunkle about the disappearance.

In every letter he shifted between anger and love for the Davies. He said his parents had instructed him not to write to the Davies, but that he did so because he still loved them. In the next sentence he begged them not to "frame" him. Still angry about the letter to the judge, he hinted that the Davies family harbored lots of secrets and that he could write a letter "Just About your Home Life. . . . There's so much you don't know about your own family Joan."

Yet after such a passage he would retreat to appeasement, urging that he and they talk and write openly to each other and stay friends.

In passages that greatly interested the BPD, Dunkle spoke of the interview in which the BPD and FBI had created their stage set with evidence from the Lance Turner murder scene. He ranted about "these sick BPD-FBI-DA," enraged that they would think he had no emotions, yet showing him photos so scary that he reached a point of not talking. Like his father, Dunkle accused alleged serial killer Charles Ng of Lance Turner's murder.

Lost in the pages and pages of rumination about having or not having a drinking problem and blaming the Davies for it, Dunkle made a remark that didn't seem significant, but later proved to relate directly to his thoughts about his crimes: "When I told you I had a Drinking Problem I really did not—The problem was trying other drugs and mixing them together. . . ."

* * *

In mid-July, Joan Davies again faced Dunkle across a small conference table, this time in an interview room in the Jamestown Prison Camp.

"Jim said to tell you he's sorry he couldn't make it this time," Joan said, though the truth was that the police, Ridelhuber, and Jim himself agreed that he shouldn't participate because he couldn't hide his rage. Also, Ridelhuber advised that Joan would be a less threatening person for Dunkle anyway, as she was a motherly, middle-aged woman, the kind of person in whom Dunkle had confided in the past. "Besides," Ridelhuber explained, "with an older woman the problem of sexual attraction won't come up."

"Gee, thanks," said Joan.

Joan started the conversation this time by commiserating with Dunkle about the troubles he was having in prison. Inmates hassled and threatened him because he was a suspect in child murders. He had written to the Davies about it. He'd written that when he reached the previous state prison, Vacaville, "two thousand" inmates surrounded him in the yard and that black and gay prisoners wanted to beat, kill, or rape him. He had been moved to Jamestown, and after three days of no sleep, he was placed in protective custody, then into a hospital unit. He applied to be moved to the California Men's Colony in San Luis Obispo, where he might be safer.

"How can I help you?" Joan asked now, and Dunkle requested that she write letters to prison authorities saying she feared for his safety and urging them to transfer him to a more protected place.

Joan pulled out some family photographs. "Here's the house we moved into after Jim went bankrupt. It's a lot smaller than the Belmont house, but we have good friends in the neighborhood."

Dunkle nodded.

"Look, this is Mark in his navy uniform."

"Wow."

Joan and Dunkle chatted about religion. Dunkle professed to read a Bible called *The Book* every day. "It helps me in this lowly place," he said. "I like the *Desiderata,* too," he added, though he couldn't begin to pronounce it.

"Yes, it's very calming, isn't it?" said Joan. "I need things to help me be peaceful these days." She began to talk about John, trying again to make Dunkle experience at least a hint of her pain. "It tears me apart not to know if he's alive or dead. Suppose he thinks he won't be welcome now? Suppose he came to the old house looking for us and now we don't live there anymore?"

"Yeah, suppose someone ran into him with their car and he forgot who he is?" offered Dunkle.

Had Dunkle killed John with his car as he had almost killed Steve Murphy? wondered Joan. Suppose John's remains still lay undiscovered down some cliff?

"Do you have any ideas about where else we should look for John?" she asked.

He shrugged. "You should ask Jim, Jr., and Mark's friends about places they used to party. Maybe someone got John drunk and left him in one of those places."

Joan and Dunkle talked almost four hours, often about safe subjects like old friends and memories; sometimes about the family's desperate need to know John's fate. Dunkle had moments of deep, sad contemplation, but did not crack.

Afterward, Bill Russell told Joan that as Lieutenant Biondi, Chief of the Sacramento Homicide Bureau, listened in on this conversation, he burst out, "I can't imagine the mother of a victim being able to stay in control like that. This woman is amazing!"

* * *

The letters kept coming. A few new elements began to creep in. Dunkle let the Davies know he wasn't fooled by their friendly seeming visits, stating he knew that because they came on a weekday and were put in a particular room that everything was staged and recorded. He was angry that she professed to care about him when all she wanted to talk about was "John T. Davies and where is he!!"

Mattei and other BPD officers believed Dunkle met with Joan despite knowing the session was bugged because he reveled in the attention and loved playing cat-and-mouse. Ridelhuber and Bill Russell agreed, but hoped another reason was that a part of Dunkle was coming closer to opening up. Over and over, he dropped hints in his letters, saying John wasn't the type to run away and that if the Davies found a body in the places where Dunkle and the Davies kids' friends used to party, Dunkle would be charged with murder and executed.

Was this often repeated suggestion to look in "parte placeis" (party places) a red herring or a clue?

Besides visiting Dunkle and fielding his onslaught of letters, Jim and Joan Davies remained active that summer in the missing children's cause. Through the Kevin Collins Foundation and Jim's own organization, PACE, the Davies and other activists lobbied and wrote letters supporting the California Missing Children's Act which was soon to be considered by the state legislature. The act would correct nearly all the errors and multijurisdictional problems the Davies and other parents of California's missing children had endured.

On August 29, 1986, the activists' efforts were rewarded: The Davis/Stirling Missing Children's Act of California passed unanimously.

Part Five

Confession
October 1986

Chapter Thirty-two

Dunkle's prison troubles did not improve and finally, in early September, he was transferred to the California Men's Colony (CMC) in San Luis Obispo, a medium-security prison housing many inmates under protective custody. There he met a twenty-year-old con named C. Louis.

C. Louis has a kaleidoscopic relationship to truth and his Dunkle tale is a work of art complete with mythological elements and shadowy implications. However, most of it can be verified.

According to C. Louis, the story begins not in September 1986 when he and Dunkle met, but three-and-a-half years earlier, January 1983, when Joan Davies appeared on TV in the recreation room of a North Carolina prison. "My son John has been missing for two years now," she stated firmly. "He was an A student, he didn't do drugs. . . ."

Inmate Louis, barely seventeen, missed his own mother, who loved him, but seldom visited because her loyalties were torn between him and her current husband. A frequent runaway as a boy, Louis says that at fourteen he told the Juvenile Court he wouldn't return to the stepfather who had broken his jaw. The family denied his charges but the court placed him with relatives, then in Juvenile Hall, and finally, at sixteen, in an adult prison on drug and assault charges.

Louis tuned in powerfully on this loyal mother Joan Davies, and when the camera shifted to the poster she held in her lap, he studied her missing son. Two years gone! The boy had to be dead.

Louis says that as he concentrated on the boy's smiling, freckled face, he experienced a rush of emotions and had a vision of a brown-haired man dressed in white, whose features increased in clarity as if in a camera's focus.

When released from the North Carolina prison, C. Louis says he was paroled to a relative in Los Angeles, where he allegedly established a complicated relationship with organized crime, became a drug dealer, and abused alcohol and cocaine himself. He describes a shoot-out among rival dealers or gangs during which "I got shot in the cheek of my ass." Another time, he reports, he struck a nonpaying drug buyer in the head and "happened to have a knife in my hand at the time." He states he was arrested for assault with a deadly weapon and other charges and tried to bargain his way out with information about the crimes of others, including a murder.

When he realized that he not only faced a long sentence, but had become a strong suspect in what officials called "the mutilation murder of a homosexual in a wheelchair," he blew. He made escape attempts and suicidal gestures. He says that because of his reputation as an informer, he was stabbed by an inmate in the Chino, California, prison and was moved to Vacaville. Then, unstable and in protective custody, he was sent to the same psychiatric wing at the California Men's Colony that would soon house Jon Dunkle.

In early September 1986, loaded on antidepressants, C. Louis wandered over to the Men's Colony chapel to catch a glimpse of a prison celebrity, former Manson family member Charles "Tex" Watson, a born-again Christian. Instead, he ran into giggly, friendly Jon Dunkle. In some versions of the story, Louis alleges that this meeting was a setup planned by prison officials and himself, but there is no way to verify this.

Dunkle and Louis sized each other up while they chatted about learning the ropes at CMC. Each had heard general gossip about the other. Louis knew Dunkle was suspected of child murders, and Dunkle knew Louis was not only a murder suspect, but was believed to be "connected." A lanky youth with a pronounced Southern accent, Louis consistently presented himself as the son and grandson of Mafiosos. With his sharp features, wiry dark hair, and heavy sideburns, he looked like a street tough. Louis was so young he still had teenage zits.

Louis amused himself watching Dunkle try to match his Southern self to the Mafia reputation. At the same time, he "saw something in Dunkle's eyes" that said violence was there.

After their first meeting, they ran into each other daily. They confided about rough times in other prisons. In the prison yard one day, Dunkle confided that he was a suspect in some murders. Louis says he asked who the victims were and tossed out names: "Bill? Joe? Mike? John?"

"Why did you say 'John'?" Dunkle asked nervously, and Louis saw "a flash of pure hate in his eyes." Dunkle demanded, "Are you a cop?"

"Hell, no." Louis stated his prison-based philosophy: "I don't care what you're here for. I take you as you are."

Though barely twenty to Dunkle's twenty-six, it was Louis who was the experienced con, the career criminal. He knew how to gain respect, score drugs, and manipulate the system. He affected a take-no-shit attitude and a cocky, teasing style. Add to that his Mafia aura and he was a youth who could easily impress a green inmate like Dunkle and bask in the hero worship.

Dunkle and Louis both had disastrous cellmates. Louis's

tried to drown himself in the toilet; Dunkle's cried for his mommy. "Hell, anyone's better than those guys!" they agreed, and they requested to share a cell.

Just before they moved in together, Louis says that Dunkle began acting weird. Overhearing Louis say on the phone, "You going up north, John?" Dunkle demanded, "What do you mean, up north? Why do you keep talking about John?"

"He's my best friend, asshole," said Louis. "You're too damn paranoid." Louis reports that as he studied Dunkle's angry eyes, he flashed back to his man-in-white vision three years earlier. "Let me see your Vacaville ID."

Dunkle became more agitated. "Fuck, no. What for?"

Louis wheedled it out of him, and there, in a shiny photo of Dunkle wearing Vacaville whites, Louis says he recognized the man from his vision.

When Louis lifted his eyes to Dunkle's face, Dunkle snatched away the card. "What are you looking at? Listen, I don't want to be cellies! It just won't work out!"

"Fine!" stormed Louis. "You're too damn weird anyway."

As Dunkle stomped off, Louis shouted after him, "I'm still your friend, asshole!"

For a loner like Dunkle the word "friend" carried great power. That night, as Louis later wrote, "We became cellmates by his doing."

Louis says that Dunkle dug out Louis's trial transcripts from beneath his bunk and was impressed that Louis's "Family" appeared to have frightened witnesses out of testifying. Louis downplays the fact that he talked to Dunkle all the time about the Mafia, a subject Dunkle would love. He does report that Dunkle tried to keep up, making claims like, "I have Mafia friends, and I was a spy for the IRS in Sacramento."

"Yeah, right," Louis would answer, unimpressed.

One evening, as they shared confidences about being murder suspects, Dunkle said, "That child murder they think I did, it was like that murder you witnessed. I just saw it happen.''

''Uh-huh.'' Louis yawned.

''This big guy on the path beat me up and ripped off my Buck knife. I saw him kill Lance with it. He left it on the ground and I picked it up and wiped it on my pants. Lance's blood was only on my pants because I wiped the knife.''

''If I was on a jury and you told that story, I'd convict you,'' Louis said.

Dunkle abruptly changed the subject. The next night, though, he brought Lance up again, circling around the events as he had with many people before. As Louis knew from personal experience, the urge to reveal one's deepest and worst acts is intense. During his first years at the Men's Colony, Louis fought his own fears and desires about confessing his part in the murder of which he was suspected. He believed, probably correctly, that in him Dunkle had found the right audience. Dunkle had to pretend to be a ''good boy'' for his parents, and a partying teen with Belmont kids, but with Louis he could take off all his masks.

Dunkle said, ''I did kill that boy. It's just hard for me to talk about it.''

Having made that disclaimer, he talked till five that morning and all night every night for the next three weeks. Once uncorked, he couldn't stop pouring out the stories. Talking compulsively, he smiled and giggled when describing the murders. His eyes remained ''flat,'' Louis later said. ''You couldn't see nothing in them.''

A couple of times, Louis says, he managed to smuggle in some booze and then ''Dunkle really babbled on and on about all kinds of bizarre shit.'' When he wasn't bragging about the murders, Dunkle confided about sex. He said his penis was only ''four-and-three-quarter inches, hard,'' and that he used to inject the suffering organ with cocaine, and once with bacon fat to enlarge it. He also alleged torment and sexual abuse by his older brother, and of incest with other relatives. He claimed that for years of his youth, he engaged in S and M, domination and bondage, with "an older Italian man." He described enticing children into "affairs."

One night, Dunkle went into more detail about Sean Dannehl. "I saw that boy ride by on his bike on the trail. It was a blue bike. I knew I was going to kill him. I rode after him and rammed him so he fell down. . . ."

Louis had been hearing these tales for over a week now. Suddenly he felt overwhelmed, as if he were looking into Dunkle's mind "like a book with glass pages." He visualized the rough chaparral where John Davies lay, the sun-dappled path where Dunkle grabbed Lance Turner, Sean's blue bike shoved beneath leaves.

Dunkle's gleeful voice didn't stop. "This boy was cooperative, so I had to humiliate him. I made him take off his clothes and I led him by the hand into the trees. I promised him I wouldn't hurt him. I made him lie on the ground and I put this two-by-four over his eyes so he wouldn't see the knife. When I stabbed him, he said, 'What are you doing? You promised you wouldn't hurt me.' " Dunkle laughed.

This was the coldest story Louis had ever heard. Some of Dunkle's other cruel statements pounded through his mind: "I had to tweeze out this piece of the knife blade that got stuck in his heart"; "I told John Davies, 'Scream all you want, no one will hear you.' "

Louis says he considered killing Dunkle. The consequences didn't matter since he considered his life ruined anyway. Yet Louis found himself using persuasion instead of murder. Some good might come to him from getting Dunkle to confess.

"If you did this shit, you need help," Louis told Dunkle. "Why did you do it? Was it sexual?"

"No, no. I don't know why I did it."

"Don't you want to stop?"

Dunkle sucked in his lower lip as if he might cry. "That

police shrink Hugh said he'd help me if I talked. But that was before Sean."

"You'll get a shrink if you confess."

Dunkle refused; he didn't want to give a thing to Belmont or Sacramento authorities. He hated them.

One night, he admitted, "I killed them for sexual reasons, but not really."

"What did you do, rape them first?"

"No. Only Sean. Sort of."

Dunkle hesitated and Louis said, "This is me you're talking to. Spit it out."

"Well, after he was naked, I shoved my cock in his mouth."

"What about Davies?" Louis believed Dunkle had taken John Davies out in order to have sex and killed him for refusing. Dunkle denied this, but as Louis later wrote, "The colder part was how Dunkle sodomized and orally copulated Davies after he killed him." Dunkle admitted he had wanted to do the same to Lance, but fled because so many people were nearby.

"You need to get all this sick shit off your chest," Louis told him.

"I can't confess. Maybe if they find the evidence—the knife I hid, or John Davies's bones. But Belmont fucked up. They never even found my blood in Lance's mouth from when he bit my thumb. I wrote to Joan to look for John's body in party places and they're still too dumb to find him."

Dunkle was on a roll. "When I get out, I'm going to kill Lisa. She was wired all those times. . . ." And off he went with a lengthy hit list that included Russell, Goulart, Bell, and about twenty others.

Inmates hate child killers but they also despise informants. Louis had little faith that corrections officials could fully protect him after he turned Dunkle in. But who cared? His life wasn't worth anything anyway. He says that he felt like if he got killed behind turning in his cellie, at least he'd die knowing he'd done one thing right in his screwed-up life. Also, turning Dunkle in gave him the opportunity to work nearly as a partner with officials.

On September 14, Louis sought out Security Squad Officer Mike Wiley. So far the redheaded officer had been straight with him; perhaps he could be trusted.

When they were in the privacy of Wiley's office, Louis blurted, "I've got to tell you about these murders my cellie committed. They're appalling."

Once Wiley realized what he was hearing, he took Louis into a conference room with a tape recorder.

Chapter Thirty-three

Sergeant Mattei couldn't believe it: On the phone a corrections officer named Wiley was saying that inmate Dunkle's cellmate had brought some information, and did Belmont have any unsolved child murders?

"Yes," said Mattei slowly. He hardly dared feel hope even now. Could Dunkle really be "leaking," as Bill Russell and Hugh Ridelhuber had predicted? Dunkle had jerked cops around so many times, had dished out so many lies. The tales with which he was regaling some cellmate might only be more twisted efforts to attract attention. And what was this cellmate after anyway? He must imagine that stepping forward would win him a reduced sentence.

When Goulart heard the news, he burst out, "Oh, God, I can't believe it!" Just a month earlier, he had told reporters he feared the case that had filled two years of his life would never be solved. Once again Goulart was glad he worked for a small department. Though back on patrol, he would still participate in the Dunkle case.

Subdued elation permeated the Belmont Detective Bureau. The cellmate's story was an exciting development, but they had no confession yet, and the road leading there was strewn with landmines of entrapment and, if illegally obtained, the confession and all evidence found to confirm it would be thrown out. The new head of the Detective Bureau, Sergeant Fogarty, contacted San Mateo County DA Robert Bishop for guidance.

On September 17, three days after Wiley's phone call, Farmer, Mattei, and Fogarty made the three-and-a-half hour drive to the San Luis Obispo Men's Colony and met with Wiley and his coworker Bill Jesus. "We're not going to give you any information about the crimes," Fogarty said, following DA Bishop's orders. "We have to protect the integrity of the information you get here."

"Right," said Wiley. Both sides carefully documented this precaution.

"Can Louis get place names, dates, specific information that we can verify?"

"He'll sure try," said Wiley. "He insists on working with us." The officers believed that Louis and Dunkle were physically involved and that Louis was enticing admissions from Dunkle with sexual favors.

"It's essential Louis knows he's operating on his own," Mattei said, issuing the same precaution he'd given Joan Davies before her sessions with Dunkle in prison: An unofficial person must in no way act in the role of a police agent. It was especially important now, with the cellmate. DA Bishop had warned that under new case law, jailhouse confessions were usually thrown out as entrapment. To prevent this, Louis's efforts must be completely independent. Even if he wore a wire, he was to do so for his own reasons.

"One guess what's motivating this guy," said Mattei. "He wants a deal. But he can't be offered one. That would taint the confession."

"He says he just wants this bastard off the streets," Wiley answered.

Farmer, Mattei, and Fogarty drove home through a landscape that alternated between dry rolling hills and clusters of lush trees, the air pungent with garlic and dung. They prayed that the cellmate wouldn't screw this up.

Louis invented a friend in the FBI. "He helped me solve a problem one time," he told Dunkle, speaking vaguely and playing on Dunkle's Mafia fantasies. It has been speculated that Dunkle soon believed "FBI friend" meant a crooked one and that for him, "solving a problem" meant hiding the murder weapon and/or the remains at the John Davies murder scene. He asked Louis to contact the FBI friend. "I'll pay anything he wants. My grandfather can sign over my interest in his motel."

"Okay, I'll talk to my friend," said Louis.

He then met with Wiley. A few days later, Louis told Dunkle, "My friend needs more to go on. How about maps?"

Dunkle sketched a trail and a hill in Redwood City's Edgewood Park. Then he drew maps of Water Dog Lake where he'd killed Lance Turner and Sunrise Park where he'd killed Sean Dannehl. Stick figures represented the bodies. Dunkle also wrote specific directions and worked long hours on what he called "papers," in which he described the three murders with many verifiable details. On them he wrote instructions reminiscent of James Bond movies: "For your eyes only destroy after reading."

That Dunkle would draw maps and write detailed confessions suggests he truly wanted to confess. Yet he had resisted doing so for five years. The official interpretation of his behavior at this point was that he could no longer bear the pressure of his secrets. He chose to talk first to Louis's FBI "friend" because he hated Belmont and Sacramento authorities and respected the FBI and would feel more at ease with someone connected with Louis.

Louis believes, though, that Dunkle still clung to the delusion that Louis's "friend" would hide John Davies's remains and the weapon. If so, he needed this fantasy in order to break through Dunkle's terror of confessing.

On September 22, when Louis took the maps and "papers" to Wiley, Wiley had managed to get hold of a surveillance transmitter and receiver through the San Luis Obispo Narcotics Task Force. Earlier, Louis had been wired one night in the cell, but the sound was so bad nothing came through. Wiley suggested they might get better transmission if Louis and Dunkle sat in a conference room.

Louis felt skeptical: Wouldn't Dunkle be suspicious? But he'd give it a try. Dunkle still seemed to trust him totally. Dunkle even believed it when Louis explained not returning the maps and papers to him. "I had to burn them," Louis said. "The guards would have took them off me."

Now he told Dunkle, "Hey, come on. I get to hang out in one of the conference rooms today." The room would normally have been off limits for inmates, but Louis conveyed the idea that this was one of many favors he received because he was "connected."

Dunkle cheerfully followed him into the room and sprawled in a chair. "Cool," he said, looking around, as he always did, for hidden bugging devices.

As they lit their unfiltered Camel cigarettes, Louis searched Dunkle's face. Did Dunkle really believe he could talk safely in here? Louis put out a feeler. "What was the name of that place you killed Lance—Piss Puddle?"

Dunkle snickered. "Water Dog Lake. There's all these neat trails and I was talking to those girls at the smoking tree and one gave me a hit off her joint after I let her sip my beer, and I saw this boy run past us on the trail. . . ."

Louis could hardly believe it. Dunkle was stupid enough to spew out detail upon lurid detail, right next door to a security squad office! He must really want to be caught.

They talked about the murders for two hours. Louis stubbed out his last Camel. "Gotta go. I got telephone time in a few minutes. Meet you back at our house."

"Okay." Dunkle walked away and Louis slipped back into Wiley's office to peel off the irritating tape.

Wiley played back a part. Through what Wiley later described as "atrocious background noise," Dunkle's "very nonchalant and very businesslike" voice repeated the murder stories. Louis could be heard "urging him to tell law enforcement," but Dunkle refused to talk to Belmont police, complaining, "They fucked up not to catch me before." He repeated that he was willing to talk to Louis's "FBI friend," but no one else.

Louis returned to his room. Though Dunkle still showed no suspicion, Louis put his senses on red alert. He wouldn't truly sleep again till Dunkle was sent away.

Farmer drove to San Luis Obispo the next day to pick up the tapes and written confessions. Back in Belmont, he and the other detectives scoured them for never-published details that only the killer could know. The officers had wanted so long to know what really happened to John Davies and how the murderer approached Lance Turner. Did they dare believe the plausible details Dunkle was giving? On his Water Dog Lake map Dunkle accurately marked the spot where Lance was found. This didn't prove he was their man: though information about the specific location had never been given to the papers, many Belmont residents knew it.

Mattei and Goulart studied the notations about "skull" and "bones" drawn on the map of what Dunkle's notes called the most "northermost" hill in Edgewood Park.

"Where the hell is that?" asked Farmer.

"Near the old Hassler Home," Mattei said. He and Farmer recalled the six fruitless weekends in early 1985 when volunteers with dogs searched around Hassler for John Davies's remains. The place Dunkle was pinpointing on his drawing was across the road and about half a mile from the area they had scoured. Apparently "the most northermost hill in Edgewood'' qualified as what Dunkle repeatedly alluded to in his letters to the Davies as ''a party place.''

Mattei began making calls to organize a search.

On October 1, Fogarty, Goulart, Mattei, and Farmer went to Sacramento and met with Ray Biondi, head of homicide, and Detective Robert Bell, the fatherly detective who had pursued Dunkle so long in the Dannehl murder. ''If he'll talk to some bogus FBI 'friend' of his cellmate,'' Goulart said, ''let's give him a bogus FBI guy.'' They tossed around what sheriff or police officer could play this role. Then they decided not to take any risk of entrapment: They'd provide Dunkle with the real thing.

On Friday, October 3, with little briefing about what they were getting into, Special Agent Hickey of the Sacramento FBI and Special Agent Payne of the Santa Maria branch came to the California Men's Colony and joined Dunkle and Louis in a conference room.

Down the hall in Wiley's office, Belmont and Sacramento detectives paced, gulping acid coffee. ''He won't talk,'' said Mattei, rigid with tension. ''He likes playing games too much.''

Farmer nodded, recalling Dunkle's cat-and-mouse games and what Whaley had always called his ''Cheshire Cat grin.'' In the conference room, Louis told Dunkle, ''This is my friend Special Agent Hickey and his partner. These are the people I've been talking to. No one else knows nothing about this.''

''I won't talk to you unless Louis is here,'' Dunkle told them.

Hickey agreed, though it was a very unusual procedure. Then he read Dunkle his rights, laying the legal groundwork for a voluntary confession. Dunkle answered, ''I don't want an attorney. I just want to get this off my chest.''

Hickey and Payne waited, pens above paper, while Dunkle giggled and cast a flirty, conspiratorial glance at his lanky cellmate, who smiled back encouragingly. Then Dunkle began to talk, presenting a vivid but nonsexual version of the murders.

Helpfully supporting his cellie through the conversation, Louis concealed his exultation. He'd done it, he'd conned a con. The stupid, murdering bastard was locking himself up for life.

When Hickey and Payne entered Wiley's office with their notes on Dunkle's confession (no recorders were used), Mattei still held his hopes in check. The pages might be nothing but hot air and lies. Impatiently he read through the agents' papers.

Then he saw: "The girls dug up a pack of cigarettes and a matchbook from a wedding."

The detail about the wedding match book by the smoking tree had never been released to the press. "This is it!" Mattei cried.

So it was as a believer that Mattei returned that day to Belmont and finished arranging the Edgewood Park search. Familiar with most of the county's trails because of his long-distance running, Mattei was the only Belmont officer who knew anything about the Edgewood area, which is many acres of California chaparral lying outside the boundaries of Redwood City and San Carlos.

He walked alone through its hilly paths. Dry weeds crunched beneath his feet. He studied slopes sparsely covered with manzanita, juniper, scrub oak, and live oak, trying to find a match for Dunkle's illustration of the "northermost hill." The drawing was confusing because it indicated that a cluster of power lines and poles were visible from the hilltop, and from many points on the paths Mattei saw two separate power plants. Eventually he found a place that seemed to resemble the drawing. It was a rounded hill. Dense shrubs covered most of one side; the other was bare except for low grass and weeds.

He climbed to the top and saw that, just as in the drawing, a power plant lay between the hill and Highway 280, with narrow Crystal Springs Road running alongside.

Mattei walked the hill's paths and poked around in the underbrush. The search would be a bitch. Coyote bush, manzanita, and scrub oak grew dense and thick, branches and leaves tangling into a nearly impenetrable wall. Mattei recalled that young John Wolfe had said Dunkle once shot a rattler here. Officers would have to bring snake guns.

Dunkle had told the FBI Special Agents Hickey and Payne that he had returned to the Davies murder scene several times. He had watched "a wolf or coyote" tear at John's body a week after the murder, and six months later, he'd found the bones scattered down the hill. His map indicated where they lay then.

John Davies had been dead five years now. Could anything possibly be left of his remains?

At ten-thirty the next morning, Saturday, October 4, searchers gathered at the upper entrance to Edgewood Park. The Belmont contingent included Mattei, Farmer, Goulart, Halleran, Fogarty, and Lisa Thomas. Because the area lay in county jurisdiction, several sheriffs were also present. Along to help also were five specially trained Explorer Scouts from Search and Rescue.

Goulart stared out in dismay. To him a park was a place like Belmont's pretty and orderly Twin Pines, and this was an untamed expanse.

After Mattei pointed out the hill and organized it into grids, the group searched the top and gradually worked down into wider and wider sections of thick growth. Soon the enthusiastic Explorer Scouts, boys ages fourteen to eighteen, dropped onto their hands and knees to inch through scrub and poison oak.

By one p.m., the group had circled the hill three times, finding nothing. Hot and tired, the officers lounged against the hoods of their trucks to eat lunch. While the men relaxed, the Explorer Scouts continued to creep through the brush on a far slope of the hill.

Officer Halleran was scratching a poison oak blister on his arm when he heard a young voice on his walkie-talkie. "I found a bone."

Seconds later another call: "I have a bone, too."

Suddenly voices crowded the air:

"A T-shirt with Kansas on the front."

"A rib."

"Blue corduroy pants."

Then: "Here's a skull!"

The area had suddenly become a crime scene that must be preserved and systematically searched. The officers hustled out the excited Explorers. To gain access to the site where the bones were, Halleran used a chain saw to cut a narrow trail through the low branches.

A park ranger ran up, his face anguished. "You can't do that! This is a preserve!"

He debated with sheriffs and Belmont officers, who informed him that investigating a crime scene takes precedence over preservation of flora. Halleran sawed his way eighty feet up the hill.

By the end of the area search, the officers had photographed and recovered twenty-two scattered bones, mostly fragments; a pair of dark corduroy pants; a well-preserved T-shirt with the name of rock group Kansas written across it; and a jawbone a couple of yards from a skull. The meticulous evidence team, Mattei and Halleran, diagrammed the exact locations of each item.

When someone held up the T-shirt, light glinted through slashes in it.

Five years before, Farmer had taken the report of John Davies's disappearance and considered him a typical runaway. He felt both sad and relieved finally to know the truth.

Lisa Thomas had put herself mentally in a "do-the-job"

mode throughout the operation. Now, for the video camera, she pointed stonily to the skull that rested on a bed of dry leaves. *God,* she thought, *it's true, Dunkle really did it.*

Mattei saw the skull's radiating fractures and couldn't help thinking of the posters that showed John Davies's freckled, smiling face.

Chapter Thirty-four

Knowing nothing of events that unfolded after Dunkle transferred to the California Men's Colony, Joan Davies gave a keynote speech at a Missing Children's Conference in North Carolina. "My son is now believed to be the victim of a serial killer," she said, "but I still maintain a shred of hope that perhaps he is still alive."

A few days later, on September 30, Governor Deukmejian vetoed the California Missing Children's Act that had passed unanimously in the state legislature. He stated that he must protect California's finances.

Jim Davies and his organization, now called the Coalition for Missing and Exploited Children, immediately scheduled a protest press conference for October 10.

Jim sat in his cluttered study on Saturday, October 4, preparing for the news conference. Joan appeared at his door. "Jim, Chief Sanderson is on his way over."

There was only one reason Sanderson would come to their home.

Joan sat down heavily. A great, dark emptiness yawned within her. Even when she had recognized the composite drawing of Dunkle and cried, "He killed my son," even when she had asked Dunkle where to find the body, she'd still half believed John was alive. Her youngest, her baby, didn't die for her and Jim till the moment Sanderson sat in their living room and described Dunkle's map and how the searchers found what were probably John's remains. Jim and Joan couldn't take in the details as Sanderson said the means of death had not been determined and that dental comparisons had to be done to verify the victim's identity.

Joan's defense system of social obligation sprang into place like scaffolding. When a family member dies, duties must be performed. "I have to notify his brothers," she said. "They're overseas with the navy. I'll need to go through the Red Cross."

"Not yet," said Sanderson. "A leak could compromise the investigation. Don't tell anyone until I give you the go-ahead."

When the chief left, Joan still didn't know why John left the house the night he disappeared or how he died. She imagined, as she had since 1985, that Dunkle had stabbed and killed John swiftly in his car before leaving their driveway, a scenario in which John suffered little.

Jim followed Sanderson to the police department, where he looked at the slashed T-shirt with KANSAS emblazoned over the chest and nodded. "It's from the only rock concert he ever went to."

Though they understood the reason for it, Jim and Joan found Sanderson's demand for secrecy unbearable. For five years they had told reporters, "No pain is worse than not knowing." How could they silence the climax of such prolonged anguish?

Soon Jim reasoned that no harm would be done if he confided in out-of-staters. He contacted friends in ISEARCH, the Illinois organization whose representatives he and Joan had met at one of the national conferences. He also left a message for John Walsh.

On Sunday morning, Joan contacted Chief Sanderson, who said the dental X rays were still being studied and a forensic anthropologist had more work to do. He could not yet give her the official notification she needed in order to have the Red Cross bring Jimmy and Mark home.

She spent the morning outlining the public memorial service that she would announce when Sanderson permitted. Later that day, she rebelled. It was inconsiderate, no, it was damn cruel, to be forced to keep the news from the family. She telephoned Grandma Bell in Colorado, and Grandma McLean in Kansas.

On Monday morning, October 6, Joan went to work long enough for friends to crowd around and give her the hugs and tears and sympathy she so desperately needed.

Later that morning, she phoned Sanderson: Couldn't she *please* ask the Red Cross to send her boys home? Again he said the announcement would be premature.

Her loathing for the Belmont Police Department was now fully reborn.

Long before dawn that Monday morning, guards escorted Jon Dunkle and C. Louis out of California Men's Colony under heavy security. They climbed into a corrections department van with Wiley, another guard, and two sharpshooters, and headed for Sacramento. Dunkle had consented to be filmed on videotape while walking, shackled, through crime sites and places he had hidden the murder weapons.

According to the testimony and written narratives of numerous officers involved, it was planned that the walk-throughs would begin with only the prison guards, Louis, and FBI agents Hickey and Payne, people whom Dunkle knew and trusted.

However, when the van stopped in the parking lot of

the Denny's restaurant outside Sunrise Park, Dunkle looked out and saw Sheriff Bell. He burst into tears. "What's he doing here? I'm not talking!"

Different accounts exist about why Dunkle reacted so strongly to seeing Bell. According to law enforcement, the problem was Dunkle's hate for Sacramento and Belmont's law enforcement. "Jon did not want to deal with either the Belmont or the Sacramento police departments," Bell later testified, "because of all the work that had been done on him."

Dunkle had experienced a particularly strong relationship with Bell, had played cat-and-mouse with him, treated him as an admired father figure, and expressed hate for him. It looked like Dunkle, who couldn't stand humiliation, was deeply ashamed to give the truth to this particular officer.

Seeing that the confession was about to be blown, the officers hastened to repair the damage. FBI Agent Hickey, to whom Dunkle had taken a liking, gently explained it was necessary to speak to the local authorities because the crimes happened in their jurisdictions.

Bell sat with Dunkle and Louis in the van. Bell spoke kindly and encouragingly. "It's an important thing you're doing here, to come forward like this. It doesn't matter that you didn't do it with me. What matters is that you did it with someone."

Louis added his own words of encouragement, "You need to go ahead now, get it off your chest, and get some help."

Careful to make no promises, Bell answered Dunkle's questions about what would happen if he confessed, adding with sincerity, "I'm really proud of you, Jon, for what you're doing here."

After half an hour, Dunkle hung his head and nodded. He'd do it. They drove to the parking lot near the bike trail in Goethe Park and on camera Bell read Dunkle his rights and Dunkle again stated he did not want an attorney.

Dunkle guided the group from the parking lot down the wooded bike trail along the river. He pointed out a picnic table near a restroom, saying that was where he had sat alone after smoking pot and drinking beer with friends until about eight-thirty the night of July 2, 1985. It was here that he had seen Sean Dannehl ride past on his blue bike, wearing shorts and a soccer shirt, a cast on his right forearm. Leading the group down the trail, Dunkle indicated where he had rammed Sean's bike with his. Then he showed them the tree whose overhanging branches had concealed Sean's body for six days. Matter-of-factly, he described shoving the pipe-cleaning tool into Sean's heart.

Bell asked Dunkle about the Lance Turner murder weapon which he told Hickey he had hidden in Sacramento.

Dunkle told the camera, "It's a Puma knife with a four-inch-long black handle that's inlaid at both ends with chrome. There's markings on the blade from Lance's chest bones. I grinded it down to make it sharper." He said he first dumped the knife along the Sacramento River around November 24, about six weeks after he killed Lance. Later, he moved it to the Girl Scout camp where he'd wandered around drunk and wounded himself the night before Whaley and Deklinski were scheduled to meet with him. He had told the FBI agents he'd stuck the knife blade up in a picnic table and fallen on it in a suicide attempt, but stopped when he found out how much it hurt.

On video, he now said he threw the knife in someone's flower bed along the picturesquely named Thistlewood Drive in a Sacramento suburb.

The group traveled to Thistlewood. On film, Dunkle stood with Bell on the sidewalk and pointed across the street. "It's near the rear tire of that vehicle over there. I've made two attempts to find it and failed." He hung his head and glanced up at Bell with a shy smile, a chipmunk-cheeked boy, humble, seeking approval.

* * *

At four that afternoon, Jim Davies received a phone call from a Department of Justice official who had worked with Jim and coalition members on the California Missing Children's Act. Jim considered the man a walking computer: Since the state lacked a sophisticated tracking system at that time, the man kept his own file of three-by-five cards on violent criminals. Whenever one was paroled, he contacted law enforcement where the criminal went, describing the person and his MO.

"I just had to call you," the friend said. "It's so great that Dunkle confessed."

"How did you know?" Jim asked. "We were told to keep it under wraps."

"Hell, it's being shouted up and down the halls of the Department of Justice! Sacramento and Belmont are giving joint press conferences tomorrow afternoon."

Jim put down the receiver before he exploded. The news was all over Sacramento, yet he and Joan were forbidden to notify their own sons? It was just like what people said at the missing children's conferences: Victims are victimized forever.

Immediately, Joan called the Red Cross.

Chapter Thirty-five

The videotaping continued on Tuesday, October 7. In San Mateo County, Belmont Sergeants Farmer and Fogarty joined the CMC guards, Bell, Louis, and the FBI agents. Farmer's casual, friendly style was finally paying off; the young, handsome officer was the only one in Belmont whom Dunkle didn't despise. Fogarty, Goulart's replacement, had no history with Dunkle, so could participate as a neutral party.

Guarding the periphery at a distance, Mattei kept himself out of sight. Goulart and Lisa Thomas stayed away altogether. The sight of either of them could blow the confession.

With the camera running, Fogarty read Dunkle his rights and Dunkle repeated that he understood them and didn't want an attorney. Farmer read aloud what Dunkle had told the FBI about Lance Turner's murder, inwardly gratified that so many details of it matched the evidence and accounts by witnesses.

The statement said that on October 2, 1984, Dunkle left his parents' Belmont home at eleven-thirty in the morning and bought a six-pack of half-quart cans of Budweiser. He walked three times around Water Dog Lake, drinking. About two-thirty, he saw four boys on the pier drinking Henry Weinhardt beer. Then he wandered up to the smoking tree and sat in one of its branches, "stabbing" the bark. Two boys approached and one "took a piss. I told him to get the fuck out of there."

Then four girls came to the tree. One dug up a hidden pack of cigarettes and two matchboxes with wedding insignia on them. While Dunkle shared his beer with them and took a few hits from one girl's joint, he saw a "young man" jog past on the trail.

When the girls left, Dunkle walked back toward the lake, found the "young man," and asked for the time. Lance acted reluctant to talk with him, but said it was three-fifty. Then he passed Dunkle, walking away.

Dunkle reached around Lance from behind and stabbed him in the abdomen. Lance cried, "Why are you doing this?" Dunkle stabbed him in the left side and in the throat. Lance dropped onto his bottom, then threw himself onto his back, curling his legs up on his chest.

Farmer thought back to Lance's autopsy. There had been defense wounds on the backs of Lance's thighs, bruises and shallow cuts all over the body. Lance had fought bitterly. Dunkle's version, which Farmer continued to read aloud in a neutral voice, greatly understated the viciousness of the attack. Dunkle claimed he just clamped his hand over Lance's mouth and told him, "Calm down, relax. Straighten your legs out." When Lance obeyed, Dunkle thrust his knife into the boy's heart. Lance's teeth clamped down on Dunkle's thumb, drawing blood; later, the nail came off.

Lance's head tilted back and his eyes rolled up—"pritty blue eyes," Dunkle had called them in his "papers."

Dunkle dragged Lance's body into bushes off the trail. Then he went straight home, dropping his bloody shirt and tennis shoes in a garbage can four blocks from his parents' house.

Finished reading, Farmer said pleasantly, "Now, Jon, we haven't made any promises or threats, have we?"

"No." Dunkle agreed that the statement was accurate as read.

At 11:43, the group walked up Water Dog Lake trail. Dunkle commented that it looked different, but with an eager-to-please attitude, he pointed out where he attacked Lance and the exact spot where he hid the body. Standing by the shrubs that had concealed Lance, Dunkle hung his head, tucked in his lower lip, and peeked sadly up at the officers. Bell later described this moment: "He got kind of emotional. There were certain things that upset him. . . . He just got very quiet, despondent, and really withdrawn."

When he had pulled himself together, Dunkle went with them up to the smoking tree, its large, low branch parallel to the earth like a cozy bench. Unemotionally, he answered questions about the Steve Murphy hit-and-run, casually admitting he had rammed Steve deliberately. When Dunkle described loading Steve into the trunk of the car, Farmer asked, "Did you know he was badly hurt?"

"Oh, I heard him moaning and groaning." Dunkle shrugged.

Early that afternoon, the group arrived at the upper entrance to Edgewood Park. Farmer again carried the audiovisual camera on his shoulder. As he followed Dunkle's lead up the dirt road toward the hill with the lopsided shrub cover, he kept the camera running. The sound track picked up Farmer's harsh breathing and the crunch his shoes made in the dry dirt.

They stopped at the bottom of the hill. As if repeating a story told so often it had become rote, Dunkle described the night he brought John Davies to this spot. He said he spent Saturday, November 7, 1981, with John Wolfe and

Brian Loftis drinking Jack Daniel's and smoking dope. When his friends went home, "I was pretty well drunk and didn't want to stop partying."

He went to the Davies' home at 1:45 a.m., entered as usual through the unlocked front door, and went to John's room. He said he noted that John was high on LSD. When he invited John to go out to drink beer, John said, "Sure." On the way to Edgewood Park, Dunkle's car skidded off the road and it took him forty minutes of jockeying and bolstering it with a two-by-four to get it back onto the road.

When they reached the upper entrance to Edgewood Park, Dunkle wanted to walk with John to the place he called "the shooting range." At this point in his narrative, Dunkle began to shake his head. "I had a paring knife in the glove compartment," he said. "I got the knife out." The officers knew that in the statement to the FBI agents, he had said that when he took out the knife, he committed himself to kill John Davies. On camera he didn't say this, but went on, "We walked up the trail to the last mountain. Since the sixth grade, I had an urge to kill. I took the opportunity with John Davies. It wasn't him personally.

"So anyway, I stuck him in the back with the paring knife. John said, 'Get that stick out of my back. What are you doing?' I told him I was mad at his father for taking the gold (the jewelry Dunkle stole from Belmont Lapidary and gave to the Davies). I jumped back a ways and thought about what I was doing.

"I picked up a rock, twelve-or thirteen-inches around and slammed it in the left side of his head three times. I still didn't think he was dead, but he wasn't responsive. I pulled him over, I left him there on the slope.

"One week later I came back. The body was there and there were animals around. An animal had flesh in its mouth."

Still showing no outward emotion, Dunkle said that he went straight home after killing John, arriving at four or four-thirty in the morning. He said he put his bloody clothes in a grocery bag. He omitted a detail he'd given to agents Hickey and Payne: When he'd arrived home with John's blood on his pants, his father saw him and asked what he'd been doing.

Finished with the story, Dunkle led the group to the top of the hill, where he stopped on the trail. "This is where the incident occurred," he said. "This is where I stuck the knife in his back." Then, gesturing toward the slope where the Explorers had found John's bones two days earlier, Dunkle said, "Over there is where I left him."

Speaking directly to Farmer, or to the camera, he said with a nearly apologetic air, "I'm telling this because I need help." He seemed sincere until he caught Louis's eye and shared a giggle with his cellmate.

That evening Dunkle and Louis were brought back to their room at CMC. Dunkle sat on one side, Louis on the other. They stayed up all night and looked at each other. According to Louis, Dunkle made only one more significant remark before he was shipped to the San Mateo County Jail: "They'll never convict me. I'll commit suicide or I'll put on a crazy act."

When Jim Davies learned from his Department of Justice friend that the Sacramento and Belmont police departments had set up a press conference, he called Chief Sanderson and asked to be included. As Jim recalls, Sanderson denied that a conference was scheduled. Furious, Jim called a Sacramento reporter and learned the conference would take place in Belmont at four p.m. Tuesday, October 7.

Jim scheduled his own news conference for five.

* * *

At four-thirty, Tuesday afternoon, Mark Davies arrived at the San Francisco airport, feeling disoriented. Maybe he had dreamed all this up and was still supposed to be in Guam. The fact that his parents weren't there to meet him disconcerted him further. *What the hell's going on?* he thought, and called home.

"My God," said Jim, "we're headed out the door to a news conference." Jim talked on excitedly, conveying to Mark that they were somehow beating out the police. "Why don't you get a taxi and come to the house? No, come to the conference, it's at the Dunfey Hotel. No wait, you might say something to hurt the case. Hold on, we'll call the Press Club."

By now Mark had his wits about him enough to pull a guilt trip: "I intentionally didn't drink all the way home," he said. Jim arranged for Mark to run a tab at the Press Club bar. Mark called several friends to prepare them for what they would soon see on the news. Then he hit the bar and watched the press conference on TV.

Afterward, Jim and Joan arrived with Mike Murray of the Kevin Collins Foundation. Having bottled up their grief and rage for four days, Jim and Joan were ready to let off a lot of steam. "We closed down the bar," Mark recalls. "We had a hell of a time."

The *San Mateo Times* October 8 headline cried, DUNKLE "POSITIVELY LINKED" TO DEATHS OF TWO BELMONT YOUTHS. Beneath the large letters were the faces of Lance Turner and John Davies, long familiar to local people; a picture of Jim and Joan flanked by microphones, Jim angry, Joan pale and solemn; and an unsmiling photo of Dunkle. Large articles about the police announcement and the Davies' statement covered most of the page.

To highlight the human-interest angle, *San Mateo Times* reporter Heidi Van Zandt interviewed Jimmy and Mark in the Davies' living room on October 10.

Asked about Dunkle's personality, Jimmy felt baffled. How could an old friend be a murderer? He said he'd always known Dunkle was "abnormal" and lacked friends his own age, but added that he'd never sensed Dunkle was strange enough to commit murder. Jimmy did not mention the dark feeling it gave him to realize it was he who had introduced Dunkle to the family in the first place.

Mark told the reporter that though John was brainy, he lacked "street smarts." Mark's eyes filled as he repeated his old sense of guilt for not protecting John.

Ms. Van Zandt entitled her article THEY'VE COME HOME TO BURY SLAIN BROTHER.

Tragedy empowered Jim and Joan. The discovery of John's remains hit the front pages just three days before the coalition held its press conference to protest Deukmejian's veto of California's Missing Children's Act.

The Davies sat on a panel with Ann and David Collins, parents of Kevin Collins; Georgia Hilgeman, leader of the Vanished Children's Alliance; and Assemblyman Lou Papan, Democrat, San Mateo County.

As John Davies's father and president of the Coalition for Missing and Exploited Children, Jim was the primary speaker. Calling for the governor to explain his "outrageous" veto of this unanimously passed bipartisan legislation, Jim read aloud a letter from John Walsh that pointed out that thirty-three states had established missing children's clearing houses by then, yet California had not, despite its being a state in which a great deal of child exploitation occurred.

A few days later, Jim moderated a bipartisan news conference on the subject in Los Angeles.

* * *

The Davies held John's memorial service in the First Presbyterian Church in San Mateo on October 18. Here, too, they carried through the themes of both grief and dedication to the cause of missing children. Jim's speech included humorous anecdotes from John's early childhood—the time at age three he solemnly held up his lunch and said, "Here you have your basic turkey sandwich," and his reaction to meeting so many divorced people in California—"These are my original parents."

Grandma Bell spoke of her love for John and her deep grief for him and for his parents and brothers during the five-year ordeal. John Walsh had sent a vintage license plate, in memory of John's license-plate collection. It was worked into the giant wreath, which also held a Garfield the Cat stuffed animal, because John had loved cats.

The written program quoted the movie *Adam:* "If his song is to continue, we must keep singing." The back page listed over a dozen San Francisco Bay Area children still missing.

"We celebrate the end of this long ordeal," Jim said at the end. Alluding to his disappointment in other parents who abandoned the cause when their own children were found, he promised he and Joan would continue fighting.

Later that day, Mark walked up the slope to the section of Skylawn Cemetery where John's ashes would be placed. He held his camera to his eye, framed the sunlit, grassy hill and captured the peaceful scene.

Part Six

Madness vs. Evil
November 1986–
September 1998

Chapter Thirty-six

On October 13, 1986, while Jim Davies was moderating the bipartisan news conference, forensic psychiatrist James Missett, working for the prosecution, drove to San Luis Obispo to meet with Jon Dunkle at the Men's Colony. He had met Dunkle the week before, on the day the police announced the confessions. The interview had taken place in a small room at the Belmont Holiday Inn. Armed prison guards lined the walls, and Dunkle and Louis wore orange jumpsuits, handcuffs, and ankle shackles. The interview had been cut short when Dunkle's parents arrived, but Missett came away with the initial impression that Dunkle could speak coherently, possessed a high-school-level fund of information, comprehended his rights and was legally sane.

Now, at the Men's Colony, Missett conducted an interview under more normal conditions. No guards attended, Dunkle and Louis wore prison-issue jeans and shirts, and the unshackled inmates lounged around chain-smoking filter-free Camels.

After the first half hour, what Missett called Dunkle's

"sidelong glances and giggles" with Louis subsided. Eventually, Louis rose, brought in coffee, and removed himself to Wiley's office. Missett and Dunkle remained together three more hours.

Despite Missett's repeated reminders that speaking to him was like speaking to the DA, there is reason to believe that Dunkle imagined that this was the beginning of getting help. But Missett's function wasn't to help Dunkle: It was to determine if Dunkle was legally sane and had been so when he committed his crimes.

Legal sanity is a much misunderstood concept, partly because the words "psychotic" and "psychopathic" sound similar, yet carry different meanings. A psychotic person may be legally insane; a psychopath isn't.

A psychotic person commits murder while ruled by visual or auditory hallucinations or irresistible inner voices. He may believe the victim has tuned a radio in on his brain or is an extraterrestrial plotting against him. He may leave a wildly disordered crime scene and make no effort to hide his tracks because, and this is the key element, *he cannot distinguish right from wrong.*

On the other hand, a psychopath, AKA sociopath, has a character disorder. Antisocial impulses drive him, and his crimes apparently cause him little or no guilt. He may not be a killer; he could be a politician, a banker, a petty criminal, a charmer running cons on wealthy women. If he is a sexual sadist, he commits crimes such as mutilation or torture murders, which the public considers crazy. Unlike a psychotic person, the psychopath knows that society considers these acts wrong and he may derive great pleasure from outsmarting authorities. He is twisted and disturbed, but, for legal purposes, sane.

Since Missett's function was to determine legal sanity, his task didn't include a search for underlying causes. He didn't pursue Dunkle's hints about family violence, hearing voices, and being a misfit, nor did he allude to the learning disabilities. For people burning to know the *why* of Dunkle, Missett's thirty-six-page report gives chilling insights, yet frustrates.

Dunkle told Missett about hurting his head in an early childhood fall from an upstairs window and his "feeling" that his brother pushed him. He claimed he "got along fine with his older brother . . . and that Jeff never harmed, threatened, or touched him," though he had told friends and Louis that his brother abused him physically and sexually throughout childhood.

He did share with Missett the fact that Jeff was arrested at age twelve or thirteen for selling marijuana and went to Juvenile Hall. He said he himself used to report his brother to the police because things were better at home when Jeff was in "Juvy." He told Missett Jeff got him drunk at age ten on whiskey and cola.

Dunkle spoke of the bad period in his family that started when he was about nine, when his parents divorced. "Mr. Dunkle attributed his parents' separation to disagreement between them as to how they should respond to his older brother's drug and alcohol problems." His father was "very strict," while his mother was "much more permissive." Dunkle told Missett that his father said, "It's Jeff or me," and left.

Dunkle said that "he first became aware that he wanted to kill someone when he was in the sixth grade . . . [after] watching a movie that depicted an older boy with glasses who was going to kill a younger boy in a field because he thought the younger boy was going to show his father a diary" that referred to a lot of murders. To Dunkle, "the point of the movie was that the more the older boy killed, the more enjoyment he got out of it." Dunkle said that as a sixth grader, he called the Belmont Police and told them he felt like killing someone, though he hung up when the dispatcher asked his name.

He told Missett that in eighth grade he overheard deacons and elders at church saying, "Sometimes when people come to our church, they become murderers." He also said that in 1974 his age-seventeen cousin " 'blew his head off with a shotgun,' " though Dunkle claimed he himself was unaffected by this.

Regarding his substance abuse, Dunkle told Missett that as a teenager " 'I was paranoid I was going to get caught partying, so would go to Vista Points or other open spots . . . where [I] could throw away the beer or joints." If high at home, he would splash warm water on his face to have an excuse for being flushed.

He said he always mixed alcohol and marijuana. He would "get a good high" from three beers, but at the same time would "be mixed up and sad" if he had too much and would "hear another voice babbling away and telling me what to do" when he combined beer and pot. At such times, he'd go to the place in Edgewood Park he called the "shooting range" and shoot his .22. (This was the area where he later killed John Davies.) He told Missett he never heard voices when sober.

Speaking about his relationship with the Davies, Dunkle focused on how their reaction to his drinking differed from his parents'. "Between 1978 and 1981, I would go over to their house and would drink with Mr. Davies." He said that in February 1981, he got drunk and blacked out and "was all mixed up . . . [about] what he said to Mr. Davies when the latter came home."

Leading up to the John Davies murder, Dunkle spoke about Youth With A Mission. "I was on a high for two weeks until I got off the train in Oregon and it was clear that I was going to have to earn it [missionary status]." He said that he quit and visited the Davies in October 1981. There he felt "pissed-off and disappointed" because Mark put "derogatory stuff" about him in the computer. Dunkle said he then went to Sacramento, where he had "only three Christian friends" and met a woman who told him he would either be in prison or dead by 1986.

Dunkle said that about a week before killing John Davies, he drank whiskey and snorted cocaine with Mark and John

Davies. In the version he gave Missett, he didn't mention spending the day of the murder with friends at the beach, getting drunk, and not wanting to stop partying; however, this information appeared in his written confession. His description of going into the Davies' home, asking John out, and proceeding with the murder matched the confession, but he added details that impressed Missett with their sadism:

"I thought to myself, You've got someone out in the middle of nowhere and here's your chance to kill someone. You've thought of killing before. I stabbed him once in the back. I was actually afraid to do it.

"He said, 'Get that stick out of my back.' He turned around and asked, 'Why did you put that stick in my back?'. . . . I told him, 'I'm going to kill you.' He asked, 'Why?' Then he started screaming. I told him, 'Scream all you want.' Then I stabbed him in the lower throat area. That didn't do any good, so I strangled him with my hands with the knife still in my hands. He stopped breathing for a while. . . . I jumped back and asked myself if I really wanted to do this, but I had told him I was going to kill him. Then I took a rock and hit him three times on the right side of his skull. . . . I saw about six to eight months later a four-inch diameter hole in his skull. I prayed for him to go to heaven."

Dunkle described visiting the body later, its look and smell, the animals tearing at it. He said he moved it and returned years later when only scattered bones remained.

Premeditation was also obvious when Dunkle described his New Year's Eve, 1982, attack on Monti Hansen. Dunkle had friends at his home. "We had beer and pot. I got crazy thoughts. I had my Buck knife on me. The thought was that I wanted to hurt someone. I had an urge. I was bored and not enjoying myself at this party with a nice steak dinner between 10 PM and 11 PM. Then I drove to Monti Hansen's house. . . . I had a one-foot-long sledge hammer in my trunk. I had on my vest and my Pinkerton jacket without the badges. I put the hammer into the vest. . . . I picked Hansen because I didn't know him that well and knew he was going to be alone. . . .''

Shorter term premeditation appeared when he spoke of the Steve Murphy hit-and-run. ''I don't know why I did it. Before I hit him, I deliberately did it. I didn't want to kill him after I put him in the car. I figured that, if someone saw it, they would think I was helping him. . . . I thought he was just hurt a little. He was still moving around even when I left him. I could hear him moaning and groaning. . . . I went back three days later to look for glass.''

He repeated to Missett his fabrication that he had been a spy for the IRS and described scams he observed.

He revealed a bit of his inner self when speaking of the day of Lance Turner's murder. When he hung out with the eighth-grade girls at the smoking tree, he ''had no thought of killing them. I just wanted them to leave. . . . I asked if they knew a Mr. Smith, who was a counselor. . . . I had talked to Mr. Smith every day because I was hyper and confused as to what was going on between my Dad and my brother. I was then almost proud of what my brother did against my Dad.'' Dunkle did not elaborate, but he was alluding to the physical fights between his father and brother, which his brother was winning. ''The girls left, I got dizzy. Lance ran by from a distance. . . . I ran or walked toward the lake but felt an urge to talk with someone. I also wanted to talk with no one. I was lonely, but drinking alone. The girls were too young to be my friends. I walked towards the school to see if I could find someone to talk to.''

Though in his confessions he said he deliberately followed or searched for Lance after first seeing him, with Missett he indicated he simply chanced upon him again: ''Walking up the hill in the ravine area, I heard something and this boy stopped a little over five feet away.''

After describing the murder, Dunkle spoke of the twisted emotions accompanying it: ''I have the same feeling now as when I asked him for the time. It's almost like the excitement at a haunted house, a scary feeling like from the visit to the old cancer hospital at Edgewood and 280, a high or excitement. I always enjoyed going there.... Another place was at the foot of La Honda, where Doug introduced me to Brian. Brian would say that the birds are talking to us. He would say, 'The birds act like they came up from the dead.' Then we went up to this house with a pellet gun and found long hair with fresh blood still on it...."

He revealed how dangerous he was to children, how constantly he had the urge to kill, after being released on bail for the Renne burglary. He harassed young boys on the park trails by the American River, the same general area where he later killed Sean Dannehl. Once he threw the bikes of two young boys down a hill. He tried to drag the boys into the river, then tried to strangle one, but stopped because too many people were nearby. "I just felt like doing something maybe somebody did to me," he said cryptically, and was not asked to explain.

He said another time he flattened the tires of two boys' bikes with his knife, then chatted with the boys, who didn't realize it was he who had done it. "I could have done anything to them. One was about ten and the other about eleven. I know I was drinking beer heavily that day. The kids were very friendly."

Missett apparently didn't ask Dunkle about events or emotions that led to Sean's murder, though it is known that he drank and smoked pot with acquaintances who grew irritated with him and left while he was in the men's room. "I was dizzy on dope with my feet on the ground but my knees up. I don't know if there were weird thoughts or not. I saw Sean go by on his bike and I knew I was going to kill him. I just had the urge to kill him."

As in his confessions, he said he chased Sean and knocked him off his bike. Dunkle told Missett, as he'd told others, that because Sean was cooperative, he had to humiliate him by making him take his clothes off. He claimed that Sean, like Lance, asked when stabbed, "What are you doing? You said you wouldn't hurt me." Again sadism came out: "I stabbed him in the heart and twisted the pick around. He looked like he was dead. I wanted to see if he was faking it, so I put my pick to each eye and pushed in, but there was no movement. . . . Sean died the quickest."

Missett concluded that Dunkle was fascinated with death and enjoyed hurting others and watching them suffer as he killed them. He also enjoyed surprising victims with his attacks. "There is also a masochistic aspect to these sadistic elements in Mr. Dunkle's personality," Missett observed, noting that Dunkle admitted that the night before Whaley and Deklinski visited him in Sacramento, he jammed his knife upright in a crack in a picnic table and fell on the blade. " 'I wanted to feel pain," he confided, "like the pain John had."

Missett believed Dunkle killed for thrills, excitement, and power: "This apparent reveling in a feeling of power over others may well have been a reaction on his part to feelings of helplessness and powerlessness in terms of his being able by himself to gain respect and responsiveness from others. His apparent emphasis on having feelings of power over others seems to be evidenced by his surprising of his victims. . . ."

Dunkle's enjoyment of inflicting psychological as well as physical pain, in particular with his deliberate humiliation of Sean Dannehl, indicated he was a sexual sadist.

Missett also pointed out that the number of stab wounds on Lance Turner suggested a symbolic sexual assault, as did Dunkle's putting the pick into each of Sean's eyes.

Missett noted that Dunkle clearly knew his acts were wrong and showed considerable skill in evading detection. He argued that though Dunkle knew that combining alcohol and marijuana released his urges to commit violence, he didn't stop using them, though once, when on probation for his DUIs, he'd allegedly quit substance abuse for almost a year. "He would thus seem to have been able to moderate his use of alcohol and marijuana when he saw it as being in his best interest. . . . In some ways, this would seem to increase the level of his conscious responsibility for his later killing of Lance Turner and Sean Dannehl in that he was certainly by mid-1983 aware of any claimed impact of marijuana and alcohol on his sensorium and its connection with acts of violence on his part."

Also, Missett noted that Dunkle showed absolutely no remorse for the murders.

All of these factors led Missett to the inescapable conclusion that Dunkle was "an extremely sociopathic and unremorseful individual who killed repeatedly for the thrill and excitement of doing so." And, the clincher for the prosecution: though Missett suggested psychological and brain evaluations to eliminate possible "organic" factors, he stated, "I found nothing in my evaluation of Mr. Dunkle to indicate that he was at the time of his [crimes] mentally ill."

Dunkle was a psychopath. Legally sane.

Yet, by the middle of the next year, he was on a psychiatric ward saying his mind was controlled by laser beams, police radar, and other powers.

Chapter Thirty-seven

When the justice system moved Dunkle to the San Mateo County Jail the end of October 1986, about three weeks after he walked through the crime sites and confessed on videotape, he was still riding a wave of euphoria.

He wrote an enthusiastic thank-you note to Officer Mike Wiley, telling the security squad officer at the Men's Colony he had been a "grate" help. To Detective Bob Bell in Sacramento, he dispensed self-important advice about the need for less "glair" in interrogation rooms so suspects could be more comfortable. He went on that officers needed to show they cared about victims and families, like Detective Joe Farmer, who Dunkle said had taken off his sunglasses and revealed tears in his eyes, after which Dunkle "cryed" for a long time.

Like a child who doesn't know when to stop showing off, Dunkle told his new cellmate in county jail about the murders. But this companion was no C. Louis. He was a young, light-weight offender who loved and protected his younger brothers. Before long, he blew up, stabbed Dunkle with a pencil, and demanded to be moved to the opposite end of the jail.

Dunkle also wrote incessantly about wanting psychiatric help. Normally inmates are not allowed to correspond with each other, but officials hoped Dunkle would further incriminate himself. In letters to Louis, he confided that he was writing down his thoughts for a psychiatrist. He alluded to what he called "patterns" that started by the time he was ten and blamed them for his troubles with reading and writing, though his next statement was that all this was the "schol's falt!"

He wrote that he committed no murder between 1981 and 1984 because there was "no pressher." (Apparently, he didn't think the Steve Murphy near-murder or his attack on Monti Hansen in the intervening years counted as murder attempts.) From 1984 on, "lots of pressher," plus something he described as a force controlling his body, the "kill Jon" related to what he referred to as the 1977 July "defect" that left him "remote" to emotions. This "defect" was an overdose and its aftereffects.

He told Louis that the killing part of his "disorder" began when he saw the murder movie in sixth grade, and also from something his father said when Dunkle was in the eighth grade, but he wouldn't write down what his father's remark was. Dunkle said that since then he'd been ill and no one could help him.

It was while Dunkle was in this frame of mind that his former school counselor, Robert Kauk, visited him.

The sight of his ex-student in orange jumpsuit and shackles caused Kauk physical pain. The teddy-bearish counselor had, in years past, given fatherly comfort to Dunkle during Dunkle's rages and crying fits.

"You tried to tell me and I didn't understand," Kauk said sadly, referring to the times Dunkle had come to Kauk's office saying, "John Davies is dead and buried where no one will find him." Kauk had lived away from the Bay Area from early 1982 till January 1985. On his return, he'd been appalled to recognize Dunkle in the composite drawing of Lance Turner's killer.

"I'm trying to understand myself," Dunkle told him, complaining that after Missett, no psychiatrist had seen him since he had confessed.

Kauk had always responded to Dunkle's neediness and, like other Belmont folks, he longed to understand the *why* of Dunkle's crimes. An educational psychologist, Kauk didn't have psychiatric training, but he did have Dunkle's trust and a strong desire to help.

Dunkle and Kauk agreed that Kauk would conduct in-depth interviews which would lead to a book. Kauk threw himself into research and prolonged, intense sessions with Dunkle and Dunkle's family. Later Kauk gave these rough notes to police.

Kauk wondered if Dunkle were a multiple personality, so much did the sweet boyish persona differ from the glassy-eyed, sadistic murderer.

For the rest of the year, Dunkle bragged in letters about "my book writer."

In spring 1987, as the furor over Dunkle's confessions shifted into tedious legal preparations, Dunkle tried to prolong the thrill confession had brought. He wrote to officers about alleged unknown murders. He claimed to know of a "dangerous suspect—Fake CIA" who killed people near Edgewood Park in 1974–1975, and that he knew this because he just happened to be there at the time. When guards shook down Dunkle's cell, they found compulsively drawn maps of roads and trails and notes in capital letters about the FBI, Feds, local maps, and demands that no attorneys come.

As the May 1987 preliminary hearing approached, Dunkle's strangeness escalated. He accused Jim Davies, Jr., and public defender Vince O'Malley of multiple undiscovered murders and claimed that bodies were buried under specific Belmont street corners. He began ascribing magical significance to police codes, badge numbers, and birthdays, and said devices like police car computers were controlling his mind. He grew despondent, writing to Louis that he might kill himself and that God no longer spoke to him. He asked Louis if God spoke to him.

During the preliminary hearing, in which the lurid details of the confession were made public for the first time, the court ordered that Dunkle undergo a psychiatric evaluation at Chope Hospital (now San Mateo General). Dr. George Wilkinson, psychiatrist, testified later that during that evaluation, Dunkle "was floridly, openly psychotic and uncontrollable in the jail setting. It's a sort of psychotic behavior that one diagnoses from across the street. . . . Most people would look at him and say, 'This guy is crazy.' "

The hospitalization and its diagnosis of "atypical psychotic disorder" gave Dunkle's public defenders Vince O'Malley and Phillip Barnett grounds to seek a psychiatric defense and/or to find Dunkle incompetent to stand trial, though the DA argued that Dunkle was simply malingering.

While lawyers argued, Dunkle remained in jail, his apparent mental deterioration continuing.

Dunkle's confession to John Davies' murder did not end the Davies' struggles with the system which Jim had publicly characterized as insensitive and cumbersome. Joan's request for John's death certificate "was another giant fuckup, somebody not moving some piece of paper. All we wanted was the lousy two thousand dollars of insurance to pay for the memorial service. Didn't those people have any compassion? Look what we went through for five years, and all we wanted was to file this lousy little insurance claim."

The coroner couldn't release the death certificate Joan needed until the police filed a report defining cause of death. The DA refused to put the cause of death into the public record prior to Dunkle's preliminary hearing due to "the sensitive nature of the confession." Postponements delayed this hearing until May 1987, more than six months after John's remains were found.

Jim and Joan didn't know what the DA's office meant by "the sensitive nature of the confession." The information they received when they met with Chief Sanderson and Sergeant Mattei didn't seem to require secrecy.

"I hope you can tell me he didn't suffer," Joan told them. "I couldn't stand it if he suffered. He was such a hypochondriac."

"The indentation on the skull indicates he was hit on the head with a heavy object," Sanderson said. "He might have been stabbed."

"How can you tell, if there was nothing left to show stab wounds?"

"There was a nick in the breastbone. That could be from a knife or from animals."

Joan said later, "I kept asking, is that all, is that all? And they said, yes. It's as if they believed I couldn't handle the reality."

Carefully providing only information that could be confirmed by physical evidence, the police didn't tell her Dunkle had described stabbing John in the back, knocking him down, beating him on the head with the rock, and then trying to strangle him. They also omitted Dunkle's alleged visits to the body. Joan learned these horrible details when the general public did, in open court during the preliminary hearing. When she heard that Dunkle told John, "Scream all you want, no one can hear you," she burst into tears under the alert eyes of reporters, providing juicy copy for that evening's articles.

The Davies were well aware that such thoughtlessness was a victims' rights issue. They informed the DA's office that they expected better treatment in the future. DA Wagstaffe made it a point, in the many future legal proceedings with Dunkle, to prepare the Davies and Lance Turner's mother for any painful testimony, at times requesting a recess to give them time to leave the courtroom.

Though Jim and Joan considered truth, no matter how awful, better than the endless speculation, it took Joan years to cope with the full content of the confessions and Missett's report. Some details kept slipping her mind and returning. For years, she periodically insisted that John died quickly in the front seat of Dunkle's car.

Other elements broke her heart. "When I heard that John asked Dunkle, 'Why are you poking me with that stick?' I thought, that's just like John, so naive and childlike. But I'll *never* believe John walked all that way up the trail willingly in his stocking feet. He had such touchy feet."

In the July 1987 Missing Children's Conference in Chicago, she mentioned these issues in a workshop called "Parent Victim: Family Emotional Needs." Later she and Jim participated in a longitudinal study, headed by psychiatrist Chris Hatcher, on the emotional impact that violent deaths and disappearances have on families.

During the same time period—1987 and 1988—Joan served on a Federal Juvenile Justice advisory committee on missing children.

A month before a preliminary hearing on the Steve Murphy hit-and-run, Dunkle's madness escalated again. In early October 1987, his attorneys requested all police records pertaining to family violence in the Dunkle home as "these relate to defendant's mental condition."

Detective Fogarty, head of the BPD Detective Bureau, visited Dunkle by invitation. "Don't read me my rights," insisted Dunkle. "No tape recorders."

"I need to take notes, at least," said Fogarty.

Dunkle grudgingly consented. "I know about two FBI agents and a probation officer who got killed in 1970," he whispered, and rattled off numbers he claimed were police codes.

"Those don't make sense," said Fogarty. "Are you okay? Are you taking your meds?"

"No. They make me slow."

"Why are you so thin?"

Dunkle shrugged. "I don't feel like eating."

A week later, Dunkle phoned BPD Patrol Officer Harnish, who had been one of the officers at the Steve Murphy scene. Dunkle asked Harnish about hand-held radar equipment and babbled about the FBI, CIA, and Air Force Security. "My lawyers are getting all these dumb fucks," he railed. "They all want to say I'm crazy and hearing voices, and I know I'm not crazy. I want that police department psychiatrist, Hugh [Ridelhuber]."

The Steve Murphy hearing had to be canceled. Dunkle again fit the description of "floridly psychotic."

Dunkle's inner darkness, bottomless pit dependency and periods of madness wore down his earnest "book writer." Taking advantage of his father's phone credit card and the jail's liberal phone policies, Dunkle phoned the Kauk residence constantly, upsetting Mrs. Kauk, who was in the early stages of a progressive illness. Then Kauk himself underwent cardiac surgery.

Kauk finally had to drop the book project. The experience had been so painful that he gave away all his notes, unduplicated, to a private detective working for an anti-death penalty organization. When interviewed a few years later, Kauk stated that a recent stroke left him unable to remember much of what Dunkle had told him. Like community members, law enforcement personnel, and anyone else close to the murdered boys, he became one of the multitude of the killer's secondary victims.

* * *

In December 1987, Jim Davies spoke at a conference entitled "ENOUGH." During his talk, he mentioned that the DA had neglected to notify them that Dunkle had again been 5150'd—put on a seventy-two-hour psychiatric hold as danger to self or others—and transferred to the locked psychiatric unit at the county hospital, which meant the murder trial had to be postponed. First Dunkle had to have a competency hearing.

Jim feared that Dunkle would keep going crazy and avoiding trial for the rest of his life.

Chapter Thirty-eight

The slow progress toward the competency hearing tried everyone's patience, including Dunkle's. When the hearing was postponed from January 1988 till April, Dunkle wrote letters referring to himself in the third person and accusing his attorneys of wanting to put him in mental hospitals and go to court every three or four months to tell "lys" about him.

Then he phoned Detective Bell in Sacramento and rambled disconnectedly. "My attorneys are running scams. I know about thirty murders, but no one will listen. Radar waves from Russia are getting in my brain—"

Bell interrupted. "Jon, I'm real disappointed. When we talked before, you admitted the murders, period. You didn't try to put them off elsewhere."

Dunkle hung up.

When at long last attorneys and interested parties like Jim Davies and Margo Turner, Lance's mother, gathered in the courtroom on April 9, the defense had to request yet another postponement: Dunkle had chicken pox. District Attorney Steve Wagstaffe told reporters how frustrated he was, saying he'd like to blame someone but whom could he blame for giving Dunkle the chicken pox?

On May 16, cured of chicken pox, Dunkle made it to court. Both sides waived a jury and squared off to lay their opposing arguments about Dunkle's competency before Judge Bulhoffer. For the court's purposes, competency meant that the defendant must comprehend the charges and their possible consequences, act in his own best interest, and work with his attorneys. The competency issue differs from the insanity defense, in which the defendant's attorneys try to prove him not guilty because he was legally insane—did not know the difference between right and wrong—when he committed his crimes. Neither side would ever allege that that was the case with Dunkle. Today's hearing was only to determine whether he was capable of going to trial.

Within minutes, it became clear that Dunkle and his attorneys, Barnett and O'Malley, were at odds.

D.A. Wagstaffe: I request that Mr. Dunkle be reexamined by Dr. Missett.

Defense Barnett: I'm not prepared to consent to that.

Dunkle: I am.

Barnett: Here we go.

Barnett pointed out that Dunkle was currently 5150'd and should have his psychotropic medication stopped "so we can see his true condition."

Dunkle said, "I want to be off it, too."

The judge refused. The battle of the experts began. Both sides presented experts who normally testified for the opposite team. All of them considered Dunkle both mentally ill and deliberately manipulative; the main difference between the sides was how they interpreted and weighed these elements.

Dr. William Horstman, a licensed clinical psychologist,

defined himself an expert in assessing competency versus insanity. Speaking today for the defense, he stated that he testified twice as often for the prosecution than for the defense.

Horstman had conducted nine interviews with Dunkle between February and May, reviewed Dunkle's medical and psychiatric records, and performed psychological testing with him.

One test used a competency tool with twenty-two test items on it, with possible scores from forty-four to zero. A score below twenty indicated incompetence.

"Mr. Dunkle scored six," Horstman testified. Dunkle lacked basic legal concepts, he said. "He thinks the DA is his friend and protector."

The Rorschach (ink blot) test supported this conclusion, Horstman added. "The Rorschach will show you whether or not a person has an underlying thought disorder, whether or not they are psychotic . . . or trying to malinger." The Rorschach revealed that Dunkle had a chronic thought disorder.

Horstman did not believe this degree of illness could be faked and cited twelve published experiments demonstrating that only fifty percent of graduate students in psychology could fake psychotic symptoms.

He described Dunkle's recent bizarre behavior: setting fires in his cell, continually talking to himself, unresponsive to high doses of medication. An hour and a half after being given a strong antipsychotic injection, Dunkle was still "incoherent, out of control," said Horstman. "He thought I had a gun in my briefcase and dove for it."

Horstman noted that Dunkle got worse when trial dates approached. "Over the past three months, he has been progressively sicker. In February 1988, he was marginally competent, with delusions about his attorney. Now he is worse. He has delusions about his family and his defense attorneys. He thinks that his attorneys are in organized crime and killed someone at Water Dog Lake."

Horstman therefore concluded that Dunkle was "a highly disturbed, thinly defended individual with a paranoid core, who is also hostilely and consciously manipulating the court system and the people within it."

During testimony, Dunkle complained that his eyes were burning, possibly a medication reaction. The judge called a recess.

During the break, Jim Davies chatted with reporters about how Americans "coddle" criminals. Lance Turner's mother told reporters she couldn't believe the last person her son saw in life was Dunkle. She commented that Lance would have been sixteen the following week. With his birthday and Mother's Day both falling in May, this was a very difficult month for her, and she visited Lance and John (at the cemetery) all the time.

The next day, forensic psychiatrist George Wilkinson followed Dr. Horstman on the stand. Testifying for the prosecution, he stated that he more often testified for the defense. He had reviewed over a thousand pages of police and medical records, spent many hours with Dunkle, and had wrestled hard with the question of Dunkle's competence.

"I think it's more likely than not that Mr. Dunkle is competent," Wilkinson testified. "However, the scales are very closely balanced, with just the slightest leaning toward competence." He felt Dunkle comprehended the role of the court and attorneys; he also found Dunkle "manipulative and subverting," both by "design and disorder."

Diagnostically, Wilkinson found Dunkle to present a "mixed and difficult picture. He wants to be found competent and is mad at his attorneys about this issue." He believed that Dunkle had an antisocial personality disorder (i.e., he was a psychopath) with transient psychotic episodes and that he was *also* a chronic paranoid schizophrenic.

"When I saw him floridly psychotic," said Wilkinson, "I don't think he could successfully get on the bus."

Wilkinson told the court that he had met with Dunkle the evening before and Dunkle told him he wanted to change his plea from not guilty to no contest. "He just wants to get this over with." Dunkle's understanding of the consequences of no contest was that he "might get sent to California Men's Colony for seven years, talk to some psychiatrists, and then get sent to the gas chamber."

The judge ruled that the request to change the plea required a separate hearing.

DA Wagstaffe emphasized Dunkle's calculated manipulativeness and apparent malingering rather than his mental illness. He called in jail employees who testified that in jail Dunkle didn't talk about the FBI or the CIA, though he did write letters to them, and that he dropped his wild behavior when he thought no one was watching. A female deputy sheriff who transported inmates testified that she'd seen Dunkle sitting on his haunches on the van's bench, alone, talking to himself, but stopped when she said, "Knock this shit off."

When Dr. George Missett took the stand, he supported the prosecution one hundred percent. To him, Dunkle's diagnosis was clear as ice. "There are overwhelming indications of sociopathy. . . . He is fascinated with killing, the enjoyment of hurting others, enjoyment of surprising them and of their injuries; he is manipulative; there is the thrill aspect; he is boastful."

Missett pointed out that when he interviewed Dunkle shortly after the confessions, there were no delusions.

"I regard their sudden appearance [delusions] as being suspicious in the extreme and highly unlikely in actuality. . . . There is nothing about Mr. Dunkle that surprises me." He stated that he did not find the Chope Hospital psychiatric records "convincing of delusions. They jump around—Mafia, CIA, lasers." He examined a letter written by Dunkle and said, "It looks psychotic, but the delusions jump around. If he is not psychotic, he is jerking a chain."

Dr. Charles Casella, a psychiatrist, was called. He stated

he had reviewed medical and psychological reports and had met Dunkle but found the case "complex and contradictory." He wanted to meet more with Dunkle before rendering an opinion.

The attorneys argued about this until the judge called a halt: "This is all in the record, and we're starting to loosely associate here."

The next day the judge declared Dunkle competent.

Around the same time as Dunkle's competency hearing, Mark Davies was participating in a Victim's Panel at an Ohio Kids in Crisis conference.

A lot had happened to Mark since Dunkle confessed, ending John's five-year disappearance and allowing the Davies to grieve and to reorganize their lives. For Mark, truth had proved a catalyst. He plunged into a final drinking crisis, but then joined AA again. In May 1988, when he stood to speak at the Ohio conference, he had achieved a year of sobriety and insight.

Mark told the Ohio audience that his family was normal until John disappeared. "I became a rebel for the cause. I was a derelict teen trying to get stopped by cops to make them know who John was. I ran from my feelings of hurt, frustration, confusion, and helplessness by drinking heavily, to hide these feelings from myself. . . . I hated it when people said, 'I know how you feel.' They *don't*. . . .

"I held on to John as hard as I could. I was prepared for him dying, but I was also prepared to see him alive. I'd carried him around like a crutch. Poor me. After another year, I decided not to carry John around anymore. Begged God to take John from me. I didn't want to carry him anymore." Finally he'd gone alone to a lake and screamed at John to go away.

"When I learned that my brother was killed by our family's close friend, I asked myself what did I do wrong to make him kill my brother?"

Dr. Chris Hatcher, who had organized the panel as an outgrowth of his study of families of missing and murdered children, put his hand on Mark's shoulder. "This is a milestone for Mark. This was his first time public speaking about his experience. His father is here in the front row."

Dunkle's attorneys scheduled a Marsden hearing (a hearing about a defendant's wish to plead guilty) on June 17, 1988. Within minutes, Dunkle interrupted proceedings: "How about this organized crime paying for this?"

When Judge Bulhoffer told him to be quiet, Dunkle responded, "I hope organized crime kills you, sir."

Bulhoffer ordered the courtroom cleared.

Dunkle then announced he wanted to discharge his attorneys. "O'Malley killed a patrolman. I'd like to plead guilty on the charges instead of having my lawyers try to indict me into a hospital or for their two hundred seventy-five thousand dollars that they are getting from the organized 432, even though they are the FBI, San Mateo County or maybe the CIA. . . . When was the last time you looked in the mirror, sir?"

"Anything more you'd like to tell me?" asked Bulhoffer.

Dunkle kept ranting about himself in the third person. "You still feel you are doing justice within Jon Dunkle's society?" he asked the judge. "Trying drug head? Make sure you're paid for all the wrong drugs you have been giving Mr. Dunkle—"

Barnett interjected, "It appears that Mr. Dunkle thinks we are operating against his interests."

Dunkle was just getting started. "Are you going to fire these two assholes, or these two gentlemen, should I say, that you call, or what do you call them, faggots? Aren't you a faggot homosexual, Vince O'Malley? Or does that make me insane to state something to such effect? . . . They didn't do their proper duty, when they come and see me on visits, Justice. They don't instruct me on the proper law instructions. They try to psych me out. . . . I am trying to get the hell out of this country. . . . They don't give me no proper legal material. I have not received hardly but one time, legal documents.''

He blathered on till the abused Vince O'Malley said, ''I think this is so incoherent that I don't believe in my own mind that Mr. Dunkle is even competent to proceed with the Marsden motion.''

Bulhoffer told Dunkle, ''There is no reason to discharge your attorneys.''

Dunkle responded, ''This is a bunch of shit right here! This judge—''

Barnett again questioned Dunkle's competence.

DA Wagstaffe argued that, based on precedent, ''merely the continuance of certain behavior by itself'' didn't justify another competence hearing. ''Instead, there must be something new to create cause to allow for another one. Otherwise, defense attorneys could forever hold up the proceedings merely by stating they have a doubt.''

Bulhoffer agreed. ''I think it's correct. Otherwise, we are going to have to go through [competency] proceedings for the rest of our lives.''

''Just the past weekend, a psychologist determined that Dunkle is completely incompetent,'' argued Barnett.

Dunkle butted in. ''I am pleading guilty to the crime. I don't need two dump-truck lawyers to tell me that. I don't need some lawyers to throw me in some hospital in Folsom Prison.''

O'Malley spoke with lawyerly reasonableness: ''If the court doesn't agree that Mr. Dunkle is at this moment incompetent, then I would suggest that it must agree that there is some breakdown in the attorney-client relationship.''

The judge did *not* agree.

Dunkle's tantrum continued. ''Why should I even cooperate with you? Just send me to the Goddamn hospital and I'll be assassinated, Vince, by thirty-two along with

President Reagan, along with Tom Wilson. We're all going to be dead anyway."

Bulhoffer again cleared the courtroom and returned to the Marsden motion. When O'Malley repeated that the attorney-client relationship was bad, Dunkle said, "No shit. I can't stand these two clowns."

"There you are," said O'Malley.

Dunkle then announced that he wanted to defend himself. Bulhoffer lectured him about the charges against him, then asked, "Do you understand that if you represent yourself, you cannot enter a plea of guilty in this charge?"

"Say what?"

"You would have to go to trial."

This was not what Dunkle wanted to hear. "I think I better talk to a better judge. You assign me to someone else."

Bulhoffer determined that Dunkle could not represent himself, but he finally allowed Dunkle to fire his attorneys and be appointed a new one.

The preliminary hearing about the Steve Murphy hit-and-run case, and the murder trial itself, now faced interminable delays.

Dunkle's new attorney, Douglas Gray, wouldn't let him plead guilty either, so within a month, Dunkle demanded to fire him, too. He and Gray appeared before Judge Bulhoffer. Gray explained to Bulhoffer that it would be improper to let Dunkle plead guilty because "Mr. Dunkle doesn't wish to discuss legal things with me," and "a defendant pleading guilty must knowingly and intelligibly" waive his rights to a public trial and examination of witnesses, intellectual feats of which Gray considered Dunkle incapable.

When Bulhoffer denied Dunkle's request, Dunkle shouted, "You tell me I have to keep this guy . . . ?" Before he lapsed into profanity, a bailiff hustled him out of the courtroom.

Outside, Gray spoke candidly to reporters, admitting that the case was "indefensible" in terms of the facts; he said he could see absolutely no defense. However, he said he would continue to defend Dunkle anyway, despite Dunkle's dislike for him. He indicated that he could care less. He didn't waste energy worrying about whether or not his clients liked him.

In August 1988, Dunkle returned to the psychiatric unit with the diagnosis of atypical psychosis with delusions.

In September, Gray noted that his client had deteriorated further. Dunkle rambled madly, wouldn't eat or bathe, refused medication, and couldn't be farther from cooperating with his attorney.

When the January 1989 trial date arrived, Gray requested a further postponement due to the clear need for updated psychiatric evaluations. Judge Judith Kemp appointed three psychiatrists to evaluate Dunkle for the court. Two of them—Charles Casella and George Wilkinson—already knew Dunkle; the third, Roland Levy, went in cold, without studying any of Dunkle's records, as he believed in judging patients in the moment.

Dunkle refused to meet with Casella, who asked Judge Kemp not to refer him again to this defendant.

Dr. Levy reported to the judge that Dunkle's mental illness was genuine, not feigned.

Dr. Wilkinson faced an ethical conflict. He now believed Dunkle was utterly incompetent and felt morally and professionally obligated to counter his 1988 testimony for the prosecution that Dunkle was "51%" competent. He wrote to Judge Kemp that Dunkle was "more disabled than before," and was changed enough to justify another competency hearing. Though facing harsh criticism as "the doctor who changed horses in midstream," Wilkinson followed his conscience and crossed over to the defense.

In February 1989, Dunkle returned again to the psychiatric unit, and in a March hearing, Judge Kemp "vacated" another trial date so that psychiatric workups could be done for a new competency hearing.

"I don't think I need any more doctors, lady!" shouted Dunkle, one of his many outbursts that day.

The frank Doug Gray told reporters that Dunkle had "shunned" him the last six times he had visited. Gray considered determining his client's competency was like nailing Jell-O to a wall.

DA Steve Wagstaffe disagreed. He told the public that Dunkle was malingering to avoid the murder trial and that if he were found incompetent, he'd be sent to Atascadero State Hospital, where he would be forced to take antipsychotic medication and be educated about the court system until declared competent, "if ever." Wagstaffe feared that by then key prosecution witnesses would be lost, which had already happened with the Steve Murphy hit-and-run case.

On July 25, 1989, Dunkle's second competency hearing began. This time Wagstaffe requested a jury.

Doug Gray's colleague Gordon Rockhill gave the defense's opening statement because, in an unusual move, Doug Gray himself would be a defense witness.

Rockhill reviewed Dunkle's psychiatric history and pointed out that numerous psychiatrists found Dunkle to be schizophrenic, psychotic, delusional, and legally incompetent.

Wagstaffe argued that Dunkle was a manipulative person who had learned during the 1988 hearing and on the psychiatric unit how to feign psychosis.

The significant defense witnesses were Dr. Roland Levy, Dr. George Wilkinson, and Doug Gray.

Levy had assessed Dunkle in jail and found him to be "out of touch with reality. Inner reality has taken over." He considered Dunkle a "classic schizophrenic" and utterly incompetent. The symptoms struck him as absolutely genuine.

Dr. George Wilkinson reviewed his two-year history with Dunkle and stated that when he met with Dunkle in the jail yard in March, "Mr. Dunkle exhibited disorganized thinking and hallucinations and other symptoms of schizophrenia. . . . He also talked, as he has with other psychiatrists, about a computer that ordered him to commit the killings." Like Levy, Wilkinson was convinced that the illness was real and that in 1988, "Mr. Dunkle's symptoms were far more under control."

When Wagstaffe asked if Dunkle could have learned the symptoms on psychiatric wards and now be using them to manipulate psychiatrists, Wilkinson said that though this wasn't impossible, "It would take a consummate actor to fake the degree of illness he now has."

On the stand, Doug Gray testified about Dunkle's refusals to work on his own defense and his increasingly bizarre behavior. As Gray spoke, Dunkle jotted notes busily on a legal pad. Rockhill tore off a page and projected it onto a screen. Gray pointed out to the jury that the notes were "gibberish, a mishmash of words and numbers." In cross-examination, Gray sternly denied ever suggesting to Dunkle that he "behave in a way that makes him appear unstable or bizarre."

The star witness for the prosecution was Dr. Missett, whose testimony became more pointed every time he appeared in Dunkle proceedings. "Mr. Dunkle's incoherent gibberish and peculiar mannerisms are part of his scheme to appear he's not in control of his thoughts," he said, adding that in his own sessions with Dunkle, "the defendant was relatively coherent for five to ten minutes, until I started taking notes. That's when the gibberish started." He called Dunkle "a master manipulator and malingerer." Under Wagstaffe's questioning, Missett described, at length, the violence and sadism against the victims which Dunkle had talked about when Missett interviewed him in San Luis Obispo.

A handsome young deputy sheriff testified that when

Dunkle talked with him, he "forgot to act crazy." The implication was that Dunkle was infatuated with the young man and wanted to impress him.

Wagstaffe also reviewed psychiatric unit records that described Dunkle lecturing other patients about the insanity defense.

In his closing argument, Wagstaffe told the jury to depend on common sense. "Psychiatry is a remarkably subjective science," he said, asserting that Dunkle had "learned the game" during the first competency hearing.

Closing for the defense, Rockhill called Wagstaffe "an angry man annoyed by all these delays. What keeps getting in his way is, frankly, the law." He accused Wagstaffe of eliciting such detailed testimony about the stabbings "to get you folks riled up enough to ignore Mr. Dunkle's incompetence." He reminded the jury that Dunkle himself wanted to be found competent and that if he were trying to avoid the consequences of his crimes, that was a strange way to go about it. "The only psychiatrist to find him competent was Dr. Missett, who is an accomplished witness hired by the prosecution."

In deliberations, the jury quickly set aside the opposing psychiatric presentations and focused on the jail and psychiatric unit records. They decided that Dunkle was mentally ill, but legally competent.

Hearing the verdict, Dunkle grinned broadly, apparently believing it meant he could now plead guilty and have done with all these court appearances. Gray quickly disabused him. He would not permit a guilty plea because he firmly believed Dunkle incapable of understanding the consequences of it.

Bitterly, Gray complained to reporters that San Mateo County juries were traditionally hostile to presentations of mental incompetence in serious cases. He asserted that the prosecution would have won, even if not one psychiatrist supported it.

Since Dunkle was judged legally competent, and since

neither side would permit him to avoid trial by pleading guilty, there were no more means, psychiatric or otherwise, to postpone the trial anymore.

Dunkle's murder trial began on October 16, 1989.

Chapter Thirty-nine

Three hundred potential jurors were handed questionnaires, and from October 17 through October 19, groups of them struggled through voir dire on issues like death penalty versus life without parole and mitigating versus aggravating circumstances.

But on the 19th, the Dunkle case was delayed again. As Doug Gray put it in chambers on the 23rd, "Since we have a record again, we ought to note that there was an interruption in the proceedings in this case, caused by what I guess is being bandied about as the Great Earthquake of 1989."

San Mateo County, much of which rests on solid bedrock, suffered less than San Francisco, Alameda, and Santa Cruz counties. The city of Oakland had experienced the collapse of the Cypress freeway overpass, which trapped and killed many people in their cars. San Francisco and the Santa Cruz area had many fallen buildings and fires. Rescue efforts continued for days and hundreds of families remained homeless for months.

San Mateo's courthouse survived, but not without damage. The trial could not resume until November 27th.

Dunkle sat quietly at the defense table. Rather than indulging in outbursts, he doodled, daydreamed, and flicked his fingers near his ears. Over the last several months, a scuzzy sort of manhood had replaced his boyishness. He had grown almost chubby and a beard obscured his lower face.

By noon of November 28, twelve jurors and four alternates were seated. Determined to lose no more time, Judge Kozlosky ruled that opening statements should proceed into the lunch hour.

"Now the trial starts," Wagstaffe told the courtroom, which included the Davies. His clear and relatively restrained opening statement set the tone for a well-organized trial with minimal histrionics or bickering.

"Ladies and gentlemen, you are going to hear evidence of evil acts, senseless acts, vicious acts. It is a trip into every parents' nightmare."

He explained that over forty people would testify to bits and pieces of the events. "There are two other people who you will not hear from in this case, of course, and they are the boys who will be known to you as the victims. What you will see is these victims in a photograph."

After describing Dunkle's friendship with the Davies and the first days of John's disappearance, Wagstaffe established a theme he would repeat throughout the trial: "Jon Dunkle looked them right in the eye and told them he didn't know a thing."

Moving on to the search for Lance Turner the day he didn't come home, Wagstaffe said, "Mr. Russell and Mr. Turner came on the most ghastly thing they had seen in their life, and that is Lance Turner precisely where he had been left after the brutal stabbing by Jon Scott Dunkle."

He held up a photograph. "This is the condition that Jon Dunkle had left that little boy in."

Wagstaffe explained how Dunkle was identified as a suspect and pursued for two years. "Throughout these two years, Jon Dunkle continued to look every police officer in the eye directly and deny it: 'I was not even there.'

"This little tiny police agency in Belmont even went so far that at the end of January 1985, they had a female police officer, Lisa Thomas, go undercover in Sacramento."

After describing Lisa's efforts, he moved on to the Davies' meetings with Dunkle. " 'Jon, we just want to give our son a Christian burial.'. . . . Dunkle would say, 'Hey, I didn't do it.' "

Wagstaffe said that Dunkle "decided to talk to the FBI while he was in San Luis Obispo." Describing the search for John Davies's remains, he held up another photo. "This is what was left of John Davies: some ribs, some vertebra, and his skull. This is what was left of John Davies five years later . . . left out in the wild, no burial, no protection, no rocks over his body in any fashion to prevent him from being devoured by the wild animals.

"Since he was in the sixth grade, [Dunkle] has always wanted to see what it felt like to kill, and after having felt it once, he decided he wanted to feel it again. . . ." Wagstaffe asked the jury to find Dunkle guilty of first degree murder "for the horrible, horrible crimes he committed."

It was Gray's turn. Months before, he had told reporters the case was "indefensible." Now he led with his chin, tacitly acknowledging this problem.

"In this case, the evidence will show that you have a very difficult job. You don't have a difficult job because there is a who-done-it. It is not. . . .

"Mr. Wagstaffe's opening statement was not easy to listen to. The evidence is going to be worse. . . . This is a case of compelling, often mind-bending sadness, and really almost overwhelming evil. . . . And yet each of you has taken an oath not to do what seems to be the very human thing, to be tremendously outraged. Each of you has said by the oath, 'I will decide this case on the evidence and the law,' and the law says you cannot be influenced by passion.

"I thank you for your attention to the evidence that is going to be presented, and really almost apologize for the fact that you are going to have to listen to it."

Joan Davies could barely believe this moment had come. Nearly eight years had passed since John had disappeared. She told reporters she felt "surrealistic" and that she'd imagined the trial would never happen. Over the years, the wait had never become easier. Her statements, along with her husband's and Margo Turner's, appeared in a *San Mateo Times* article called "The Long, Winding Road to Justice."

As the first prosecution witness, Joan's role was to lay some bricks in the prosecution's foundation. Responding to Wagstaffe, she described her family and home before the disappearance. "By 1977, Jon Dunkle was like another son. He called us Mom and Dad."

She emphasized that the front door was locked the night John had vanished, though locking doors had not been the Davies' custom, and her statement contradicted Dunkle's confession of entering through the unlocked door "like always." But the Davies had endured years of criticism, veiled and direct, for befriending Dunkle, drinking with him in their home, and not perceiving that he was dangerous. The unlocked door symbolized that they'd allowed this evil into their lives. Joan's memory could not unlock that front door the night Dunkle took her son.

Cloaking love in unsentimental remarks, she explained why she'd known immediately that John hadn't run away. "I am his mother. He was a wimp . . . he would say he could never understand how anybody would run away. He was going to live with us until he was twenty-four and got out of medical school. So we used to laugh a lot about how he wanted to make sure that he was supported in the style in which he had become accustomed to living. . . . The week before he disappeared, he categorized his collection of one thousand license plates. You had to have known this kid to understand this."

She described how he liked to sit in the driveway and listen to music with Dunkle in Dunkle's car.

Gray asked no questions.

Jim Davies confirmed his family's close relationship with Dunkle, then described his own efforts when John vanished—the frantic calls to friends, making up the posters, searching mud flats, Hassler, Vista Points, and so on. He described Dunkle's single visit during the first week. "He called me Dad," Jim said bitterly. "Until November 1981."

FATHER OF ALLEGED DUNKLE VICTIM: HE CALLED ME "DAD" said that night's headlines.

Mark Davies, home on leave to testify, described for Wagstaffe the activities he and John had done with Dunkle, especially listening to music in Dunkle's car and partying near Hassler.

The next witness was Sergeant Tompkins, the first detective to handle the disappearance, retired since 1984. Wagstaffe used Tompkins to establish the theme of Dunkle's denials. Describing his meeting with Dunkle at Toys "Я" Us the first week of the disappearance, Tompkins stated, "He had no knowledge and he had no idea where John Davies was."

Jim and Joan glanced at each other. They, along with Bill Russell, believed that Tompkins had blown the investigation by thinking of Dunkle as John's friend rather than as a suspect in that first contact.

Detective Farmer testified that after taking the report that John was missing, he sent it up to the Detective Bureau. This version left out certain intervening variables, such as

Jim Davies phoning the BPD the morning after Farmer took the report and learning that no officers knew his son was missing.

Jerrold Whaley took the stand. After thirty-one years as an officer, his ulcers, a torn rotator cuff, and stress had forced him to retire from the department in 1988. He now worked on a switchboard for a busy Silicon Valley company. His testimony revealed his anger and frustration.

He said that early on he followed up with "fifty people plus students at Serra High School" while carrying "at least forty other cases." He "eventually put out John's flyer all over California and registered him in NCIC."

Questioned about considering John a runaway, Whaley said, "At that time most missing person reports involving juveniles were handled more as a runaway because that's the way, during those years, most of the kids did turn up as runaways." He admitted that this idea led to conflict with the Davies.

> Wagstaffe: They felt that wasn't the way their son should be categorized?
> Whaley: That is correct.
> Wagstaffe: Who made contact with the FBI?
> Whaley: I did.
> Wagstaffe: Why did you decide to bring in the FBI?
> Whaley: Two reasons mainly. The case had gone far beyond that of what a normal runaway juvenile would be considered. The second was at the insistence of the Davies.

Gray questioned Whaley about the disagreements with the Davies. Whaley responded, "They felt that we should be doing a lot more than what we were doing. I believe that they had the feeling that I should be working solely on John's case and drop all my others."

Whaley described the "Cheshire cat grin" Dunkle wore

when questioned. "It wasn't like he was worried about John Davies. He was having fun with us."

After Whaley came Special Agent Deklinski, who listed the significant "can't remembers" Dunkle ran on him and the many discrepancies between Dunkle's stories and the Davies'. Deklinski said, "After that, I felt strong in my mind that the defendant had been lying to me."

Having laid the groundwork about Dunkle's suspected involvement in John Davies's disappearance, Wagstaffe presented Lance Turner's murder. Here, too, the first witness was the victim's mother. "It's been totally nerve-wracking—all the delays," Margo Turner said, and now described the night Lance didn't come home. "I was walking up and down that house like crazy, I just didn't know. . . ." Her husband had returned from the search at about nine p.m. "He said, 'He's dead.' " She ducked her head, shielding her eyes, and Wagstaffe quickly said she didn't need to describe any more.

The three boys who had accompanied Lance to the soccer field testified next. All were now athletic and handsome high school seniors, preoccupied with girls and college applications. Seeing them brought Margo Turner bitter sadness. Lance should be one of them.

The boys described their activities with Lance the day he died, and Thomas Russell spoke about searching for him with his father and Mr. Turner.

Before the medical examiner, Dr. Peter Benson, was allowed to testify, Mrs. Turner left the courtroom and the attorneys and judge met without the jury to determine which autopsy photographs could be admitted into evidence. Gray was concerned about "the cumulative effect" but had to withdraw part of his objection because photos A through M depicted separate wounds. The attorneys agreed that Dr. Benson could not show more than one picture of each injury.

Though Gray elicited the fact that Lance died quickly and that some of his scrapes probably came from being dragged into the brush after death, he could do little to dilute the impact of the brutal injuries that the photos depicted.

Three of the smoking tree girls testified. Eighteen now and in college, they were embarrassed to admit smoking and talking with the stranger they'd met the day Lance Turner died. "I told him my name," one said. "I was young. I wasn't afraid to meet anyone."

Mike Brent, now seventeen and living in Canada, had been badgered by the police after Lance's death because he'd kept denying that he drank and smoked cigarettes near the place Lance had died. When he took his turn on the stand, he said of Lance, "He's just real athletic," still using present tense for his dead friend.

Officer Pat Halleran presented photos of the scene and of Lance's body in situ. He described the evidence found at the smoking tree, especially the "blue matchbook with silver writing—Cindy and Eric, August 25, 1984." He emphasized that information about this matchbook was never made public, laying the foundation for verifying Dunkle's confession later, in which Dunkle had spontaneously described this matchbook.

Goulart described investigating hundreds of possible suspects, narrowing them down to Dunkle, and the series of interrogations in which Dunkle denied everything. "At one point we got very terse with him."

Goulart clarified the term "terse" by saying, "Very direct. We called him a liar, telling him we were getting frustrated because we knew he wasn't telling us the truth."

When asked Dunkle's reaction, he answered, "He had a funny laugh. To me it was a nervous laugh. And he tried to change the subject at that point. . . . He tried to tell us it could have been hundreds of different kids."

Goulart made it clear that there had been no physical abuse of Dunkle, nor any violation of his rights. His testimony went up to the time of the undercover operation.

Now it was Lisa Thomas's turn. By now she had been

an officer for more than seven years. She testified in careful detail about her undercover work with Dunkle, including the fact that Dunkle had often talked about being suspected of killing Lance Turner. "On February second, he showed me a news article with a picture of Lance and of himself. He laughed. It was an inappropriate laugh, a nervous laugh. He would laugh at odd times, when one wouldn't normally think something was funny." She described the time he showed her a picture of Lance and joked, "Ugly, huh." He made fun of the police and joked about lying to confuse them. He tore up cigarettes and crushed beer cans to avoid leaving fingerprints on them.

Her testimony ended without mention of the burglary arrest, which had to be withheld during the guilt phase of the trial.

That night a big *San Mateo Times* article appeared : "GIRLFRIEND" SAYS DUNKLE LAUGHED OFF POLICE. In the picture, Thomas smiled directly into the camera, her hair long and curly, her features attractive. The article made her a heroine, yet she felt more shame than pride. The years since she'd worked on Dunkle had been filled with pain and humiliation. Another year would pass before she gained insight into why this was so.

Lisa Thomas's testimony was followed by California Men's Colony officers William Jesus and Michael Wiley. Since Dunkle's imprisonment couldn't be mentioned, the men presented themselves as law-enforcement officers, not prison guards. Each told the story of C. Louis coming to them to report Dunkle's confession. "He was appalled by the crimes," Wiley testified. "He insisted on working with us."

Wiley produced exhibits 17 and 18, the maps Dunkle drew showing where John Davies's remains lay and where Lance Turner died. Wiley then described the tapes obtained when Louis wore a wire while Dunkle talked about the murders. "Mr. Dunkle was telling Mr. Louis very nonchalantly and very businesslike, that in 1981 he killed John Davies. . . . He also told Mr. Louis that he killed Lance Turner in, I believe it was 1984, and he described some pretty graphic detail. . . . He gave no indication as to any motive." Wiley said Louis "convinced Mr. Dunkle" to confess to the FBI.

After this testimony, Gray spoke to the court out of the presence of the jury, explaining for the record that Wagstaffe had used many leading questions with Jesus and Wiley, and that this was all right with Gray. "Mr. Wagstaffe and I had fully discussed it in order to avoid any reference to the incarceration of Mr. Dunkle and thus have the jury speculate as to what that would be for . . . which would have been prejudicial. . . . I simply didn't want somebody to think that I'd either left the room or fallen asleep."

The natural next step in the progression would have been to put C. Louis on the stand. However, Louis had finally confessed to Wiley that he'd played a role in the mutilation murder of which he'd been suspected for so long. At the time of Dunkle's murder trial, Louis was involved in his own.

Officer Halleran returned to describe the search for John's remains based on Dunkle's map. "We found clothing, bones, a skull, which we turned over to the coroner."

After the chief investigator for the Coroner's Office testified about how these sixteen pieces of evidence were bagged, sealed, and stored in a locked refrigeration unit, establishing that the chain of evidence had been preserved, Coroner Dr. Jose Ferrer took the stand.

He stated he had found a depressed fracture in the upper part of the skull, a fractured right cheekbone, and some other indentations, leading him to "guesstimate" a total of five fractures consistent with blunt trauma as from a rock. He explained in dark detail how the head blow would have driven bone into the brain, causing lacerations and hemorrhages. The brain would have swollen and compressed "vital nerves" leading the heart and lungs, causing coma and death. The victim would have lived a maximum of half an hour.

Gray asked how one could determine antemortem versus postmortem injury of the skull. Ferrer explained that a postmortem fracture would have a "shattering" effect, while an antemortem one would be "like a green stick fracture." He conceded that the injuries could have been inflicted while the victim was unconscious or barely dead. This information didn't make Dunkle look any less vicious.

Rodger Heglar, forensic anthropologist, took the stand next. Using a plastic skeleton, he pointed out "some areas are missing [from Davies's bones] which are typical of animal chew." He explained that he ruled out environmental cause, however, for the skull injuries; blunt trauma had caused those.

John Davies's orthodontist testified that the skull's and mandible's teeth were John's.

After the jury had heard more than they wanted to ever know about John Davies's bones, they heard again from his mother. Joan testified about two long conversations with Dunkle without stating they had occurred after his burglary conviction. Though she presented herself as a tough woman who would never weep in public, she alluded to her own grief in describing what she'd told Dunkle about how the disappearance had devastated her family emotionally and financially, and had explained what Mark had gone through.

"And at that point in time," Joan testified, "because I was getting rather emotional . . . Jon [Dunkle's] eyes started to cloud up—and then it quickly passed."

Wagstaffe followed up on this emotional impact by calling Dr. Missett to testify about the cold cruelty Dunkle had revealed to him.

Wagstaffe next introduced a series of witnesses to lay the foundation for the confession videotapes: Mattei; Farmer;

Bell, who described Dunkle leading him to the Lance Turner murder weapon while being filmed by Farmer; and the FBI agents to whom Dunkle first confessed.

Prior to showing the videotapes, Gray stipulated, with the agreement of the judge and Wagstaffe, that the young man (C. Louis) who appeared in the tapes was "an acquaintance of Dunkle's, who is unrelated to the commission of the crimes."

Dunkle would not testify, but the jury now watched and heard him. They saw the police on the Edgewood Park hill where they searched for John Davies's bones, saw Lisa Thomas point out the skull where it lay in brush; then they saw and heard Dunkle lead officers up the same trail the next day, with remarks like, "This is where the incident occurred. This is where I stuck the knife in his back." They observed Dunkle's moment of emotion as he stood by Lance Turner's murder site, agreeing with Farmer's reading the confession of Lance's murder, and peeking up at officers like a child seeking approval. They saw him point out shrubbery in a Sacramento suburb where officers found the Buck knife he'd used to kill Lance.

With this climax to a devastating presentation, the prosecution ended.

Gray stood. "The defense rests," he said.

The court heard the closing arguments the following morning—December 6, 1989.

Wagstaffe told the jury, "Every parent's nightmare came true in this case, as you heard. You . . . are now a part of this nightmare."

He discussed different degrees of guilt, arguing that Dunkle committed the murders with intent, premeditation, and deliberation. He reminded the jury that they should not decide the degree of guilt through sentimentality or speculation. For example, Dunkle had claimed that

John Davies was on LSD the night he died. "Now you can sit there and speculate about what in the world is involved there. [But] you only use items of evidence as they fit into the case and they are proven by the case." Nor was the jury to speculate about what testimony was omitted by witnesses like Dr. Missett, who had been asked only for some "very narrow statements" to which he had been held by rules of evidence.

Wagstaffe reminded the jury that he was not required to prove Dunkle's motive.

"Both murders have premeditation, deliberation, overwhelmingly." Wagstaffe argued that by picking John up late at night, taking him away without John wearing his shoes to a remote area, taking the knife from the glove compartment, walking a long way along a service road—all these factors proved premeditation, as did the attack itself and Dunkle's "lifelong desire to kill."

Wagstaffe argued that Dunkle was not impaired by alcohol at the time of Lance's murder, since he was able to remember it in clear detail. "He could remember it because he enjoyed it."

Wagstaffe asked the jury to find Dunkle guilty of first-degree murder.

Gray rose to perform his unenviable task, the closing argument in the face of his client's overwhelmingly obvious guilt.

"This is an awful case," he told the jury. ". . . . Mr. Wagstaffe said you will be considering guilt or innocence, but you will be considering no such thing. There is no innocence in this case."

He told them not to waste their time with the verdict cards that said innocent nor with any other matters except the issue of premeditation and deliberation. "Mr. Wagstaffe says there is no question that there was deliberation and premeditation. That is nonsense. Obviously, there is a question or he wouldn't have talked to you about it for over an hour."

Gray pointed out that all the factors Wagstaffe used to prove Dunkle's premeditation relied on Dunkle's own statements. "[Dunkle] is not only a seriously disturbed individual, but a pathological liar and megalomaniac, an individual who lied repeatedly year after year after year. . . . Anyone who accepts anything that Jon Scott Dunkle says that cannot be independently corroborated is a fool."

He reminded jurors that Dunkle loved being the center of attention.

"We will know simply by the result whether you were carried away with emotion or whether you followed the law. Because if you follow the law, they are second-degree murders." Gray said that Wagstaffe's use of words like "evil" and "vicious" evoked emotion, not law.

Gray asked the jury to practice courage, "grace under pressure," as had the Turners and the Davies, who "in a system that has occasionally ignored them, in subtle ways abused them, and has probably dragged all of this out in interminable fashion, they have managed to put aside what must be unbelievable rage and unfathomable emotion and they have comported themselves with magnificent dignity.

"If they can do that, then it seems to me the least we can expect of you is the same."

In his rebuttal closing argument, Wagstaffe said, "Ladies and gentlemen, you just heard something that might be unique by and large in our system. You heard the defense attorney get up and say his client is a 'liar,' 'don't believe him.' That is different.

"However, the defense attorney in this case has a very difficult task during this guilt trial. He has nothing. This evidence provided him with nothing."

Wagstaffe then pointed out, "The law says you can rely on the statement of a defendant," and he reminded the jury of the elements of deliberation he had listed earlier. "The defense counsel presented the best picture that can be presented of the defendant, but the fact is that this is overwhelming. This is overwhelming. The defendant is clearly guilty of two first-degree murders."

Within two hours, the jury returned with the verdict Wagstaffe requested: Guilty of first-degree murder, two counts.

Chapter Forty

In the penalty phase, the prosecution would argue for the death penalty, and the defense would advocate life without parole. No other options existed.

DA Wagstaffe could now present the jury with prejudicial information that he was required to withhold in the guilt phase. "November of 1981 was the threshold crime of Jon Dunkle," Wagstaffe told the jury. "In November 1982, Jon Dunkle attempted to murder Steven Murphy, and through no fault of Mr. Dunkle, Mr. Murphy is alive today. . . . He is a survivor."

No trial about Dunkle's crime against Steve Murphy had ever been held. Hammering a couple of nails into Dunkle's coffin for John and Lance brought Murphy as close to personal justice as he would ever come.

Now twenty-three, he described the night when he was sixteen, when he and his friend Kelly Moroney walked home from a party, "tipsy," and Murphy left Moroney's porch to walk half a block home. "My next memory is opening my eyes and I saw a big round dirt area. I guess that's after I climbed up the cliff. . . . And the next thing

I remember after that was waking up in the hospital.'' He described his injuries: ''Fractured ribs. My skull is—as of today, I still have lumps and dents in it. A broken pelvis bone. And they took out a kidney and a spleen.''

He testified that he had never known Dunkle and had no memory of him from the attack.

Murphy stepped down from the witness stand, passing Dunkle at the defense table on his way to the aisle. ''Happy New Year,'' said Steve scornfully.

''Happy New Year,'' muttered Dunkle.

Dr. Bruce Allen testified, ''He was fortunate to survive. He was in poor condition when he arrived in the emergency room. . . . Most likely because of his youth, he was able to survive these injuries.''

He explained that without a spleen, Murphy could be subject to ''overwhelming infection,'' and that losing a kidney left him in danger of needing dialysis later in life if his diabetes damaged his remaining kidney.

A jail nurse testified that Dunkle threatened her life when she tried to give him prescribed medication.

Gray cross-examined for the first time, eliciting that it was a medication for mental illness that Dunkle had refused.

Now Wagstaffe presented Dunkle's attack on Monti Hansen. The San Mateo police hadn't taken Hansen seriously at the time. Now he had an audience that did. Like Murphy, Hansen was now twenty-three, and was sixteen when Dunkle attacked him. He described the New Year's Eve when Dunkle beat him in the head with a two-by-four. ''His body raised . . . with his arms very high in the air . . . he struck me with a good amount of force, where his intentions were obvious that he was not just trying to knock me out, but rather a blow strong enough to kill me. . . . The other thing I recall during the actual assault was the stare that he gave me. He stared directly into my eyes and gave me a rather Satanic look that really, really scared me. It was a combination between, it was a serious—he was looking very serious, but he was smiling. It was a light smile." Hansen's voice trembled.

Goulart followed to testify about Dunkle's break-in in Sacramento while Lisa Thomas was working undercover with him. Goulart had stayed by the back fence, knowing Dunkle was inside the house. "I was worried about what he was going to do . . . just steal something or was he going in there to hurt somebody. . . . I was also trying to make a decision whether I should go in after him or wait outside. And as the minutes kept on ticking by, it almost got to the point where I was going to go in."

Lisa Thomas and Mr. Renne, the homeowner, were supposed to testify next, but Wagstaffe disrupted his orderly progression to accommodate Sacramento Coroner Dr. Robert Anthony, who was on a tight schedule.

Dr. Anthony testified that on July 8, 1985, he was called to a crime scene in Sunrise Park. "There was a great deal of concern about a boy who was missing in Sacramento. A body was found in the park that was of appropriate size to be an adolescent male, but everyone thought that the child was black, and they wanted my expertise at the scene to see if this could have been a Caucasian child. . . ."

Wagstaffe showed three photos of a bloated, blackened body beneath a tree. Dr. Anthony pointed out the insect larvae which indicated that the body had lain there several days.

He described the autopsy, the puncture wounds that matched Dunkle's pipe cleaning tool, and the head wound that matched the nail in the board at the scene. This information evoked Hansen's recent testimony about Dunkle hitting him in the head with a two-by-four.

Next, Sean's father, Guy Dannehl, took the stand. Living and working up in the Twain Harte area, Dannehl didn't get papers that carried news about the case. After Dunkle's confessions had thrust Dannehl into a flurry of media coverage in Twain Harte, he had heard nothing more. He was unaware that the trial was happening until Wagstaffe phoned to ask him to testify in the penalty phase and filled him in on the competency hearings and the progress of the murder trial.

Now Dannehl recounted his search for Sean in the 106-degree temperatures. "The heat was so extensive, I just felt, 'If he has been here since he turned up missing, there is no doubt that he is dead.'"

As he testified, his wife, Debbie, sat in the courtroom directly behind Dunkle, close enough to touch him. Her body remained immobile while her thoughts ran along furious lines. She could easily understand how a grieving parent would want to lash out at such a person.

Sean's mother, Ellen, wept as soon as she took the stand. Judge Kozlosky called a recess, after which Ellen haltingly repeated the story of Sean's bike ride through Sunrise Park at dusk to say good-bye to a friend, his failure to return, the police officer who told her he couldn't do anything officially till twenty-four hours had passed. "Sean didn't like the dark," she said.

Now Wagstaffe brought in Lisa Thomas to produce Dunkle's statements about the Steve Murphy hit-and-run, the Monti Hansen attack, and the Renne break-in. The jury heard Dunkle's recorded voice bragging and joking ghoulishly about beating Monti with the two-by-four and ramming Steve Murphy with his car.

Lisa Thomas described the night Dunkle got very drunk with her at the Wits End Bar and talked about robbing houses. "And he brought up the subject about a twelve-year-old child, that if there is a twelve-year-old child there . . . he said he could tie them up, make them tell where stuff is. If he's dead, he can't make a composite." She said he talked about breaking into houses at night to learn the layouts. He claimed he'd broken into his own former home in Belmont after it was sold.

Wagstaffe saw that Lisa was trembling and near tears. The powerful content of her testimony was clearly making an impact on the jury. The tape that scratchily reproduced everything Thomas and Dunkle had said up to the moment she notified Goulart that Dunkle had entered the Renne house was played. Then Lisa stepped down, casting a haunted glance toward Dunkle, who stared down at the table.

Next Mr. Renne narrated the events of that night. It was clear that while the couple was making love, Dunkle had prowled through their house and entered their children's rooms.

Then Wagstaffe presented Sacramento officers who testified about the Dannehl crime scene. He held up aerial photos of the American River, crossed by Sunrise Bridge and the tiny wooden bridge Sean had bicycled across. A red circle showed where his body was found.

Sheriff Ron Goesch described his undercover effort, when he masqueraded as a tough biker and told Dunkle he'd seen him hit Sean Dannehl with the board. Dunkle "didn't say much," Goesch said, and didn't come to their assignation.

Detective Bell described how he and Homicide Chief Ray Biondi had shown Dunkle a videotape of Goesch telling police he'd witnessed Sean's murder. Bell told how Dunkle almost opened up after seeing that video: "He began phoning me and asking what would happen if he confessed, what if he did see the kid, and the kid was screaming, alive or whatever, but that he, Jon, did not take any action to save the child, would he be in trouble . . . ? [In Bell's office] Jon paused for a great period of time and it was real apparent . . . that he was seriously considering telling me about what had happened. He subsequently terminated the interview. . . ."

Bell spoke of joining Dunkle and FBI agents in Sunrise Park the day Dunkle confessed on videotape. When Dunkle got upset at seeing him, Bell had sat in the prison van with him "to reestablish rapport. I thanked him. I told him even though he didn't come forward to me, it was important that he did come forward and I was proud of him for what he had done." Bell raised his eyes to Dunkle's. "And still am."

Now came the climax: the videotapes of Dunkle confessing to Sean Dannehl's murder and the Steve Murphy hit-and-run.

The accumulated testimony, backed by the audiotapes and videotapes, was devastating.

The next morning Doug Gray would fight back with the only weapon possible: Dunkle's mental illness.

Dr. George Wilkinson hauled his stacks of data to the stand.

"Doctor, I know you have a lot of records," said Gray. "Let me get this [water pitcher] out of here and you will have a little more room."

"Thank you. Is this fresh or is this just here?"

Judge Kozlosky said, "Drink it at your own risk."

Gray intervened. "Let me remove the temptation then." He ogled the mountain of files. "This is amazing."

Wilkinson recounted his many hours of contacts with Dunkle, beginning in December 1987, when Judge Kemp had first asked him to evaluate Dunkle's competency. He had collected "all available records—school, employment, probation, police—nine hundred pages of material. It was both the circumstances of the crimes . . . as well as a past history of mental difficulty."

Gray stipulated, "The . . . voluminous medical records . . . are being used to explain his testimony, not as hearsay. These are allowed in as expert opinion."

Wilkinson stated that his first long session with Dunkle, January 9, 1988, had posed a problem. Dunkle had spoken of disordered thoughts, hallucinations, and delusions, but had not seemed to experience them during the session. "So I had to consider malingering—voluntary, conscious deception."

Wilkinson explained that Dunkle tried to fool psychiatrists; he very much did not want to be seen as mentally ill. "He would tell me there was nothing wrong with him and yet describe these bizarre and psychotic symptoms."

Wilkinson argued that Dunkle's low-normal IQ would prevent him from being able to effectively fake such symptoms.

He stated that his observations of Dunkle over time brought him to form a clear diagnosis. First, Dunkle had "an antisocial personality, meaning an inability to control his impulses, apparent inability to learn from past conflict with the law." Dunkle saw people as objects to use and manipulate.

But, Wilkinson said, a person can have two diagnoses, and he now understood that Dunkle also met the criteria for "chronic paranoid schizophrenia." Dunkle believed his thoughts were controlled by computers, espionage, the FBI, and so on. This meant that though Dunkle might realize his crimes were wrong, he might not "appreciate" that it was he, not the computers, who would suffer the consequences. Dunkle also believed that the DA would help him more than the defense attorney, and that the Sacramento judge (an African-American) was his relative.

In July 1989, Wilkinson went on, he had met with Dunkle three times, finding him still worse. Dunkle then believed his parents were fakes who looked the same, but were different. He had expressed similar delusional ideas about his victims, saying John Davies was really a sixty-two-year-old man.

Wilkinson explained that "schizophrenia is a very severe mental illness that I believe . . . is a biological or neurological illness with psychiatric symptoms." Dunkle's way of rubbing his fingers near his ears was a ritualistic behavior characteristic of this illness. He said Dunkle's mental course was downhill, characteristic of severe paranoid schizophrenia.

Wagstaffe challenged Wilkinson: Why hadn't Dr. Love, who evaluated Dunkle in Kaiser in 1983 when Dunkle had injected his penis with fat, and Dr. Ridelhuber, who evaluated Dunkle for the police in 1984, found him psychotic?

Wilkinson responded, "I feel that if they saw him today, they would agree with me." He cited several psychiatrists who did: Fricke, in 1987: "Mr. Dunkle is a fragile individual with psychotic material present"; Horstman who in 1988 found Dunkle incompetent; and San Mateo County Hospital psychiatrist Richard Komisaruk who diagnosed him a chronic paranoid schizophrenic in September 1989.

Wilkinson referred to a school psychological testing Dunkle had at age ten which found him both dyslexic and emotionally disturbed, with the emotional disturbance being the most prominent problem.

Wagstaffe had Wilkinson clarify that dyslexia was a learning problem, not mental illness nor a condition that causes criminal conduct.

Wilkinson explained again the ways he'd seen Dunkle change over three years. Wagstaffe suggested that Dunkle had learned better how to malinger by hearing Wilkinson testify in 1988.

"What's the goal of malingering?" asked Wilkinson. "Some theories would be to delay the trial, put off judgment—"

Wagstaffe pounced. "And he's had success in that, hasn't he, Doctor, through these last three years?"

"Now, wait!" The kindly Dr. Wilkinson could get angry, too. He argued that Dunkle's illness was not primarily a "conscious endeavor to delay things. I think his illness really was starting to come to the fore. The process could have been speeded up if he had been sent to the state hospital for a thorough evaluation . . . which was one of my recommendations, which was refused."

Wilkinson reiterated that at Atascadero State Hospital Dunkle could have been evaluated thoroughly and "returned to competency."

Later Wagstaffe asked, "Isn't it true that Mr. Dunkle

went to Chope Hospital in February 1989 for a rest instead of psychosis?"

Gray objected. "Mr. Wagstaffe makes it sound as if Sheriff Cardoza was running a hotel on the fourth floor. People in and out at their option. It's very clear that people go to Chope when they're in custody because some mental health professional has sent them there."

Wagstaffe produced a passage in the hospital record stating that at admission Dunkle said he "was glad to be in the hospital; now he could get some rest."

Next they argued about Dunkle's mixed bag of delusions. "Doesn't it have to be a fixed delusion to qualify as paranoid schizophrenia?" Wagstaffe demanded, pointing out that Dunkle's had changed from mind control by synthesizers and police radios to computers and other machines.

Wilkinson bristled. "It's just this problem that the American Psychiatric Association realized was going to occur, which is exactly the one that is occurring. In the book *[The Diagnostic and Statistical Manual]* they say don't use this in court because this is a clinical description of clinical cases, and when you start using it in legal things, you're going to come to a lot of cross purposes." He added that the *DSM* was not a cookbook. Wilkinson explained that as a person gets sicker, his delusions progress into a fixed pattern; they are not fixed in the beginning.

On redirect, Gray elicited from Wilkinson the information that a person can be very mentally ill and at the same time also be manipulative.

At this point, Judge Kozloski excused the jury. Dunkle had been muttering to Gray, who needed to address the judge. "No plea of not guilty by reason of insanity has ever been entered," he said.

"Well, I don't agree with you!" cried Dunkle.

"Do you want to talk to your lawyer, Mr. Dunkle?" Judge Kozlosky asked. "Don't talk to me. Don't talk out loud."

Gray and Dunkle left for a few minutes. When they

returned, Dunkle told the judge, "Oh, I had nothing really much to say. He's handling it the way he wants to. He's responsible for his perjury that he denounces himself of. Same for you, ma'am."

"All right," she said.

"And the DA and the Belmont Police Department—"

She reminded him that he was not to have outbursts.

"I'm not going to no hospital. You can continue with your job."

"You will be removed from the courtroom if you continue your outbursts," she said firmly.

The jury returned and Wagstaffe presented his rebuttal witness, Dr. James Missett.

Over the years Dr. Missett had grown increasingly outspoken about Dunkle. Now he reiterated what he'd said in the competency hearings about Dunkle's fascination with death, his desire to kill since the sixth grade and his ability to conceal the murders for years. Missett said that at the times of the murders, Dunkle had "a mixed personality disorder: antisocial, borderline narcissistic, and sexual sadism." Missett had seen no evidence of schizophrenia when he met Dunkle in 1986, though he admitted that Dunkle did speak of hearing voices when using alcohol and marijuana.

Missett had not interviewed Dunkle again until July 1989 (when many other doctors found Dunkle a paranoid schizophrenic). Though Missett found Dunkle "markedly different" then and given to periods of "gibberish," he did not believe Dunkle was truly psychotic. "The presentation . . . was a conscious and intentionally devised one . . . for the purpose of getting me to conclude that he was seriously mentally ill." Missett considered the gibberish to be "intentionally disruptive."

Missett then presented his clincher: "There was one period of time where he smiled. And it's an extraordinarily difficult thing to describe in words, but it's the kind of smile where it's an exchange between two people—I was smiling and he was smiling . . . like, 'C'mon now, we know what this is all about'—not a smile you'd see with an individual who is preoccupied with their thoughts or is schizophrenic."

Paranoid schizophrenics don't smile or make eye contact, Missett said. He argued that schizophrenics don't "just arise out of the ground without earlier indicators." He felt the odd finger movements occurred at deliberate moments.

To Missett, Dunkle's case was "one of the most flagrantly presented and pushed attempts at malingering that I've observed inside or outside of the criminal justice system."

When Wagstaffe said, "You heard Dr. Wilkinson refer to the defendant as crazy; do you agree with that?" Missett responded, "Like a fox."

Gray opened his cross-examination with that nonpsychiatric term the next morning. "What do you mean by . . . 'crazy like a fox'?"

Missett said Dunkle had been very cunning to avoid detection and responsibility for his offenses "without remorse" for several years.

Gray asked why Missett disagreed with Wilkinson, "who has struggled with the question of malingering and decided on a combination of malingering with mental illness."

Missett answered that he saw a little mental illness and a lot of malingering and pointed out that Wilkinson "didn't have the benefit of seeing Mr. Dunkle prior to the onset of these symptoms."

When Missett gave the same response when asked why Dr. Levy also considered Dunkle mentally ill, Gray challenged, "Is that the common thread of all these psychiatrists who disagree with you, Doctor? Dr. Casella, Dr. Horstman, Dr. Lewis, Dr. Wilkinson, Dr. Levy, Dr. Komisaruk . . . they did not have this six-hour advantage that you talked about?"

Wagstaffe objected that this misstated the situation and

Gray withdrew the question, switching to a discussion of Dr. Missett's payment—over $6000—for his work with Dunkle. He brought out that Missett's specialty wasn't forensic psychology but philosophy, in which he had a Ph.D.

When Gray asked him to explain what he thought Dunkle's motivation was for malingering and not cooperating with his defense attorneys, Missett launched into a lecture about how Dunkle's treatment of the Davies family ("shining them on, jerking them around") did not differ from his treatment of his victims.

"Excuse me, Doctor—" said Gray.

"No, I will finish my answer first, Mr. Gray, and then I will go on—"

"Just a moment, just a moment," interrupted Judge Kozlosky.

Gray complained that Missett's answer was nonresponsive. "I specifically asked what the doctor perceived to be the goal with respect to the relationship between me and Mr. Dunkle, which clearly did not begin in 1980."

The judge allowed Missett to continue. The psychiatrist explained that Dunkle hated people that he also liked and respected. A prime example was how Dunkle had once turned away from Dr. Wilkinson and urinated, "an indication of contempt on Mr. Dunkle's part for an individual who is otherwise trying to be decent and nice to him, and quite frankly I know few people whom I regard as more decent or nicer that George Wilkinson. . . ." He went on a good while longer.

Finally Gray said, "Have you finished?"

"Yes," conceded Missett.

"Would you please now answer the question, which was—"

Wagstaffe leaped up. "Objection! Argumentative!"

"Sustained."

Gray tried again. "What is his goal in not cooperating with me at this stage—"

More objections came, this time because Gray hadn't

presented evidence about Dunkle's behavior toward him. "I assure you that there will be," said Gray, and finally he got the question in.

Missett said Dunkle's mental illness and noncooperation won him privileges, allowed him to escape responsibility for his acts, and delayed trials. He predicted, accurately, that Dunkle would have more trials, and his current "pattern of behavior" was calculated to enable him to avoid execution.

Missett also disagreed one hundred percent with Wilkinson on the fixed delusion issue. "Mr. Dunkle is the first person in medical literature to go through a series of five different controlling machines." Missett had once told Dunkle, "You are demeaning yourself by acting crazy. . . . You're a man, not a boy, and you are able to act like one."

Then Missett pounded in his final nail: He said that Dunkle was evil.

"Isn't that a moral judgment, Doctor?" demanded Gray. ". . . Is evil a psychiatric term?"

"I think some psychiatrists would work overtime to avoid it," Missett joked.

Gray pushed. "Is evil a term from the *DSM*?"

Missett conceded that a philosophy textbook would call the disregard of other people's rights "evil," while a psychiatry text would classify it as "antisocial."

The closing arguments ran long but predictably, with Wagstaffe reviewing Dunkle's many vicious crimes and arguing that these aggravating circumstances justified the death penalty. Gray acknowledged that aggravating circumstances outweighed mitigating factors, but asked the jury to consider Dunkle's mental illness. He closed with a few remarks about Dr. Missett.

"Some people faced with a fact situation like this who are supposed to approach it in a professional manner succeed, and some do not. I think that Dr. Missett did not.

Dr. Missett was an advocate, not just an expert. . . . He's the kind of witness people want to get because he has that sense of advocacy. . . . Dr. Missett told you that Jon Dunkle was evil. So did Mr. Wagstaffe. Mr. Wagstaffe's entitled to, he's an advocate, he represents the people of the state of California. . . . Dr. Missett was going well beyond the bounds of psychiatry and into the area of morality when he decided to issue that opinion from the witness stand."

The jury deliberated through the afternoon on January 9 and all the next morning. During that time, they requested portions of the transcripts, especially the psychiatric testimony. They asked whether there had been any testimony about Dunkle's state of mind at the time of the murders. They also wanted the definition of sadism and to know how many times Dr. Wilkinson had met with Dunkle.

At 1:40, they emerged. Several were tearful. They had reached their decision: death.

Epilogue February 1990–Fall 1998

Jon Dunkle in Sacramento

By the time Dunkle reached San Quentin Prison's Death Row in February 1990, Sacramento officials had decided to try him for the murder of Sean Dannehl. Sacramento DA John O'Mara explained to the media that Sean Dannehl's family was relieved about the San Mateo County sentence, but that they were still entitled to their own day in court on behalf of their son.

Behind the scenes, Sean's Dannehl's divorced parents, Guy and Ellen, were divided on this subject, a disagreement that would become more acrimonious as time passed. Sean's mother desperately wanted Sean's—and her own—day of justice in court. Sean's father preferred a longer term strategy: He wanted to hold off on the Sacramento trial so that if the San Mateo death penalty should be overturned, Sean's trial could be used to reinstate it.

When reporters contacted Jim Davies about the Sacramento trial, he said he felt that not only did the Dannehls deserve the satisfaction of a trial but that Dunkle deserved the additional punishment of sitting through it.

These arguments were destined to remain moot for four years.

Receiving the death sentence in San Mateo had worked no miracles on Dunkle's sanity, and Sacramento would have to replay San Mateo County's battles over his competency.

In 1992, two full years after Dunkle's Sacramento arraignment, court-appointed psychiatrists found him incompetent to cooperate with his own defense or to comprehend the proceedings. The court ordered him transferred from San Quentin to maximum security Patton State Hospital, where he was to be educated about the courts and medicated into sanity—a plan Dr. Wilkinson had recommended years earlier during the San Mateo County competency wars.

After battles among his defense attorneys, the DA, and San Quentin officials, Dunkle was returned from Patton to San Quentin in February 1994, allegedly now sane, though a string of psychologists and psychiatrists continued to evaluate him. They testified in a competency hearing that occurred in bits and pieces from July until October, fighting over issues San Mateo County knew only too well: The prosecution considered him to be hiding behind a performance of insanity, while the defense considered him psychotic and utterly unable to participate in his own defense.

As the drawn-out competency hearing ended, defense attorney Jim Ramos described Dunkle as "a lump of flesh" whose brain did not function. He criticized the low standard of psychiatric evaluations performed on Dunkle at San Quentin and accused San Quentin officials of interfering with the appropriate processes by their political maneuvering to have Dunkle returned prematurely from Patton State Hospital.

DA Kit Cleland appealed to the court's common sense.

He argued that "meddling and muddling" psychiatrists ignored the horror of Dunkle's crimes. He said Dunkle poured forth "psychobabble," yet at other times behaved calmly. County jail and state prison staff who observed the defendant offstage, so to speak, were aware of his "hidden agenda," Cleland added. He presented testimony from San Quentin guards supporting this position.

After what seemed an eternity—four and a half years since Dunkle was arraigned for murdering Sean Dannehl—Sacramento Judge Connelly reached the same conclusion that juries and judges had ultimately reached in San Mateo: Dunkle was crazy, but legally competent, schizophrenic, but also a deliberate malingerer.

Ultimately, though, Dunkle did not have to endure another trial. His being adjudicated legally competent gave him and the attorneys a window of opportunity and they leaped through it. On December 31, 1994, the court permitted Dunkle to plead guilty to Sean Dannehl's murder in return for life without the possibility of parole.

Sean's mother, Ellen, who had waited a long time for her day in court, made a furious and anguished Victim Impact Statement, screaming that Dunkle should rot in hell and his soul should never rest.

Judge Connelly told Dunkle his crime was utterly "despicable." He then passed the sentence he and the attorneys had agreed upon: life without parole plus (using legal guidelines) an additional year for committing the murder with a knife. Dunkle waived his right to appeal this sentence.

Sean's father, Guy Dannehl, states that neither his ex-wife Ellen Dammen nor the Sacramento District Attorney's office notified him of this hearing. He learned of it in March 1995, when he received a note from DA Kit Cleland. When he complained to Cleland about not having been informed about the hearing, where he would have liked to make his own Victim Impact Statement, Dannehl reports that the DA said he didn't have to notify him because he was not the custodial parent. Dannehl, with whom Sean had lived for the last two years of his life, vehemently disagreed. He remains in contact with Citizens Against Homicide, a victims rights organization.

The Dannehls still live in Twain Harte. They now have two daughters, thirteen and nine, both born at home. A framed photo of Sean, grinning in a baseball uniform, sits in their living room, and the little sisters he never knew mention him as casually as any other close and familiar relative.

The People

While the psychiatric war limped along in Sacramento, Belmont citizens and officers tried to put their lives back together.

In May 1990, Bill Russell and three other Belmont Oaks fathers put on a banquet to distribute the Lance Turner Reward Fund. Russell announced that half the money would go to C. Louis. He stated that it didn't matter that Louis was a criminal; what mattered was that Louis solved the case by persuading Dunkle to confess.

When the trial had ended, Russell had received calls from Louis's attorney, who demanded that Louis be given the reward. "I absolutely agree," said Bill. "Have him call me himself." When Louis developed a collect-phone-call relationship with Russell, Russell enjoyed the inmate's intelligence, irreverent humor, and grandiose Mafia tales.

Louis instructed Russell to send him the $7500 reward via his girlfriend/wife (he used the terms interchangeably, as near as outsiders could tell). Louis later said he quickly spent it on legal fees in his Los Angeles murder trial.

The next largest award, $2000, went to Jim and Joan Davies for their painful sessions with Dunkle in prison, which had helped loosen him up for confession.

The two smoking-tree girls who had helped most with the composite drawings each received $1250.

Dunkle's former school counselor and "book writer," Robert Kauk, was awarded $500 for giving helpful information to police about Dunkle's character, family background and mental illness.

The reward fund also paid for Dr. Hugh Ridelhuber's consultations with Belmont police and the Davies and his three-hour interview with Dunkle in his car.

Lisa Thomas could not be given a monetary reward since her undercover work had been part of her job, but Jim Davies, as president of the International Organization for Missing and Exploited Children (evolved from his prior group PACE), presented her with a certificate entitled "The Child Safety Award" in behalf of Dunkle's living and dead victims.

This made the fifth award Lisa had received for her role in the case. By now Hollywood had noticed her.

When trial publicity glorified Lisa Thomas as "the killer's girlfriend," a Belmont woman with Hollywood connections had gotten in touch with her. "I was just doing my job," mumbled Lisa when the woman suggested a TV movie. Still, she grudgingly agreed to meet with producer Joni Marks when she went to L.A. to attend a conference in her new position as the department's education officer.

The conference topic was post traumatic stress disorder in police officers, and there Lisa suddenly learned why she'd been so depressed and self-destructive after her work with Dunkle. Though she hadn't witnessed or directly experienced violence with him, she'd existed in a hypervigilant mental state twenty-four hours a day for two months, had been alone with him in places where her backup officer could not quickly get to her, and had reincarnated her hated former self, loser Lisa Davis, for her role as Dunkle's girlfriend.

She'd received no debriefing or counseling when that role abruptly ended with the Renne break-in. Instead the department had punished her for the emotional and social problems she developed.

Then Dunkle had killed Sean Dannehl. Lisa Thomas had felt sad, but numb. Now she realized her numbness masked an agony of guilt and failure. If she had developed deeper intimacy and trust, wouldn't he have confessed to her instead of killing another child? Yet while working on him, she'd played on his neediness, even talked about getting married in Tahoe, when her true goal was to put him in the gas chamber. She'd struggled with the immorality of it, the sense that with the intentional deceit she'd betrayed herself as well as Dunkle. Yet at the same time, she'd hated herself for not conning him well enough to stop him, and the last time she'd seen him in court she'd seen nothing in his face but "pure evil."

In order to educate the public about post traumatic stress like hers, Lisa sold her story to Hollywood. Much fictionalized, and with PTSD changed to Adult Child of an Alcoholic syndrome, *In the Company of Darkness* made its debut January 1993. It starred Helen Hunt as Lisa's character and Steven Weber as Dunkle's.

An injury prevented Lisa Thomas from returning to active duty when she rotated out of her stint as education officer. She has since married, left the police department, and moved out of state.

John Davies's disappearance directly influenced changes in San Mateo County police procedures in missing person cases. In 1986, the Belmont PD rewrote its general order on the handling of such cases and its policy became the blueprint for San Mateo County's Model Missing Person's Order.

The California Missing Children Act that Governor Deukmejian vetoed in 1986 later passed and found funding. Jim Davies served on task forces to program the statewide computerized clearinghouse, which became operational in 1991.

Sergeant Jim Goulart rose in the Belmont Police Department, first to commander and finally to chief.

Sergeant Don Mattei has risen to commander.

Officer Pat Halleran, still a dog-handling officer and a meticulous evidence tech, is now a sergeant.

Detective Joe Farmer left Belmont several years ago and is a police officer in Guerneville, California, along the Russian River.

Bill Russell continues to practice law in San Mateo County. From 1996 to the present, he has worked actively behind the scenes on another Belmont disappearance and remains in contact with an FBI profiler who meets with Dunkle at San Quentin. His son Thomas, who was present when Lance Turner's body was found, is now in the sales division of a major company.

Steve Murphy currently has a job he loves and is living a relatively normal life, other than being very careful with his diabetes, more brittle since Dunkle ran him over and destroyed his spleen and a kidney.

C. Louis was convicted of manslaughter in his Los Angeles trial in 1990 and had twenty-seven years added to his sentence. He may be considered for parole around 2003. He remains at the California Men's Colony, where he has a clerical job and spends his free time painting with acrylics. He states he has been drug free for quite a while now and hopes to lead a peaceful life when he is freed.

Mark Davies married a childhood sweetheart and remains in the navy. He and his wife, Anne, live in Connecticut with their dog family, which ranges in number from three to ten. His bumper sticker announces that he is a CLEAN AND SOBER PARTY ANIMAL.

Jim Davies, an expert with both IBM and Apple computers, repairs and programs computers and teaches. He still appears in public service spots about child safety and missing children.

For the past several years, Joan Davies has led organizations that work to prevent substance abuse in youth. Jim and Joan participated in the enormous volunteer effort that occurred when Polly Klaas was abducted in Petaluma, California.

Jon Dunkle in 1998

In his original confessions to Louis and the FBI, Dunkle made vague, tantalizing references to a fourth murder, a boy he allegedly met in Golden Gate Park and threw off the Golden Gate Bridge. Officers immediately thought of Kevin Collins, whose February 1984 disappearance (eight months before Lance Turner's murder) became a national cause célèbre and a focal point for the missing children's movement. It has been argued that when the eleven-year-old disappeared from a street corner opposite Golden Gate Park's panhandle, Dunkle was working in San Francisco, and although he had no driver's license and his father had sold the white Honda Civic, he could have had access to a vehicle and snatched, killed, and disposed of Kevin.

Initial investigations into this possibility turned up nothing substantive. Investigators still periodically question Dunkle about Kevin Collins, as well as other unsolved missing/murdered boy cases. He remains vague and usually babbles about lasers and computers controlling his mind.

As of September 1998, Dunkle's mental state precludes his mandated death penalty appeal process from moving forward. His competency must again be adjudicated in a hearing, or series of them. Responsibility for these hearings has devolved back onto San Mateo County, where DA Steve Wagstaffe will again represent the prosecution. First, though, two defense attorneys unfamiliar with the original case must review thousands of pages of documents. Sometime in the future, Dunkle and the attorneys will appear before Judge Judith Kowalski to weigh Dunkle's sanity versus his evil.

Victims' Families

Margo Turner seldom speaks of Lance's murder, and when she does, she experiences it as if it happened yesterday.

Guy Dannehl says he has been changed forever by Sean's murder. For him, as for Jim Davies, pain and rage burn unquenchably side by side.

One day when Joan Davies heard an old song on the radio, she commented, "John liked that."

Her mother, Grandma McLean, looked up in surprise. "You still think about him?"

Joan glanced toward nearby shelves loaded with family photos and answered as all the other victims' parents would: "Mother, I remember him every day."

Acknowledgments

This is a true crime book and a labor of love. I lived with the events as they happened.

I attempted to tell the whole story, its whats and whys, but pages can't capture reality. They distill truth drawn from a hundred hours of interviews and thousands of pages of police records, trial transcripts, and news accounts.

I have changed several names and modified identifying information at times to protect certain individuals.

I am very grateful to the many people who contributed their time and stories. They include:

Victims and their families:

Jim, Joan, Mark, and Jimmy Davies, who gave me many hours of painful interviews, plus boxloads of clippings, notes, videotaped TV specials, and photographs. Without the Davies, this book would not exist.

Margo Turner, who was dignified and gracious in all our contacts.

Guy and Debbie Dannehl, who spoke candidly and forgave me for waiting so long to meet them.

Steve Murphy and his mother, Deanna Baldwin, who told me their stories and supported this project.

I was unable to locate Monti Hansen or Sean Dannehl's mother, Ellen Dammen.

Law enforcement:

The Belmont Police Department, which gave me access to the case files, plus a desk where I could read them for six weekends.

Chief James Goulart, Commander Don Mattei, Sergeant Pat Halleran, former Sergeant Jerrold Whaley, Officer Lisa Thomas, and Sergeant Joe Farmer, now working in Guerneville, CA, who gave me terrific anecdotes and inside information. I'll never forget how, after I despaired of ever getting my hands on any original photos of Dunkle, Chief Goulart dropped nine of them into my lap.

District Attorney Steve Wagstaffe, who provided a desk and a roomful of transcripts and gave me easy access to court exhibits.

Community people:

Bill Russell, the hero behind the scenes, who provided great information and insights, as well as helping in many other ways. I appreciate also Thomas Russell's input and Juanita Russell's hospitality.

Dr. Hugh Ridelhuber, who shared his unusual story and insights about Dunkle.

Robert Kauk, who met with me despite still finding the subject of Dunkle painful.

Belmont Oaks head coach Ray Williamson and his wife, Carole, who told me some moving stories.

I also appreciate the people who spoke with me, but did not wish their names used, including Belmont folks who knew Dunkle, forensic psychiatrists, Carlmont High School staff, and people who were minors when these events took place. I appreciated their information and incorporated it indirectly.

And others:

The inmate who is called C. Louis in these pages was a fascinating and colorful interviewee, as well as playing a key role in the case.

Paul Ciotti, author of "The Killer's Girl Friend," *San Jose Mercury News,* 12/90, encouraged me to take on this project and provided some good information.

I was fortunate in my agents Lettie Lee and Andree Abecassis of the Anne Elmo Agency. Editor in Chief Paul Dinas and Consulting Editor Karen Haas have been great in working with me as a first-time author.

My writing friends/critiquers endured this very long haul with me: Betsy Roeth, Carole Girvan, Cheryl MacKenzie, Matt Carvalho, Cleo Jones, Kaa Byington, Beth Jacobs, Bud Gundy, and Dave Lara.

And finally, there are my terrific and supportive kids, Scott and Dana Phelps and Jeanie Phelps Touchstone, and my patient buddy Roy Wellman.